# Media and Public Spheres

# Media and Public Spheres

Edited by

Richard Butsch
*Rider University, USA*

First published 2007 by
PALGRAVE MACMILLAN
Houndmills, Basingstoke, Hampshire RG21 6XS and
175 Fifth Avenue, New York, N.Y. 10010
Companies and representatives throughout the world

PALGRAVE MACMILLAN is the global academic imprint of the Palgrave
Macmillan division of St. Martin's Press, LLC and of Palgrave Macmillan Ltd.
Macmillan® is a registered trademark in the United States, United Kingdom
and other countries. Palgrave is a registered trademark in the European
Union and other countries.

ISBN-13: 978–0–230–00721–5    hardback
ISBN-10: 0–230–00721–X        hardback

This book is printed on paper suitable for recycling and made from fully
managed and sustained forest sources.

A catalogue record for this book is available from the British Library.

Library of Congress Cataloging-in-Publication Data

Media and public spheres / edited by Richard Butsch.
    p. cm.
  Includes bibliographical references and index.
  ISBN-13: 978–0–230–00721–5 (cloth)
  ISBN-10: 0–230–00721–X (cloth)
    1. Mass media and culture. 2. Mass media—Political aspects. 3. Mass
media—Social aspects. I. Butsch, Richard, 1943–

P94.6.M4246 2007

302.23—dc22

                                                            2006051577

10   9   8   7   6   5   4   3   2   1
16   15   14   13   12   11   10   09   08   07

Printed and bound in Great Britain by
Antony Rowe Ltd, Chippenham and Eastbourne

*Thanks to Ava*

# Contents

# Notes on the Contributors

**Michael Bailey** teaches media history and cultural theory at Leeds Metropolitan University. He is currently working on an edited book entitled *Narrating Media History* (forthcoming), and has recently been awarded a Higher Education Funding Council for England (HEFCE) fellowship researching, 'Mediating Faiths: Religion, Community and Culture'.

**Richard Butsch** is Professor of Sociology, American Studies and Film and Media Studies at Rider University. His is author of *The Making of American Audiences from Stage to Television, 1750–1990*. He is currently completing a book on the history of politicized representation of audiences as crowds, publics and individuals. His studies of class and gender in five decades of American sitcoms have been reprinted several times.

**Nick Couldry** is Professor of Media and Communications at Goldsmiths College and was previously Reader in Media, Communications and Culture at the London School of Economics. He is the author or editor of six books, most recently *Listening Beyond the Echoes: Media, Ethics and Agency in an Uncertain World*.

**Peter Dahlgren** is Professor of Media and Communication at Lund University, Sweden. His research focuses on democracy, the evolution of the media, and contemporary socio-cultural processes. Most recently he has been looking at how young citizens make use of new communication technologies for democratic engagement and identity work. He has published on journalism, television, the public sphere and civic culture. His forthcoming book is *Media and Civic Engagement*.

**Todd Fraley** is an Assistant Professor in the School of Communication at East Carolina University. His research interests include popular culture, politics of representation, political economy, democratic communication, and alternative media. He co-edited *Media, Terrorism, and Theory* with Andy Kavoori.

**Lewis A. Friedland** is Professor of Journalism and Mass Communication and Sociology at the University of Wisconsin-Madison, where he directs the Center for Communication and Democracy and its Madison Commons Project. He has written on the theory of communicative action, the public sphere, civic innovation, community integration and network structure, and public and civic journalism. He is currently working on citizen journalism.

**Sofia Johansson** is a lecturer in Media Studies at Södertörn University College, Stockholm. Her PhD thesis examined tabloid newspaper reading. Her research interests cover print journalism, media audiences and popular culture. She has written a number of articles on popular journalism and is a board member of the journal *Westminster Papers in Communication and Culture*.

**Nakho Kim** is a PhD student in the School of Journalism and Mass Communication at University of Wisconsin-Madison. His MA thesis was on the history of the Internet and social movements in Korea, and he has worked on several projects on Korean civil society and media.

**Michael J. Kramer** is the J.N.G. Finley Postdoctoral Fellow in the Department of History and Art History at George Mason University, Virginia. He is currently working on a book, *The Civics of Rock: Musical Experience and Public Life in the Counterculture, 1965–1975*.

**Stephen Lax** is a Lecturer in Communications Technology at the Institute of Communications Studies, University of Leeds, UK. His research interests are in the social role of communications technologies. He is author of *Beyond the Horizon: Communications Technologies Past Present and Future* (1997) and editor of *Access Denied in the Information Age* (Palgrave, 2001).

**Sonia Livingstone** is Professor of Social Psychology in the Department of Media and Communications at the London School of Economics and Political Science. Her current work concerns domestic, familial and educational contexts of new media access, use and regulation. Recent books include *Audiences and Publics* (ed.) (2005) and *The Handbook of New Media* (ed.), Sage (2006).

**Christopher C. Long** is a PhD student in the School of Journalism and Mass Communication at University of Wisconsin-Madison where his research interest is the interaction between mass media, community, and civic engagement. As a journalist, he was New Media Director at C-SPAN and an editor and reporter for various news organizations, including Newsday and UPI.

**Peter Lunt** is Professor of Media and Communications at Brunel University UK. His research interests include consumption studies, audience research and social theory. His books include *Mass Consumption and Personal Identity* and *Talk on Television*, both with Sonia Livingstone. He is currently conducting a study of the new approach to the regulation of financial services and communications in the UK with Sonia Livingstone and writing about regulation and social theories of subjectivity.

**Tim Markham** is Lecturer in Media (Journalism) in the Faculty of Continuing Education, Birkbeck College, University of London. Previously he was

Research Officer in the Department of Media and Communications, London School of Economics. His research has examined war correspondence in relation to the sociology of journalism and the rise of the journalist as moral authority.

**Virginia Nightingale** is Associate Professor in the School of Communication Arts, University of Western Sydney, Australia. She is author of *Studying Audiences: The Shock of the Real* (1996), and co-author of *Media and Audiences: New Perspectives* (McGraw-Hill, 2003). She is currently investigating the relationships between affect, audience and disturbing imagery.

**Tobias Olsson** is a postdoctoral researcher at Lund University, where he works on the project 'Young Citizens, ICTs and Learning' (funded by the Swedish Knowledge Foundation's research programme Learn-IT). He is also a lecturer in Media and Communication Studies at Växjö University. He has published a number of journal articles, book chapters and reports, as well as made a number of presentations at international conferences.

**Henrik Örnebring** is Senior Lecturer of Television Studies at Roehampton University, London, UK. He has published several pieces on the history of television and the history of journalism, including journal articles in *European Journal of Communication and Journalism Studies*.

**Mervi Pantti** is Communications Research Fellow at the University of Amsterdam, where she is focusing on the mediatization of emotions. Recent publications include 'Talking Alone. Reality TV, Emotions and Authenticity', *European Journal of Cultural Studies* (2006); 'Do Crying Citizens Make Good Citizens?', *Social Semiotics* (2006); 'Masculine Tears, Feminine Tears – and Crocodile Tears', *Journalism: Theory, Practise and Criticism* (2006).

**Cornel Sandvoss** is Head of Media, Cultural and Communication Studies at the University of Surrey, UK and co-editor of *Popular Communication International Journal of Media and Culture*. His past publications include *A Game of Two Halves: Football, Television and Globalization* (2003) and *Fans: The Mirror of Consumption* (2005).

**J. Zach Schiller** is an Assistant Professor of Sociology at Kent State University, Stark. He has a co-authored piece on starting a community radio station in *Be the Media*, an encyclopedia of independent media (forthcoming). He is also the Moral Economy Project Coordinator at The Longview Institute, a progressive think-tank based in Berkeley, CA.

**Shawn Shimpach** is an Assistant Professor in the Department of Communication at the University of Massachusetts, Amherst. His work on cultural and institutional aspects of media and media audiences has appeared in such journals as *Social Semiotics* and *Cultural Studies*.

**Yong Jun Shin** is a PhD student in the School of Journalism and Mass Communication at University of Wisconsin-Madison. His MA thesis was on workplace community and information seeking.

**Tanjev Schultz** has a PhD from the University of Bremen. He is currently a science and education editor at *Süddeutsche Zeitung*. He is author of *Geschwätz oder Diskurs? Die Rationalität politischer Talkshows in Femsehen* as well as several articles on media and the public sphere.

**Hartmut Wessler** is Professor of Mass Communication at International University Bremen. He is author of *Offentlichkeit als Prozess*, co-author of *Transnationalization of Public Spheres*, and co-editor of four other books, as well as many articles on media and the public sphere. His work centers on political communication and internationally comparative media research.

**Yan Wu** recently completed her PhD thesis 'From Teahouses to Websites: Can Internet Bulletin Boards Construct the Public Sphere in China?', in the School of Journalism, Media and Cultural Studies, Cardiff University. Her research interests include new media and deliberation, citizen journalism, media and diasporic culture in the context of globalization. She co-edited *International Journalism and Media Studies*, published in Chinese in 2002.

# 1
# Introduction: How Are Media Public Spheres?

*Richard Butsch*

Through the twentieth century, in scholarship and in public debate there have been recurring worries about the impact of mass media upon civic practice. Instead of enabling a public sphere, as print had done in the late eighteenth century, some argue that the new mass media of the twentieth threatened to subvert the public sphere and democracy. Movies, radio and television became large and concentrated industries or government agencies that reached millions of people. They had great propaganda potential to truncate the range ideas in the public sphere and restrict debate.

The success of World War One print propaganda stirred debate among intellectuals. George Creel who had been in charge of US wartime propaganda, published a book boasting about how effective it was on Americans. While some 'realists' such as Walter Lippmann, argued that propaganda was necessary to channel the choices of the masses, many others, including John Dewey and many ordinary Americans, who were the target of the propaganda, were disturbed (Gary 1999, 3). These concerns grew in the 1930s as democracies succumbed to fascism in Europe. New theories of mass culture and mass society explained the vulnerability of modern democracies and the power of radio and film as tools for propaganda (Swingewood 1977, 10ff; Sproule, 1987; Lacey 1996). Central to such theory was the use of media for propaganda to bind the population to the fascist state.

Post-war political theorists continued this work, and began to question whether publics and even democracy could survive in the heightened mass media environment. By the 1950s, right, left and liberal critics all feared that mass mediated culture was overwhelming the common man's ability to play his part in democracy, although they differed on what that part was (Adorno *et al.*, 1950; Rosenberg and White, 1957; Jacobs, 1959; Kornblum, 1959; Giner 1976). Television bore the brunt of this criticism, but everything from comic books to kitsch took a beating from these critics. It was in this era that Jurgen Habermas began his habilitation thesis on publicity and public sphere and the part played by mass communication.

These concerns were supplanted by the upheavals of the civil rights protests in the US, then by Vietnam and the student movements in North America and Europe. The concerns resurfaced only in the 1990s, when there was increasing concern about the 'dumbing down' of public discourse, about the concentration of media ownership and the formation of international media conglomerates, and when that German thesis was translated into English.

Public sphere is, of course, the term used for *Offentlichkeit* in the English translation of Jurgen Habermas' *The Structural Transformation of the Public Sphere* (1989). Published three decades after the original, the translation spawned a voluminous literature in English on this subject. Habermas' theory of the bourgeois public sphere is part of the tradition of Enlightenment liberal political philosophy. It addresses questions about what makes democracy work. Its primary focus is the origins of a bourgeois public sphere in eighteenth century social institutions and political philosophy, from which Habermas draws a normative model of the public sphere. Recent scholarship responding to Habermas is similarly rooted in the scholarly discourse on political theory and political philosophy, leavened with history.

There is a second tradition, of publics, rooted in social rather than political concepts and theory, framed in terms of different issues and questions, but also placing mass media at the center of the idea of publics. Unlike the liberal tradition of public sphere that focuses on deliberation, this tradition considers what actions follow from deliberation. This approach originated with French theorist, Gabriel Tarde, who contrasted publics to crowds in late nineteenth century theory of crowd psychology (Tarde, 1969). About the same time as Tarde wrote, American sociologist Robert Park completed a German dissertation on the same subject, contrasting crowd and public (Park 1972). Tarde and Park wrote at a time when the principle mass medium was the daily metropolitan newspaper, and both considered it central to the functioning of a public. Returning to the US, Park founded the sociological field of collective behavior that included the study of crowds, publics and other collective gatherings. Crowds were masses in action, and the tradition would turn increasingly to talk about masses – and mass media audiences – in contrast to publics, with the advent of radio (Cantril, 1935, 1940). The linking of publics to crowds emphasized a social rather than political approach, contrasting a constructive role in society for publics to the supposed destructive role of crowds. Related to this tradition is the American debate about publics between Walter Lippmann and John Dewey in the 1920s (Gary, 1999). Lippmann considered the mass incapable of performing its role as a 'true' public and in need of guidance through propaganda, i.e. mass media messages, by an educated elite (Lippmann, 1925). Dewey, on the other hand, conceived publics as the natural emergence of community efforts to solve shared problems, with solutions then institutionalized in government (Dewey 1927, 112–13, 149).

Both traditions of the concepts of publics and public sphere include media as a necessary element for public deliberation. But the media presumed in those traditions were subsidiary to the public sphere. By contrast, given the growth in media variety, size and convergence in the late twentieth century, media have become the primary focus and force for today's public sphere. We now find ourselves in a time of intense debate: What media provide what kind of public spheres? Scholars still disagree about the impact of existing media institutions on the public sphere, as well as about the ideal structure of the public sphere. The recent work on public sphere has generated numerous criticisms and multiple versions of the concepts of public and public sphere. Issues of the media and public sphere revolve around the central axis of whether media enable or undermine a healthy public sphere with widespread participation. Debates about the good or bad impact of media institutions parallel past splits between political economic and cultural studies approaches to media institutions and culture (Clarke, 1990), and between mass culture critics and those who downplayed the effects of media. But what role media play and how effectively they do is still the subject of much discussion and few answers. The debates have produced fewer answers and no consensus on what is a public sphere, or whether or in what form it exists. It has generated relative less empirical investigation into actually existing public spheres.

It is the purpose of this book to explore these questions empirically. These collected chapters present case studies, surveys and interviews, as well as reviews of previous research on media ranging from newspapers to the internet, to ask what kind of public spheres do these media sustain. In the process, the studies suggest a range of inductive definitions of public sphere. The hope is that these inductive definitions will open up further questions and examinations about the nature and the possibility of public spheres in our mediated world.

A systematic examination of the concepts and literature concerning media and the public sphere would require a lengthy book. There are several schema of criticism available in recent literature (Calhoun, 1992; Dahlgren, 1995; Weintraub and Kumar,1997; Curran, 2000; Hill and Montag, 2000; Crossley and Roberts, 2004; Livingstone 2005; McKee, 2005). Therefore to introduce these chapters, I will confine myself to two works, one on public sphere, the other on media, in order to set the stage for the relevant issues raised in them. But first, I will review Habermas' concept of public sphere.

## Habermas: liberal political theory and the public sphere

The Western idea of citizens participating in their governance through public discussion originates in ancient Greece and Rome (Weintraub, 1997). Its modern revival was incorporated in liberal political theory of the eighteenth century that addressed the relations between the state and its citizens in a democracy. Jurgen Habermas' *Structural Transformation of the Public Sphere* (1991), in this tradition, is an historical exploration of the development in seventeenth and eighteenth century Europe of public institutional space between the state and the private world of the family. As Habermas interpreted the history, mercantile capitalism required a public space where information could be freely exchanged. This would become, according to Habermas, the bourgeois public sphere, where not only information about business, but about culture and politics might also be freely discussed (1991, 14–26). From this historical analysis, Habermas extracts the characteristics of the public sphere that work to advance a democratic state. Within evolving bourgeois public sphere institutions, such as the coffee house, salon and the press, he finds conversation among equals whose private interests and inequality are temporarily suspended, which in turn allows for rational discussion and debate on questions of state policy and action.

Habermas then assesses modern mass media as a public sphere environment. In this he seems to shift to the social theory tradition of publics, reflecting the mass culture critique of his Frankfurt School mentors, Max Horkheimer and Theodore Adorno, a critique of twentieth century mass-produced and mediated culture as ideological domination rather than as public sphere (Jay, 1973). The large scale media of monopoly capitalism transforms what had been a political public sphere into a medium for commodity consumption. Bread and circuses replaces the forum. A healthy public sphere requires small scale media not motivated by commercial interests (Habermas 181–88).

Commercialization is the result of economic self-interest taking precedent over the collective interest. As media require greater capital investment and as larger and more economically powerful and oligopolistic organizations supplant smaller competitive organizations, power supplants equality and reason as the identifying characteristics of this new mediated public sphere that becomes representational rather than political. Consequently, Habermas refers to the re-feudalization of the public sphere, returning to its function as a place for public display rather than public discourse and debate.

## Criticism of Habermas: Bourgeois vs alternative public spheres

The characteristics of the public sphere have been the subject of debate and controversy: there is no equality; reason is not the necessary foundation; twentieth-century mass media have not destroyed the public sphere. The principle criticism of Habermas has been focused on his historical public sphere (before modern mass media) and this bourgeois public sphere's exclusivity (Negt and Kluge, 1972; Calhoun, 1992). Such critics introduced the ideas of alternative and multiple public spheres.

One of the most influential criticisms after the publication of the *Structural Transformation* in English, was by philosopher Nancy Fraser who noted the absence of subordinate groups, including women and lower classes in these bourgeois public sphere institutions (Fraser in Calhoun, 1992). Fraser disputes four assumptions of Habermas which she identifies: that it is possible 'to bracket status differentials and to deliberate as if they were social equals';

that a single public sphere is preferable to multiple spheres ; that private interests must be excluded from the public sphere; and that the public sphere must be clearly separated from the state (117–18). Fraser's contention is that the public sphere did not exist, in the form Habermas claims, in the eighteenth century any more than in the twentieth.

Fraser's response to these assumptions is, first, that bracketing does not work, inequalities continue to operate through cultural hierarchies of everyday habits, for example as described by Bourdieu (1984). Rational deliberation and debate are bourgeois individualistic social practices; other classes are less at home in these practices, putting them at a disadvantage in such situation. In effect, a formal presumption that inequality is bracketed merely masks the actual operation of inequality within the public sphere and gives the impression of universality where it does not exist.

Second, given the weakness of the bracketing assumption, Fraser argues that in a stratified society, 'arrangements that accommodate contestation among a plurality of competing publics . . . come closest to the ideal' (122) In this context, Fraser introduces the concepts of alternative publics and 'subaltern counterpublics' (123, 125). The terms evoke Raymond Williams' concepts of alternative and oppositional cultures that were woven into cultural studies in the conception of resistance to cultural hegemony (Williams, 1977; Hall and Jefferson, 1976). What does it mean for spheres to be alternative? Like Williams' alternative cultures, it implicitly defines each sphere as an identity-based, homogeneous group, rather than a diverse deliberative body (Warner, 2002). Identity (and contestation) also utilize emotion. These all diverge from Habermas' normative rational public sphere.

The idea of multiple spheres raises the issue of the relation among them. Sociologist Graham Murdoch and historian Geoff Eley independently formulate an ideal in which these alternatives are 'staging areas' where different interests prepare their case/voice for presentation in an overarching public sphere (Murdoch in Skovmand and Schroder, 1992; Eley in Calhoun 1992).

Pertaining to the relationship, Fraser disagrees with Habermas' third assumption that deliberation in a public sphere is to seek and advance the common good. Fraser contends that in a stratified society there is limited shared interest and common good. Stratified societies are zero sum societies in which what is good for one group is bad for another. The purpose of deliberation is futile (129, 131).

Consequently, Fraser accepts the idea of competition of interests among publics. In defining their relation to each other as 'contestation' Fraser reintroduces power as a factor. Fraser abandons the method of deliberation that Habermas considered essential and adopts Eley's and Murdoch's proposal of an overarching 'structured setting' in which differences between unequal publics are resolved through contest or other means, but not necessarily deliberation.

As soon as we accept contestation, power and interests as legitimate in the public sphere, collective actions intended to register opinion with the state, in addition to deliberation, fall into the purview of the public sphere. Suggesting this, Eley makes a stronger assertion, that the relation between publics 'was always constituted by conflict' (Eley in Calhoun, 1992, 306). More recently, Hill and Montag criticize Habermas for opposing reason to force and speech to action (2000, 6). Like Fraser, Murdoch and Eley, they argue for an expanded conception of public sphere, inclusive of force and action as well as reason and speech.

This redefinition opens entirely new vistas for the concept of public sphere, to collective actions based upon solidarity more than individualism, including social movements, union actions, and civil disobedience. The scholarly literature on crowds and social movements then becomes a resource for exploring these enlarged definitions of publics and public sphere. At the very least, such proposals introduce whole new possible forms of public sphere, beyond reasoned deliberation. It also opens it to emotion in public discourse, a motivator to participation and a concomitant of group solidarity and contestation, and to a reconsideration of the very dichotomy of reason versus emotion.

Eley fits his conception of the public sphere to Gramsci's concept of hegemony. Hegemony, according to Gramsci, was achieve not through overt ideas and propaganda, but through the 'whole lived experience' (Williams 1977), thus through persuasion rather than suppression, and it is never complete but always challenged and in process. It is in Eley's public sphere that the lived experience, both persuasion and contestation occur. But balancing Eley's emphasis on the contested nature of hegemony is Williams' idea of incorporation. In that respect, inclusiveness, when not resolving the inequalities Fraser addressed concerning the first assumption, can simply be a veiled form of incorporation. Again the extension of the concept of public sphere raises additional issues for rethinking the public sphere.

Fourth and last, Fraser rejects the idea that public spheres should be free from the state, characterizing it as a *laissez-faire* policy and arguing that, to the contrary, some form of state regulation is necessary to avoid one interest consistently prevailing over others and short-circuiting democracy (133). In the eighteenth century, the center of power was the state, compared to which private organizations (businesses) were small. The need for separation was a need to insulate the public sphere from state control. Today, two centers of power stand on either side of the public sphere, the state and corporations. Either can threaten the public sphere. State owned and operated media run the risk of reducing it to a representative public sphere serving the state rather than the people. Alternatively, corporate-owned media run the risk of serving the interest of private corporations over the people. Both distancing the state from public media and regulating private media then become important to the continued health of the public sphere. This raises concerns about the relations among the state, private economy and the public sphere that are more complicated than simply a hands-off policy (Curran 2000).

## Twentieth century mediated public spheres

Having discussed versions of the concepts of public and publics sphere before the rise of pervasive mass media, we now come to the core issue of the book, the significance of mediation. Traditional liberal political theory claims three positive functions for media in a democracy: to act as watchdog over the state as an independent fourth estate; to act as an agency of information and debate for citizens to participate in their democracy; and to act as the voice of the people to the state (Curran in Curran and Gurevitch, 2000, 121, 127,129). In such theory, media are cast as allies of citizens in their role of supervising democratic government through public opinion.

The theory is rooted in an eighteenth century reality in which communication media (the printing press, handwritten notes and the human body) were accessible to many citizens. Hand-operated printing presses were relatively inexpensive and not greatly different in influence than the voices of other citizens (Lee 1937, 167). Likewise, the eighteenth century public sphere encompassed a rather small, exclusive and intimate population engaged in face-to-face interaction and handwritten letters (Darnton, 2000). Today, large populations make media necessary to the public sphere. Media also are different, owned by corporate conglomerates, and pervasive in our everyday lives, available or intruding wherever we may go.

These changed conditions raise entirely different issues: how can media serve the public sphere when also powerfully pulled to serve the state or profit. Perhaps more fundamental today than issues of rational deliberation or inclusion, is this question of how to position and control the means of communication *for* the public sphere. How do we contend with corporate mass media's potential to dominate the public sphere with its own voice or that of the state, drowning out all others. Alternately, how do we utilize new media technologies and niches such as the internet, low power radio, or public access cable tv, to create alternative mediated public spheres.

To understand today's mediated public sphere, Peter Dahlgren (1995) suggests examining four dimensions: media institutions, media representation, general social structure, and face-to-face interaction. With the advent of broadcasting, states took responsibility for establishing media institutions to serve the public sphere. European governments established semi-independent public media, funded by or through the state. Government funding or control, of course, creates the possibility of media used for propaganda and paternalism rather than public service. In the US, commercial media were regulated by the state. Since the 1980s, ideological forces advocating the market over public service, and new technologies, particularly transnational satellite broadcasting, have led to considerable growth of commercial media that is large and wealthy enough to compete with public media. Deregulation has accelerated this by promoting global economic concentration of media corporations (Curran 2000, 121–2).

Commercial media present different problems for a public sphere. Their first master is the drive for profit, which conceives media in relationship to consumers in a market rather than to citizens in a public sphere. It provides what sells rather than what informs and enables public discussion, often two different and competing types of programming, squeezing out the public sphere.

This problem is exacerbated by the growth in size and power of mass media, constituting a formidable political force in a public sphere. Today's giant media corporations now present similar dangers as the state in controlling the public sphere for their own interests. The sheer scale of modern media corporations overwhelms the relatively minute institutions of the public sphere, as a skyscraper enshadows a small public park.

Consequently, the issue today is less whether subordinate groups of citizens have a voice in the public sphere, and more whether any but a very few citizens have a voice and whether the public sphere is simply 're-feudalized', as Habermas characterized it, into a representative public sphere, because the fundamental institution of the public sphere, media, has been captured by the state and/or commercial corporations.

The potential of such domination is to reshape media representation, Dahlgren's second dimension, in two senses of the term. As the principal source of information for citizens, law and regulation of media have focused on ensuring a wide range of opinions to be expressed in the public sphere. Both the principle of a free press and limitations on private media ownership have had this purpose. Also, the balance between media presentation of entertainment or information is important for reducing the quality of information and the value given to civic participation. Critics equate entertainment with appeals to pleasure and emotion, and contrast it to information equated with rational deliberation.

As media grow in scale and centrality in the public sphere, the degree to which media representation displaces active participation of citizens in the public sphere becomes an issue. Representatives, such as journalists, political figures, academic experts and even ordinary citizens, stand in for citizens to speak and debate in the media, with citizens reduced to passive audience observers. Media simply provide information and surrogate debate, which citizens then use as *individuals* to vote. Does this eliminate the interactive and collective dimensions of the public sphere, reducing public opinion to polling statistics and vote counts?

Dahlgren's third dimension, social structure, concerns the scale and structure of the public sphere and its congruence with political and other institutions. This addresses several of the concerns mentioned above: the idea of multiple public spheres and their relation, such as the relation between alternative media and the dominant media outlets. It also addresses the newer matter of media globalization.

Dahlgren's fourth dimension concerns face-to-face interaction, or assembly. The questions above about media representation creating a passive subject position, become more important as media audiences are dispersed and as places for public assembly and discourse, such as Parisian cafés or English coffee houses, disappear from the social landscape. These institutions of communal sociability are the basis for the social tradition of the concept of public in Tarde (1969) and Park (1972). It is the concern about the decline in public assembly that concerned mass society theorists and recently Robert Putnam's *Bowling Alone* (2001).

We might think of Dahlgren's dimensions as stages in the process of the public sphere. Media are the institutional infra-structure for modern public sphere, they produce media representations, the information and models of deliberation necessary to a public sphere. Finally, public places enable citizens to assemble and engage in discussion about public issues. It is collective citizen participation that is the realization of the public sphere and of democracy. To assess the efficacy of any public sphere, we need to know how much do people do this and who is included. The other dimensions are means to this end. We need to know how well they enable the latter.

Dahlgren frames these four dimensions in terms of civic culture, a set of values, public trust, identity, knowledge and practices that form the cultural substratum for this citizen participation (see Chapter 16 in this volume). The four dimensions can sustain or undermine this culture, which in turn sustains adherence to the rules of an egalitarian deliberative public sphere that itself feeds back upon the culture and the four dimensions.

## The chapters and their issues

The overall impression of the chapters in this book confirms the criticisms that few public spheres meet the standards of Habermas. But there are many public spheres of varying sorts and qualities. If we relax the criteria of reasoned deliberation among equals for a common good, and we accept the presence of multiple public spheres, then we find public spheres of all sorts in many places, included, abetted or unrestrained by today's pervading media. We have tended to ask whether there is or is not a public sphere; but perhaps we should instead acknowledge, through a broader definition, the existence of an on-going institutional public sphere, but one which varies in attributes, so that it's what we do with that space that we need to understand and evaluate. What these chapters offer is a nuanced understanding of a variety of actual, existing public spheres, the varying degrees to which they work effectively, and the dilemmas and difficulties that people encounter as they participate in these public spheres.

The question then becomes, are these public spheres enough to make a difference? Readers will disagree, some seeing the glass half empty, others half full. That is not a satisfying and conclusive answer, but it is closer to the messiness of the real world. This may reflect what Sonia Livingstone says, that media audiences,

> sustain a modest and often ambivalent level of critical interpretation, drawing upon – and thereby reproducing – a somewhat ill-specified, at times, inchoate or even contradictory sense of identity or belonging which motivates them toward but does not enable the kind of collective and direct action expected of a public (Livingstone, 2005, 31).

Livingstone proposes an intermediate concept of civic culture, such as Dahlgren's formulation, between audiences and publics (32). How much then does participation in mediated popular culture constitute sufficient political significance to qualify as a public? And how much is it too 'watered down' to be of significance politically?

The chapters are roughly arranged in a sequence that begins with examinations of cross-media issues, such as the criterion of rational deliberation, people's experience of the mediated public sphere generally, the intersection of media and community as foundations of public sphere, and proceeds to studies of specific media, from the press to movies, radio, recorded music, television and the internet. The general issues reappear in various combinations in these media specific studies.

We begin with an examination of Habermas' criterion of rational deliberation. Hartmut Wessler and Tanjev Schultz examine news media as a model representing deliberative debate to the public. Critics have argued that news, especially broadcast news, in recent years has been degraded by commercialism into emotion-based entertainment. After laying out an argument for the importance of deliberation, Wessler and Schultz review research on German newspapers and television news talk shows to assess its presence today. They conclude that in these news genre, journalists, academic experts and public intellectuals continue to practice deliberation in the spirit of a model public sphere.

But does such a model rub off on the audience? Nick Couldry, Sonia Livingstone and Tim Markham ask another baseline question: How much do people attend to deliberative media and engage in rational deliberation about public issues? Ultimately this is the outcome we wish to know about: do citizens participate in the public sphere, however well or poorly it is institutionalized? To explore this question, they interviewed Britons of differing classes. Most people attend to media presentation of public issues and talk about them with others, but they do so using different media and genres. Contrary to stereotypes, the less educated are engaged with public issues and discuss what they read. Even working class women who express reservations about their understanding of public issues still have something to say. They mention the barriers of literacy and self-confidence that make them reluctant to read or to talk about public issues, and read tabloids to reduce these barriers and present the option of an alternative public sphere.

Lewis Friedland and Christopher Long, with Yong Jun Shin and Kim Nakho look at the intersection of the institutions of media and the public sphere in a local community, using John Dewey's concept of the public based in the American social tradition. Dewey understood publics not in terms of discourse among strangers, but as based upon social networks rooted in physical communities, including informal groups, voluntary associations, businesses and other organizations. This allows them to develop an understanding of publics as a form of action rather than as a form of discourse or identity. In effect they continue beyond where Habermas leaves off with the concept of publics as discourse, by tracing them into the sphere of action. In their case study, two opposed publics contest local school referenda, with traditional media allied with one, and the internet effectively used by the other.

Cornel Sandvoss takes an ethnographic approach to assess ordinary peoples' engagement in the public sphere, by extending the public sphere into seemingly un-political discourse of the everyday, as suggested by Couldry, Livingstone and Markham. He interviews football (soccer) fans and observes their on-line discussions, finding politics embedded in sport discourse. While media have taught us to expect fierce team loyalties and even 'hooliganism', Sandvoss also hears them debate the nationalism and localism implied by team loyalty, as well as issues of race, class and gender. A search for a pure political public sphere would miss much of what is political in everyday conversation and thus may qualify in some senses as a public sphere.

Henrik Ornebring addresses the institutionalization of a particular kind of media representation incompatible with a deliberative public sphere, the news. Habermas argued that commercialization of the newspaper in the nineteenth century undermined the public sphere by turning the press from a political institution into a business, and replacing information with entertainment. Ornebring goes beyond this analysis, presenting a complex argument that the form of news itself as a narrative of facts, and the practices of journalism to create informed citizens, are actually inimicable to a deliberative public sphere. Critiques of commercialism that contrast rational informative media to sensational entertainment media miss this deeper problem.

Fact based news is considered raw material to rational deliberation and is contrasted to sensational entertainment media. Sofia Johansson interviewed readers of British tabloid newspapers, to test the widespread assumption that these sensationalist newspapers undercut the public sphere. She asked if tabloids work as an alternative public sphere for subordinate groups, speaking to them in a language of their own. Her interviews reveal that readers accepted the predominant criticism of tabloids and claimed limited interest in public affairs news. Nevertheless, they did express a desire to know what's going on and considered the papers accessible, stimulating talk about news in the everyday. Moreover, the newspapers fostered a sense of common identity among fellow readers and with their preferred newspaper, a basis for an alternative public sphere.

Shawn Shimpach explores how representations of the audience shaped the public sphere of the movie theater. Building on Warner's identity based public sphere, Shimpach examines how Progressive descriptions of nickelodeon audiences effectively represented the audience to itself. In combination with the rise of narrative film and reforms of theaters, this transformed the vocal nickelodeon counter public audience into a disciplined public sphere defined by middle class decorum. Shimpach's approach raises questions about the cultural construction of the public sphere, about the relation between reform, cultural uplift and public sphere, and about the multiple meanings of media and representation in the public sphere.

Michael Kramer looks back at the inspiration for the term counterpublic, the counterculture of the late 1960s and whether it constituted a public mediated by rock music. Focusing on a particular rock tour of 1970, Kramer uses quotes of people of the time to examine the contradiction in that era's rock music culture as both a commercial enterprise and an expression of the countercultural public. In this peculiar combination the counterculture also blended cultural and political publics. Blending Habermas' and Dewey's concepts, Kramer frames this public as one based in a strong sense of community that was characteristic of the era, and uses it to explore the problems of a public in a mass culture.

Michael Bailey examines the history of the early BBC. Publicly funded media have been justified on the ground that they are a public good, too important to leave to the vagaries of the market. But what if, instead of the media providing a public sphere, they operate as technologies of governmentality, to use Foucault's term? Bailey argues that, rather than creating an inclusive public sphere to allow a diversity of voices, BBC adopted a cultural uplift policy to educate the public and to counter the supposed degenerative effects of mass culture. Bailey explores the recurring tensions between two camps with more or less faith in the masses' capability for public sphere participation, the pessimist advocating media as an educator and guide, optimists seeing media as enabling their participation in the public sphere.

Stephen Lax explains the implications of new digital radio technology and policy in the UK. Smaller local stations, more community oriented and thus more suited to a public sphere are being displaced by larger 'quasi-national' stations. The expansion of the number of stations made possible by digital technology has not resulted in greater diversity of 'voices', but rather the concentration of radio station ownership in the hands of a few large broadcast organizations that deliver national programming with little local content, a refeudalization resulting in a diminution of the public sphere. Lax argues that a combination of market forces and government policy favorable to commercial broadcasting and deregulation have undercut the possible benefits of digital radio for the public sphere. The study indicates the importance of insulating the public sphere from both commercial and government distortion.

J. Zach Schiller studied a low power US radio station as an alternative public sphere. This gives us a glimpse of a mediated public sphere beyond the concentrated media that Habermas and others see as the downfall of the public sphere, one closer to the localized printing presses of the eighteenth century. Providing richer insights, debates about policy and programming between two factions within the radio station, consciousness-raisers and inclusivists, reveal many complications. Within this alternative public sphere are all the issues of the Habermasian public sphere: inequality, exclusion, who controls the medium and for whose interest. The case also explores implications of an alternative public sphere that is homogenous and based on identity compared to one that is diverse and focused on political deliberation; these options also parallel the definition of the station as part of a public sphere or a social movement, raising questions about the relation between these two phenomena.

Peter Lunt and Mervi Pantti address the question whether emotion-based popular culture can be a public sphere, through their study of sensationalist television talk shows and reality TV shows. Their analysis explores dichotomies implicated in this question, between reason and emotion, deliberation and identity, inclusion and exclusion, free expression and script, spectacle and rationalization, entertainment and civic duty. For example, these shows are exceptional in their inclusion of ordinary people in the mass mediated public sphere. In addition, their study raises other interesting questions: is it the voices of these people or that of the producer and the network that come through in this dialog? Is it a counter-public or a corporate representational public sphere.

Virginia Nightingale examines the implications for the public sphere of the transformation of television from a stand-alone medium to its convergence with several new digital video media, including internet and mobile phones. Broadcast television through its concentration and national audiences created public spheres through imagined communities. It was funded or regulated as a public good to serve this national community. Convergence of media such as tv, internet and mobile phone, has resulted in strategies to develop new markets and new audiences. Two recent marketing strategies, enhanced tv and branded tv have replaced free tv with pay tv and produced 'brand-based affiliations', positioning viewers even more as consumers and less as citizens than broadcast television had.

Todd Fraley documents an example of a counter public medium compatible with Fraser's and Eley's ideas of contesting counter public spheres. Fraley describes the goals, policy and programming of an American satellite and public access cable television network, Free Speech TV, that provides an alternative mediated public sphere to progressive groups and social movements. This case study demonstrates the implications of redrawing conceptual boundaries so that contestation and social movements are included as part of the public sphere, and raises the question of where such practices lay what is their relation to the public sphere if excluded from the concept. Finally, the study raises the question of the relationship of this counter media to

mainstream media and to the larger population. Is it isolated, is this counterpublic still marginalized even with its own media outlet, or somehow
integrated into the overarching public sphere?

Peter Dalgren and Tobias Olsson's study of Swedish internet use explores
what Dahlgren has called civic culture, the values, trust, affiliative feeling and
identity as a citizen that motivate, and the knowledge and practices that enable
people to participate in a public sphere. Most particularly, they examine the
role of internet institutions in sustaining this civic culture as well as constituting a public sphere. They interviewed young Swedish activists who use the
internet as a resource to build and sustain the elements of civic culture. From
the internet, these activists gain knowledge of their society and the activities
of their allies and opponents. They engage in public sphere practices of discussion and debate, and coordinate their activities. The youth choose the
internet as their public sphere medium because they distrust the traditional
mass media as biased. By contrast, they trust their peers with whom they
interact and other sources of information on the internet.

There has been much theory about the internet's promise, based upon its
technological capabilities, particularly its open access, making an egalitarian
and inclusive public sphere a reality, and moreover one that extends beyond
national borders. Yan Wu examines the consequences of this in rapidly changing China. Here the traditional media are tightly controlled and function as
a representational rather than deliberative public sphere. Wu examines how
Chinese inside China and among the diaspora use Chinese internet bulletin
boards as a public sphere to discuss political issues within China, countering
government control of other media.

# 2
# Can the Mass Media Deliberate?: Insights from Print Media and Political Talk Shows

*Hartmut Wessler and Tanjev Schultz*

One of the most important values of a democratic public sphere lies in its capacity to facilitate public deliberation. Public deliberation, broadly speaking, transforms social and political conflicts into argumentative debates in which claims are not just made but can be problematized and discussed. Such debates are public to the extent that they are openly accessible to citizens. Public deliberation, then, is an open, collective process of argumentative exchange about issues of societal relevance. In modern societies such a process will necessarily rely mostly on the mass media (see Page 1996).

There remain a number of theoretical and empirical questions that revolve around the notion of public deliberation. It is embedded in normative theories of both democratic politics and media performance. What kind of normative claims should we make with respect to 'good' public deliberation? What kind of gains can we reasonably expect from public deliberation? And which conditions are conducive to the flourishing of public deliberation? These are the kinds of questions we wish to address in this chapter.

In the first part we propose a model of public deliberation that evaluates and revises normative claims made in the literature. The normative standards we formulate turn out to be lower and sometimes also of a different nature than the ones associated with an ideal speech situation as defined by Jürgen Habermas (1984). This is because we take into account the basic structural characteristics of mass-mediated communication in modern democracies. In the second and third part we probe this revised normative model in two real-world contexts by reviewing studies about public discourse in the print media and about deliberative characteristics of political talk shows.

## Public deliberation: what it means, why it is important

Public deliberation can be distinguished from non-public or less public forms of deliberation as well as from non-deliberative forms of public communication. Structurally, the public sphere consists of many ranging from small encounters through public meetings and events up to the mass media

(Gerhards & Neidhardt 1991). The mass media have become the most important forum for truly *public* deliberation in modern societies. Media genres that contain public deliberation to varying degrees include news and commentary, talk shows, discussion programs and interviews. In this section we offer what we consider to be reasonable normative expectations rather than maximum demands. We proceed from considering the input of mediated public deliberation, to reflecting on its internal workings (throughput) and finally to its desired output.

## Open access for issues and ideas: the input dimension

Mediated public deliberation is essentially delegated deliberation (Page 1996). Everybody can observe it (in principle) but very few speakers can participate. But who, then, should participate? Following Peters (2001; 2002) we contend that neither a simple standard of equal participation by everybody nor a standard of representative participation of certain groups or camps is appropriate.

For one, the sheer number of possible participants makes it unfeasible that all those who want to say something can get an equal share of attention. And it contradicts two other important standards of public deliberation, namely competence and innovation. Even if it were possible for everybody to speak equally, some utterances are based on deeper knowledge and better understanding of the subject matter or they offer new perspectives (see Schultz 2006).

Proportional representation in public discourse (see, for example, Gerhards 1997) does not seem to be a plausible standard either because it is unclear on what grounds these groups would be chosen (and by whom), and how their respective share of attention should be defined (see Page 1996: 123). Positions and perspectives are not always fixed a priori but are developed in public discourses so that a fixed set of representative actors would endanger the innovative function of deliberation. For mediated public deliberation, a standard of 'openness or equal opportunity for topics, perspectives, interpretations, ideas and arguments' is more appropriate (Peters 2002: 14) because it would ensure that new ideas and ideas held by minorities get a chance of being heard.

But how can such a standard of openness be effected? In free democratic discourse there seems to be no other way than to leave it to public discourse itself to criticize instances of exclusion of relevant issues and ideas. '[T]he identification of partisan selectivities in public discourse, ignoring or stigmatizing certain positions and arguments, would not appear to be unsolvable – corresponding criticisms are indeed always a constituent part of public discourse' (Peters 2002: 14). In addition, comparisons of public discourses on the same topic in different countries may yield insights into the relative selectivity of national public spheres (see Ferree *et al.* 2002).

## Justification and civility: the throughput dimension

What should happen to positions and opinions once they have found their way into the public sphere? How should they be presented and how should they relate or be related to each other? It is this throughput dimension on which the desired deliberative nature of public discourse is most clearly articulated by normative theories of deliberation. The basic idea here is that claims are not just made but can be problematized and discussed. This can be achieved by giving good reasons for one's own claims and demanding reasons from others (justification), and by weighing arguments in a climate of mutual respect and civility. Deliberative communication aims at persuading addressees with convincing arguments.

In many accounts this notion of argumentative exchange is derived from or associated with the more demanding model of communicative action oriented toward understanding rather than success (see Habermas 1984). It is plausible to assume that an orientation toward understanding on the part of discourse participants will enhance their willingness to learn and, if need be, to be persuaded by the arguments of their opponents. This willingness in turn will increase the sophistication of their own justifications and thereby the rationality of the discourse. But what if participants are not oriented toward understanding and, for example, simply want to maximize the number of their followers? After all, it must be remembered that deliberation in the mass media is not directed at the mutual persuasion of the deliberators. Rather it has a trialogical structure (Jorgensen 1998): The deliberators discuss with each other in order to persuade the audience. So strategic intentions will always play a role, too. Does this mean that mediated public deliberation misses the core criterion of deliberativeness?

We do not think so. The substance of justifications advanced in public discourse (with whatever intention) deserves to be taken seriously precisely because audiences observe such discourse rather than engage in it. An argument advanced with strategic intentions may be just as cogent and valuable and persuasive to members of the audience as one advanced with the intention to foster understanding (Schultz 2006). We concur here with Jorgensen (1998) who, revising Walton's (1989) typology of argumentative exchange, has argued that debates held in front of an audience, if they adhere to their own normative standards, may be just as enlightening as dialogical discussion. And civility is precisely one of those standards. Uncivil debates degenerate into quarrels. But if deliberators refrain from personal attacks and inflammatory speech debates can constitute valuable instances of public deliberation even without the honest intention to learn.

Authors such as Young (2003) and Dahlgren (2002) have criticized the deliberative tradition for being too rationalist and excluding those actors and groups that engage in emotional protest and accusation or in public testimony concerning their grievances and demands. Such legitimate forms of public utterance can indeed clash with the standard of civility in deliberation. However, this seeming contradiction can be resolved by distinguishing between different process types or functions in public communication.

One function lies in the discovery of issues and problems, the building of the media agenda. Social movement research shows that it is this function that civil society groups or organizations fulfill best (see, for example, Gitlin 1980; Wolfsfeld 1984; Friedrichs 1994). In this stage attention-gaining techniques are legitimately used that may not adhere to the civility standard. Outrage, protest, scandalization can be vital in order to fulfill the input criterion we have defined, i.e. to ensure that particular problems and concerns are not completely forgotten or marginalized. But agenda-building is not everything.

Once a problem has reached the public agenda, claims-making activities ensue that advocate opposing positions (see Gerhards 1993; Tarrow 1994). It is here that conflict is transformed into debate. Debate is essential in order to problematize claims, even those of oppressed groups, as well as their foundations and justifications. And in this context of contention and justification the deliberative qualities of debate hold the promise of particular epistemic and social gains. By focusing on justification and the weighing of arguments public deliberation promises to foster deeper understanding as well as stronger recognition of and respect for the legitimate interests of opponents. Therefore, we contend that agenda-building and public deliberation are two separate and legitimate components of public communication. Both processes should be allowed to follow their own rules and the justification, civility and respect standards applied to public deliberation in the throughput dimension should not be invalidated by hinting to the more impassioned practices of attention-gaining. The real exchange of arguments is too valuable to let it drown in clamor.

### Innovation and reasoned dissent: the output dimension

What kind of outcome can be expected from processes of mediated deliberation? Should we expect that public deliberation leads to consensus or at least a higher level of agreement on the issues discussed? This may well be a reasonable expectation in dialogic and smaller settings where deliberators are faced with higher pressures of mutual accommodation, for example in order to arrive at a common decision. But for large-scale public deliberation in the media the triadic and competitive structure makes consensus unlikely. In such a setting deliberators try to convince the audience, in most cases not even the entire audience but those segments that belong to their own camp and maybe a few undecided groups. (see Peters *et al.* 2005: 155).

If this description is correct, is there room for a normative perspective on the outcomes of public discourse? We believe there is because it makes a difference whether dissent is enlightened or not. Public deliberation may be able to clarify the grounds on which disagreement builds up as well as discredit a few arguments generally deemed unacceptable. In this sense the desired outcome of public deliberation would be reasoned dissent rather than a consensual solution (but see Ferree *et al.* 2002, 221 and 229).

While reasoned dissent seems achievable in the short to medium run, the long-term gains to be expected from public deliberation should be conceptualized 'more as a *shift* of the opinion spectrum, rather than as a *contraction* of this spectrum' (Peters *et al.* 2005: 156). The long-term sedimentation of generally acceptable public knowledge may lead to societal learning processes as a desired effect of deliberation. But the judgment about whether a certain shift in conviction constitutes learning in an emphatic sense must itself be demonstrated argumentatively. It cannot be shown by applying methods of media content analysis alone. Therefore, we leave the question of long-term learning processes aside in the following and concentrate on some elements of public deliberation that can be studied in content-analytic research.

To conclude, public deliberation in the mass media appears to be a competitive process of argumentation whose democratic qualities rest on three normative pillars: (a) equal opportunity for access of issues, ideas and arguments; (b) reason-giving and weighing of arguments in a climate of mutual respect and civility; and (c) innovation and the achievement of reasoned dissent in the short and medium term. Empirical studies using these criteria are few. But the existing results attest to the fact that the mass media indeed partly conform to these norms and that instances of public deliberation in the desired sense do exist.

## Public deliberation in the print media

### Forms and formats of deliberation

In newspapers, news magazines and journals of opinion, deliberation surfaces in at least three forms: Argumentations of various social actors are reported or quoted in news articles and news analysis; they are presented in interviews with question-and-answer sequences; and they are contained in opinion pieces such as commentary, op-ed pieces and guest commentary as well as letters to the editor. While these formats are quite universal nowadays, there are national differences in the discursive styles of print journalism, particularly concerning the degree to which facts and reported statements are mixed with elements of interpretation and opinion in news stories. Hallin and Mancini (2004: 99) report that in the French newspapers *Le Monde* and *Le Figaro* roughly two thirds of the paragraphs of news stories were devoted to reporting facts and statements only whereas in the *New York Times* this was the case in 90 per cent of paragraphs. Conversely, the French news stories contained higher doses of interpretation and opinion interwoven with the still dominant reporting function. This shows that despite an apparent change in European print journalism in the direction of information-oriented journalism, French quality newspapers still exhibit a more interpretive variant of journalistic expression than their American counterparts.

Anglo-American mainstream journalism also has a stronger tradition of couching public deliberation in the form of 'debate style articles' with arguments from opposing camps or actors being presented in the same article. Ferree *et al.* (2002: 240), in their comparison of abortion discourse in US and German quality dailies, find that 42 per cent of abortion coverage in the US and 25 per cent of the German coverage were characterized by such debate style articles. The majority of the German articles presented arguments from one side only.[1] Systematic comparative data on the style of public deliberation for a wider array of countries is not available at present (see Wessler 2007).

When we leave the more aggregate level of the article behind and look at the individual utterances advanced or reported in print articles (as well as radio and television) interesting deliberative features emerge. In an average of 40 per cent of such utterances speakers support their claims with justifications (Kuhlmann 1999, 248; Gerhards *et al.* 1998, 143). Thus, one central claim of the normative model of public deliberation developed above is met to a considerable degree in the news media. The same holds true for the climate of civility in which public deliberation flourishes best. Even in the case of a hotly debated and strongly value-laden issue such as abortion only a small proportion of speakers appearing in quality newspapers use what Ferree *et al.* (2002: 239) call ' "hot button" language, that is words that are likely to outrage opponents such as accusations of murder, persecution, or barbarity'. This was the case for 5 per cent of the German and 4 per cent of the US speakers.

## Types of actors and the role of journalists

Public discourse typically features a spectrum of different types of actors that assume different roles. Apart from politicians different kinds of advocates (professionals concerned with an issue and often speaking on behalf of those affected by a problem) as well as experts and intellectuals contribute to mediated public debate. Journalists, in turn, play a special role due to their double function as participants and mediators of the debate. The exact composition of the collectivity of speakers depends on the topic of debate and in itself does not tell us much about the deliberative character of public discourse. But there are interesting differences in the character of the utterances made by (or attributed to) different types of actors as is shown in a study of public debate on drug policy in Germany (Wessler 1999).[2]

For one, actors differ with respect to the number of ideas they advance in one utterance, a measure of the complexity of argumentation (see Table 2.1). The highest complexity is found in the utterances of journalists, followed by members of the judiciary as well as experts and intellectuals. These types of actors seem to contribute most to providing a complex picture of the issue, while politicians (especially parties' representatives) and those directly concerned with the problem under discussion offer the least complex interpretations.

Second, as argued above, public deliberation will flourish if actors take other actors' ideas seriously by incorporating them in their utterances (without necessarily endorsing them). In German drug policy discourse (as probably in many highly polarized public debates) the vast majority of utterances contained ideas that support only one camp. The number of utterances that simultaneously contained ideas identified as core arguments of both camps was small (1.6 per cent on average). But again, journalists occupy an exceptional position.

*Table 2.1:* Utterance profiles of various types of actors in the German drug policy debate

| | Complexity: no. of ideas per utterance* | Opposing ideas: Utterances with 2 or more opposing ideas* | | Weighing judgments: no. of ambivalent policy assessments** | |
|---|---|---|---|---|---|
| | | % | N | % | N |
| *Actors of the political center* | *1.4* | *1.0* | *16* | *0.3* | *5* |
| Executive/ administration | 1.4 | 1.1 | 9 | 0.4 | 3 |
| Legislative/ political parties | 1.0 | 0.7 | 4 | 0.2 | 1 |
| Judiciary | 2.6 | 1.1 | 1 | 0.0 | 0 |
| Law enforcement | 2.0 | 2.1 | 3 | 0.8 | 1 |
| *Actors of the periphery* | *2.2* | *2.9* | *21* | *2.3* | *11* |
| Helping professions | 1.4 | 0.9 | 2 | 0.6 | 1 |
| Experts/ public intellectuals | 2.5 | 1.9 | 3 | 0.0 | 0 |
| Those affected by problem | 1.1 | 0.0 | 0 | 3.4 | 1 |
| Journalists | 3.0 | 5.6 | 15 | 6.7 | 9 |
| Other civil society actors | 1.8 | 1.8 | 1 | 0.0 | 0 |
| *Total* | *1.7* | *1.6* | *38* | *0.8* | *16* |

*Notes:* * Basis: total of 3,929 ideas expressed in 2.374 utterances
** Basis: total of 2,011 policy assessments
*Source:* Wessler (1999), pp. 167, 171, 197.

They are the only type of actor with a share of 'opposing ideas utterances' that is worth mentioning (5.6 per cent, See Table 2.1).

This also holds true for a third measure of deliberative quality, i.e. the extent of policy assessments that discuss both positive and negative aspects of a given policy proposal. Again, the vast majority of policy assessments in speakers' utterances clearly favors or opposes a proposal. Judgments weighing positive and negative aspects are rare and where they occur, they are mostly advanced by journalists (see the ratio of 6.7 per cent in Table 2.1). Of course, the absolute numbers for these measures of deliberativeness are rather small and can probably be attributed to the highly value-laden and polarized character of this particular debate. Still the fact that journalists come out on top consistently shows that their performance is pivotal for achieving elements of public deliberation in a normatively demanding sense (see the corresponding finding in the section on talk shows below).

## Phases of discourse

What is the dynamic of a public debate on an issue, particularly when it is not associated with a shift in public policy? Does deliberation inject new problematizations and innovative ideas into the public realm? In the study on German drug policy discourse already mentioned this process dimension has been analyzed as well. The debate, stretching out over six and a half years, exhibits a characteristic sequence of three climaxes associated with specific events and longer phases of little media attention before, between and after theses climaxes (Wessler 1999, 155).

Most ideas were present in all seven phases, while others only surfaced in those phases without much media attention to the issue. A third group of ideas entered the debate at some stage and stayed whereas a forth, very small group dropped out of the debate altogether (Wessler 1999: 207). During climax phases of high media attention actors tend to rally around the flag of their camp. Not much innovation is taking place in those phases. But about 10 per cent of the ideas expressed by both camps of the debate constituted innovations in the sense that they entered the debate at some stage and became permanent ingredients of the argumentative repertoires. In addition, about 10 per cent of the ideas expressed by members of the liberalization camp only surfaced in low-impact phases while they were absent in climax phases. This finding points to the importance of low-impact phases of debate for the innovative function of public deliberation. There clearly is an increase in the variety of ideas, particularly during phases of relatively lower media attention. To some degree, therefore, public deliberation flourishes in the interstices left by heated media activity.

## Political talk shows – reasoned debate or clamor?

Like print media television offers various settings for public deliberation. Newscasts do not only report events but also inform the audience about actors' claims and justifications. In addition, talk shows have become a common and popular segment in television programs. They can serve as fora for deliberation by gathering different actors who bring forward claims and reasons (Herbst 1995). Talk shows allow for immediate challenges and responses so that the audience gains more vivid insights into the constellations and dynamics of public controversies.

However, the explosion of talk shows in the USA and in many other countries has also triggered concerns about an alleged 'talkathon culture' (Kurtz 1997). Media critics blame the shows for a degeneration of public debate. In Germany, for example, the currently most successful political talk show, 'Sabine Christiansen', is an object of harsh attacks (see Rossum 2004). Critics lament the restricted circle of participants and complain about the rise of a 'punditocracy' in which only a few opinion leaders and prominent news shapers influence the public (Alterman 1992; Soley 1992). They also question the substance of the conversations claiming that talk shows hardly enable a thoughtful exchange of arguments, but limit themselves to showmanship, mere confessions, assertions and attacks. Talk shows, it is claimed, become an arena for verbal combat, voyeurism and entertainment rather than for some form of rational deliberation (see Gitlin 1991; Gamson 1999; Liebes 1999; Plake 1999).

These criticisms are to be taken seriously even if we lower the normative criteria for mediated deliberation as we have done above. Yet the empirical base for such general reservations is limited at best; critics rarely refer to systematic analyses and data. Moreover, when evaluating talk shows and their capacities to foster public deliberation one has to pay attention to different forms and formats and distinguish between various types of actors. In this context, the role of journalists who serve as hosts is especially important since 'television talk is host-centered' (Timberg 1994, 273) and the hosts' performance is likely to have an effect on the overall quality of the talks.

### Show formats and the role of entertainment

Over the years, many different types of television talk shows have been introduced (see Timberg 2002). Their potential for public deliberation mainly depends on their profiles with regard to participants, topics, and styles of moderation (see Murdock 2000; Mittell 2003; Schultz 2006). Much of cultural critics' disgust for the genre goes back to daytime confession shows in which lay people discuss problems of their private lives and lifestyles (see Greenberg *et al.* 1997). Most of these programs use elements of audience participation. On the one hand, these shows raise worries about a 'tyranny of intimacy' (Sennett 1974), a loss of shame and an abuse of lay people by the media (see Tolson 2001). On the other hand, it has been argued that some of these shows give ordinary people a voice, involve them and their experiences in public debates and revaluate the life-world (Livingstone and Lunt 1994; Leurdijk 1997).

This dispute cannot be resolved here as we narrow the focus down to political talk shows that explicitly deal with public affairs. But political discussions also differ with respect to their participants. Some programs restrict themselves to politicians and lobbyists, others present journalists or experts from think tanks and academic institutions. Chances of civil society actors to be invited into popular political talk shows are fairly poor in the USA and in Germany (see Nimmo and Combs 1992; Schultz 2006). Finally, some political discussion shows attempt an involvement of laypersons by offering phone-ins or selecting citizens who interview politicians.

Political talk shows are sometimes seen as entertainment (see Postman 1985; Dörner 2001). But this view ignores the differences between types of talk shows and puts sedate and issue-oriented shows on the same level with personality-oriented chats. Second, it ignores the (more or less sophisticated) elements of deliberation in the conversations. Third, there is evidence that citizens learn something from talk shows and televised political debates – that they gain political knowledge and may be encouraged to think and discuss about public affairs (Abramowitz 1978; Drew & Weaver 1993; Chaffee *et al.* 1994; Benoit *et al.* 2002). Certainly, the dynamics and visuality of talk show communication can be quite entertaining, at times it can also be distracting from the substance of argumentation. But deliberation and entertainment are not *per se* mutually exclusive. Nor can their relationship be understood as a zero-sum game. Baym (2005) has recently argued that a blending of comedy, parody, news, and public affairs discussion – as is typical for hybrid programs like 'The Daily Show' in the USA – establishes an alternative journalism that indeed enacts a model of deliberative democracy. Satire is indeed a good means for criticism and can stimulate discussions. But deliberation is still dependent on explicit reasoning and argumentation.

## Types of actors

Content analyses reveal significant differences in the 'deliberative profile' of the various talk show participants (Schütz 1995; Schultz 2006). According to an analysis of 40 broadcasts from four different political discussion programs in Germany, politicians, show stars, lobbyists and businessmen show significantly weaker efforts to back up their claims by arguments than academic experts and journalists (in their role as participants of discussion, not as talk show hosts) (see Table 2.2).[3] Furthermore, academic experts and journalists bring forward more sophisticated deliberative threads. They frequently weigh up different views and arguments while other participants are more likely to apodictically stick to one-sided views. About one third of journalists' and experts' argumentative turns include counterarguments (running against the speaker's position) and elaborations that explicitly take into account other views

*Table 2.2*: Argumentative efforts of various talk show participants (measured by turns in conversations of 40 political talk shows in German television)

| | Turns that lack considerable argumentative efforts (%) | Turns that include considerable argumentative efforts (%) | Not to determine (%) | Total (%) |
|---|---|---|---|---|
| Politicians | 40.8 (256) | 50.3 (316) | 8.9 (56) | 100 (628) |
| Journalists (in participant's role) | 20.3 (70) | 75.9 (261) | 3.8 (13) | 100 (344) |
| Academic experts | 13.3 (12) | 81.1 (73) | 5.6 (5) | 100 (90) |
| Lobbyists and businessmen | 39.4 (84) | 50.7 (108) | 9.9 (21) | 100 (213) |
| Artists, celebrities | 39.5 (17) | 51.2 (22) | 9.3 (4) | 100 (43) |
| Military personnel | 44.4 (16) | 55.6 (20) | – | 100 (36) |
| *Total* | 33.6 (455) | 59.1 (800) | 7.3 (99) | 100 (1354) |

*Note*: Chi-Square: 90.68; $p < 0.001$.

on the matter. Such balancing is rare in politicians' contributions and was found only in 17.5 per cent of their argumentative turns (Schultz 2006: 260).

Apart from the overall level of deliberativeness, the professional groups that appear in political talk shows also differ in their argumentative style. Here, some cross-cutting patterns are especially conspicuous (Schultz 2006: 252–8): Politicians and journalists often use elements of accusation as well as moral judgment and condemnation (on average, in every third turn, while only 18 per cent of experts' turns included such a pattern). As can be expected, academic experts by contrast use more scientific modes of argumentation – they frequently point to empirical data, determine causal connections, draw analogies and conclusions from international or historical experiences. In almost two thirds of their turns at least one such element of 'scientific' argumentation was found. At times academic experts also make predictions or discuss other actors' (particularly politicians') motives. But overall, prognostic and psychological arguments are most often used by journalists (39 per cent of their turns). In comparison to the other groups, artists and celebrities are most likely to rely on anectodal evidence and contribute personal experiences to the deliberation.

**The role of the hosts**

Political talk show hosts have the capacity to structure and guide the conversations by their questions and interventions and to stimulate more or less substantial argumentation. The performance of the hosts and their contribution to the deliberativeness of the programs can be assessed on four dimensions (see Schultz 2004): (a) the hosts' general level of activity, (b) the extent of criticism in their questions (including the share of questions asking for the justification of claims), (c) the substance of their questions, and (d) the responsiveness of the interviewees (as an indicator of the effectiveness of the questions, see Bull & Mayer 1993).

According to critics, hosts of political talk shows carry out their job insufficiently because they frequently miss the opportunity to corner their guests and involve them in substantial argumentative communication (see Weischenberg 1997; Tenscher 1998). But the performance of talk show hosts differs significantly, as the analysis of their contributions in German discussion programs has shown. For example, the host of Germany's currently most popular political talk show, Sabine Christiansen, less often challenges her guests and asks for justifications than Maybrit Illner, the host of another popular German show called 'Berlin Mitte' (Table 2.3). The following are examples of questions eliciting justifications: 'Your party has now presented new plans to reform social security. But doesn't this come far too late?'; 'You said that the country cannot give up nuclear power plants. So you don't care about the risks attached to final disposal sites?'[4] The differences in the use of questions eliciting justifications between the shows verify that the genre allows journalists considerable latitude. Hosts can increase the shows' deliberativeness by an adequate training and commitment.

*Table 2.3:*   Aim of hosts' questions in different political talk shows in Germany

| Talk show | Eliciting expression (%) | Eliciting information (%) | Eliciting opinion (%) | Eliciting justification (%) | Total (%) |
|---|---|---|---|---|---|
| 'Sabine Christiansen' | 6.6 (20) | 15.8 (48) | 51.2 (155) | 26.4 (80) | 100 (303) |
| 'Berlin Mitte' | 3.3 (11) | 16.6 (56) | 41.7 (141) | 38.5 (130) | 100 (338) |
| '19:zehn' | 3.0 (9) | 19.9 (59) | 56.9 (169) | 20.2 (60) | 100 (297) |
| 'Presseclub' | 0.5 (1) | 13.1 (26) | 66.7 (132) | 19.7 (39) | 100 (198) |
| *Total* | 3.6 (41) | 16.6 (189) | 52.6 (597) | 27.2 (309) | 100 (1136) |

*Note:* Chi square = 58.14; $p < 0.001$.
*Source:* Schultz 2006: 227.

## Conclusion

The most important conclusion to be drawn from the empirical literature is that public deliberation in the mass media does exist. However, it remains difficult to systematically assess the quality of such public deliberation because we lack data on the whole range of normative criteria defined above. This is particularly true for the input dimension where the existing studies that use a public deliberation framework do not offer clues concerning a possible systematic exclusion of issues, ideas or arguments.[5]

The situation is different for the throughput dimension for which some data are available by now. We have seen that speakers in public debate do offer justifications for their claims to a considerable degree and that journalists, experts and public intellectuals engage in argumentative efforts more strongly than other actors in both print media and political TV talk shows. Journalists also display higher levels of weighing ideas and judgments than all other types of speakers in the print media, a feature that was even more pronounced for academic experts in TV talk shows. However, as talk show participants journalists also used as many elements of accusation and moral judgment and condemnation as politicians did – and more of these than other actors. In their role as talk show hosts, on the other hand, they command particular leverage in eliciting more deliberative forms of utterances. Nevertheless it is plausible to speculate that print media and television perform complementary roles in public deliberation with print media offering better opportunities for developing arguments richly and TV talk shows being more suited to challenging views spontaneously and insistently.

On the output dimension, again, systematic insights are sparse. There is an indication that over the course of an issue-specific debate new ideas will find their way into the public realm, particularly during phases with less media attention. Whether such discursive innovation is coupled with a more reasoned understanding of inescapable dissent is unclear, however. And the role of public deliberation in the long-term sedimentation of generally acceptable knowledge also needs more systematic attention.

The current state of affairs, thus, suggests that a lot of further research is needed in order to fill the gaps in knowledge and to bridge the still yawning divide between the normative literature on deliberative democracy and empirical studies on qualities of media discourse. In fact, it seems that the genuine contribution of media and communication scholarship in this area could lie in the development of media- and setting-specific criteria of deliberativeness that can be applied in empirical studies. We have gone a number of initial steps in this direction.

However, we would like to suggest even bigger tasks for future research. Apart from an empirical investigation of normative criteria, we propose to use such results in *explanatory* frameworks more often and more consistently than in the past. This could be done on three levels: (a) by studying the relationships between different partial features of public deliberation and thus contributing to a deeper understanding of the inner workings of public debates in various media settings; (b) by linking measures of deliberativeness to characteristics of national media and political systems in an attempt to structurally explain different levels of performance; and (c) by asking whether specific deliberative qualities are appreciated by audiences and have effects on their deliberations in everyday life. A long and interesting road lies ahead.

## Notes

1. Stripping news articles of all interpretation and opinion can weaken their value for the public sphere. See Ornebring in this volume. This is particularly true when facts are presented as isolated bits and pieces and statements from political actors are couched in 'horse race' terms rather than linked on substantive grounds.
2. The study analyzed the entire coverage on the drug policy debate in daily and weekly newspapers as well as news magazines in Germany for a period of six and a half years (September 1988 to February 1995). During this period a possible liberalization of prohibition of cannabis and heroin was discussed in Germany (with no resulting policy change).
3. The study covered four German talk show programs: 'Sabine Christiansen', 'Berlin Mitte', '19:zehn', and 'Presseclub'. All of them were broadcast weekly on public television in the format of a group discussion. 'Sabine Christiansen' and 'Berlin Mitte' usually present top politicians, but also participants from other professional groups. In '19:zehn', less prominent politicians appear in addition to experts, journalists and artists. 'Presseclub' gathers only journalists from various print media. From each show ten broadcasts were randomly selected between June 2001 and July 2002 for a quantitative content analysis.
4. Hosts of 'Presseclub' and '19:zehn' use even less 'justification questions' than Christiansen. This is due to the fact that these shows feature no or less politicians. Challenging and face-threatening questions mainly target politicians.
5. Of course, journalists' preference for well-established (e.g. government) sources generally limits the range of issues reported and may serve to privilege the position of such sources. The question remains, however, whether this leads to wholesale exclusion of certain ideas and arguments from the public sphere.

# 3
# Connection or Disconnection?: Tracking the Mediated Public Sphere in Everyday Life

*Nick Couldry, Sonia Livingstone and Tim Markham*

The decades-long debate on media and the public sphere has primarily been normative, rather than empirical, in character. We especially lack empirical research detailing how the mediated public sphere is enacted (*if* it is) in everyday life. There has been, we would argue, a significant gap in studying the experiential dimensions of citizenship (what it actually *feels* like to be a citizen (cf. LeBlanc, 1999)): indeed what *are* the practices which link private action to the public sphere, beyond the obvious act of walking down to the polling station to cast your vote?

Deliberative democracy theory (Benhabib 1996; Cohen 1996), growing out of a critical engagement with Habermas's model, lies somewhere in this gap, as does the tradition of analysing the relations between conversation, public opinion and the mass media stemming from Tarde's early social psychology (Katz 1992). We are interested in the possibility that, as several scholars now argue, the problem with contemporary democracies lies in the displacement of public discussion (Mayhew 1997; Eliasoph 1998). Not everyone, of course, is so negative. The growing literature on Internet-based civic practice is well-known (Graber *et al.* 2004; Kahn and Kellner 2004). The American sociologist Michael Schudson argues more generally (1998: 298–9) that 'civic participation now takes place everywhere'. But significant concerns about the distribution of opportunities to participate in deliberation remain.

More recently, writers have begun to move beyond theoretical models of deliberative democracy towards detailing more precisely the practical preconditions for an effective democratic politics, bringing out the mediating role of everyday thoughts, conversation and activities that may, under certain conditions, bridge the private and public spheres (Livingstone 2005). Drawing on a well-known but in many ways unsatisfactory earlier literature (Almond and Verba, 1963), Peter Dahlgren has recently re-examined the notion of 'civic culture' as the key concept underlying the daily experience of citizenship (Dahlgren, 2003). What is most striking about Dahlgren's model of civic culture – a 'circuit' of six interlocking processes: values, affinity, knowledge, practices, identities and discussion (see Chapter 16 in this volume) – is the multiple *and often uncertain* relations it suggests between the imagining and understanding of civic life and its practice (both acts and talk). Since talk is only one of the model's dimensions, it is the articulations of talk to other elements that is crucial, as we shall examine in what follows.

## The UK 'public connection' project[1]

Our research question in the 'Public Connection' project is best explained in terms of two connected and widely made assumptions about democratic politics that we have been trying to 'test': First, in a 'mature' democracy such as Britain, most people share an orientation to a public world where matters of common concern are, or at least should be, addressed (we call this orientation 'public connection'). Second, this public connection is focussed principally on mediated versions of that public world (so that 'public connection' is principally sustained by a convergence in what media people consume, in other words, by shared or overlapping shared media consumption).

These assumptions are detachable from each other. Some believe the first without the second, because they argue public connection is unlikely to served by people's use of media (Robert Putnam's 2000 well-known *Bowling Alone* thesis takes that position in relation to television). Generally however it seems to us that many writers assume both, even if only tacitly – or at least that is our contention (there is no space to defend our view of the literature here). Consequently, our concern is with the empirical question: can we find evidence for those assumptions in how UK citizens think about their own practice?

The first assumption is important because it underlies most models of democracy: informed consent to political authority requires that people's attention to the public world can be assumed, or at least one can assume an *orientation* to the public world which from time to time results in actual attention. When in this project we talk of '*public*' connection, we mean 'things or issues which are regarded as being of shared concern, rather than of purely private concern', matters that in principle citizens need to discuss in a world of limited shared resources.[2]

We have been careful not to assume that a decline in attention to 'politics' in the traditional sense means lack of attention to 'politics' in general, let alone apathy. People's understanding of what constitutes politics may be changing (Bennett 1998). The *media* landscape that may enable public connection is also changing. The multiplication and intense interlinking of media and media formats through digital convergence may lead to an intensification of public connection, as people become more skilful at adapting their media consumption to suit their everyday habits and pressures. Or it may lead to the fragmentation of the public sphere into a mass of specialist 'sphericules' (Gitlin, 1998) that can no longer connect sufficiently to form a shared public world. In this context, the question of where and how, and for what purpose, talk oriented to a public world occurs (including talk that might fit within the theoretical model of a public sphere) becomes crucial.

Our working assumption, then, is that the public/private boundary remains meaningful in spite of many other levels of disagreement over the content and definition of politics. But our understanding of the public/private boundary is not prescriptive. The point of our research has been to ask people: what makes up *their* public world? How are they connected to that world? And how are media involved, or not, in sustaining that connection to a public world (as they understand it)?

These are the questions we aimed to explore: first by asking a small group of 37 people across England to produce a diary for three months during 2004 that reflected on those questions; second by interviewing those diarists, both before and after their diary production, individually and in some cases also in focus-groups; and finally by broadening out the themes from this necessarily small group to a nationwide survey (targeted at a sample of 1000 respondents) conducted in June 2005. The survey provided data on media consumption, attitudes to media and politics, and public actions, and also the contexts in which all of these occur.[3]

The diaries were produced weekly for up to three months. We encouraged open reflection and avoided specific signals as to what people were to comment on. The diary data are particularly complex, our intention always being that the diary material would be 'triangulated' by interview data. For ease of exposition, we will draw mainly from the interview data in this chapter. Each diarist was interviewed face to face in their home by a member of the research team, both before and after the completion of the diaries, using a fairly open-ended interview schedule focused on questions of media consumption, daily activities, and political or civic interests. First, however, we will provide some context for our discussion of individual diarists by reviewing briefly the overall trends of our nationwide survey.

## The mediated public sphere in action: survey background

In our survey age is by far the most significant demographic influence on media consumption, though class and gender do play a part. While newspaper readership does not vary according to class, television viewing is much higher among people from classes C2DE (semi-skilled and skilled workers and the unemployed), and internet use is very significantly higher among those from ABC1 households (business, professional and administrative classes) and also among under-35 year old respondents. Men are more likely to read newspapers and access the internet than women, but read books less on average. Notably, radio consumption is not dependent on any demographic factor.

The types of public issue people say that they 'keep up with' vary more by demographic than any other factor – especially by age and gender – although some issues such as the environment (70 per cent of all respondents), crime (67 per cent), Iraq (63 per cent) and health (66 per cent) are heavily reported across all groups. The under-35s report following music, fashion, celebrity and reality shows more than older respondents, who favour more traditional issue categories such as Westminster politics, the economy and local politics/ services. In terms of socioeconomic status, people from ABC1 households are more likely to follow international politics, the economy, health and European debates. More men than women follow trades unions, sports, international events, Iraq, the economy, Westminster and European debates, while women are more likely to follow celebrity gossip, health issues, fashion and reality shows, confirming broader arguments about the gendering of the public sphere.

Respondents overwhelmingly report that watching the news is important and a regular practice for them, while also agreeing that there is often too much media and that politics is too complicated. However, age makes a difference: a feeling of duty to follow the news increases with age, as do practices of regular news consumption and understanding of issues. As to class, those from C2DE households exhibit a distinctly higher tendency to agree that there is no point in following the news, that politics is too complicated and that they have no influence over political decisions. Men are more likely to say they have a good understanding of issues and actively compared news sources, while more women than men agree that politics is too complicated to understand. People from ABC1 households tend overall to find media relevant, and agree that different sources of news give different accounts of events, while those from C2DE households are more likely to agree that media are irrelevant to their lives. Respondents over 55 and from ABC1 households are far more likely to agree that they know where they could find the information they needed about issues important to them. Once again, the general features of the mediated public sphere seemed stratified by gender, class and age.

Finally, as to talk, 85 per cent of our respondents say they regularly talk about issues to friends and 72 per cent to family about issues. More broadly, we identified social expectation (which implies some form of discursive context in which issues are discussed, and in which a level of proficiency is expected) as an important contributing factor, if not for public actions generally (beyond the minimal action of voting), then certainly for engagement with the public world. In addition, although there is no room to discuss the detail here, although there is no room to discuss the detail here, we found that news engagement (not just news consumption but the 'value' of keeping up with the news) was a significant contributor to political interest.

Our sense, then, from our survey data, is not only do people acknowledge social reinforcements to follow a public world through media, but that engagement with media makes an important contribution, alongside the expected demographic factors, to explaining political interest. This broadly positive picture is useful context for the more uneven picture we gained from the qualitative data obtained from our diarists.

## The mediated public sphere: diary data

Our data from the diary phase, as with our survey, covered a wide variety of themes, of which talk and the enactment of a mediated public sphere was only one. We were however interested from the outset in people's opportunities, through talk, to link their individual practices of media consumption to what other people do and think. Most of our diarists said they talked about the public-type issues that they raised with us in their diaries: this broadly confirms our survey findings, but with an often fascinating degree of detail. For example this account of almost a mini-public sphere in a West London newsagents' shop which one diarist ran:

> It's like a village shop, so I know my customers, they know me. . . . And you talk about the weather, and what's been done and . . . ask about the family, they ask me about my family. . . . And what's the main issue, everyday issue. . . . So we discuss all sorts of things. (woman, 51, shop owner, suburban West London)

There were many other positive accounts of talk with family friends and at work about public-related issues.

However, the detailed picture is more mixed. For some people the absence of others with whom to discuss the type of issues they wrote about was a constraint, for example this man with a masters degree in politics:

> It's a sad point, sad state of affairs but I've been in situations where people you know, you speak about politics at work and then people get on their high horse. . . . it's quite scary to see how people are disinterested in it, particularly this generation. (man, 23, university administrator, West London suburb)

In some cases it was a more general social network that was missing. These are some issues to be borne in mind when considering the four diarists that follow.

They have been chosen to give an insight, through two contrasting pairings, of how possibilities for talk are always embedded in the context and constraints of people's everyday lives. We have chosen pairings whose diarists share some important things in common (the first pair – gender, retired status and at least a reasonable degree of privilege in socioeconomic terms; the second pair – gender, being at work and poor), while being sharply contrasted in other ways. In this way, we hope to take further the broader points that emerged from our survey discussion.

### First case study

We first want to contrast two retired men,[4] both from north of England suburbs who had very different relations to the mediated public sphere.

John was a retired chief executive of a major subsidiary of a publicly quoted financial services company. An early retirement package enabled him to buy a medium size house in an elite suburb of a major Northern city. While he was working, he had no time for media except the financial news; it was only in retirement that he had the time to consume news more broadly. His clear preference was for newspapers, with television being mainly relaxation. He strongly disliked new forms of television entertainment such as reality TV and celebrity-related fiction – 'every time you see the trailers for all these pro-grammes, it's not life remotely as we live it' – and required media to keep him informed about the world:

And I'm just interested in what happens to the financial world in general, just to see what's developing. And I'm not a political animal but I'm inter-ested in the country and the politics of the country and so forth. And world-wide events. I like to keep up to date and see what's going on. And I find that the newspaper generally gives you a more balanced coverage than television.

Expressed clearly here is a sense of a 'world' that exists independently of media, about which media, if carefully selected, provide a flow of information. The financial aspects of that world were something in which John still regarded himself as involved:

I read the business section everyday and I read all of it, partially because I'm interested and there's people who I still know and so forth. But also I still have money invested and I'm interested in how that's doing.

The 'public connection' sustained for him by media is not one *generated* by media. The same was true of the other dimension of his public world, his voluntary service as a magistrate judge in a local magistrates' court. This role required him to keep informed about aspects of government policy about which he had previously known little. It was a further incentive to consume media news more broadly.

Alfred's overall orientation to the mediated public sphere was quite different. He was a printer who had done well from his job and who lived in retirement in a comfortable but not elite suburb of another major Northern city. His man-ual occupation carried with it into retirement no status within a wider public world, nor did he have any official voluntary role in retirement: his occupations were being a grandfather and everyday tasks 'household activities you know, quite boring really'. In terms of media, his preference was for television and radio, not newspapers. Like John however he was interested in the factual dimension of media:

I like documentaries, I like the history, the history channel, I like anything to do with nature, geography, things like this stimulate me. I need to be stimulated and drama in particular, particularly, doesn't stimulate me because I don't, and for that reason I don't really read fiction. . . . To me it's, I like reading about real people and what people have done.

He also took great pleasure in talk radio, especially one presenter on a local radio station:

> I'm an avid listener now. . . . He finds the alternative argument, whether he believes it or not, whether it's his thoughts on something or not, if somebody comes along waffling about certain issues he will very, very quickly find the alternative argument to it and argue it out with them and he very often wins. He more often than not he wins and he'll tell somebody eventually that frankly you're a pillock and get off my show, you know. (laughs). . . . Yeah, it's quite informative.

For Alfred, then, the public world to which media sustain his attention *was* the world presented by media: he has no independent access to a public world. That does not mean he had no interest in taking action on public issues: he intended to lobby for speed restrictions on his road to protect schoolchildren, and he had a civic sense that, if no one else did, he at least would sweep up the rubbish and leaves on the street near his house. But these were small scale actions, carried out with no link to anyone else. They did not alter the fact that for him the world of public issues was accessed almost entirely through media.

How were these broad contrasts reflected in these diarists' opportunities for talk themselves about public issues (vicarious talk alone cannot meet the participative ideal that underpins the public sphere model)? Here there are both sharp differences and similarities between the two diarists. John, as we saw, was disappointed in his children's lack of interest in the public world (at least as he defined that world); nor it seems could he generally talk to his wife about that world, although it seems they did debate the rights and wrongs of the 2003 Iraq war. Other general opportunities for talk were limited to occasional discussions with friends: he was involved in various amateur sports networks but here talk about public issues was largely excluded:

> The only topic that comes up when we play golf, holidays and that sort of thing tend to be talked about, but the only other thing and it invariably comes up is somebody will comment on something in the paper, involving crime, and the question of crime and punishment comes up. Ahh, people do talk about that.

Similarly, 'conversations with neighbours tend to be trivial'. He did however have one significant outlet for discussion on public issues, the times before or between cases at the magistrates court:

> I've discussed a lot at the magistrates. I usually go down and get there about half an hour before the court starts and everyone has a cup of coffee and you have a chat and there's about an hour and a half over lunch time and inevitably you lunch and generally talk to the people you've been sitting

with. But you get a good cross section of views there cause there's all sorts of people magistrates. And it's very interesting to hear people's views.

These discussions involved, he said, a wide range of classes and occupations and provided clear opportunities to display knowledge about public issues.

This was what Alfred, equally clearly, lacked. He made no mention of discussions about public issues with family, even though he appeared close to his family. Most of his friends were at a local club he visited once a week, but there he had no scope to raise his interests in the environment, the Iraq war, pensions reform or the dangers of religious extremism:

> Well, there's a lot of sport talked about you know and I'm not particularly sporty so I can't involve myself too much with that and a lot of people talk about holidays. I find that type of talk very shallow. I tend to back off a bit, it's not deep enough for me. I don't have great, I'm not really endowed with great wisdom or original thought or even much of a wordsmith really but I do find certain subjects a bit shallow.

It is easy to see why he appreciated the chance through talk radio to listen in on debate: the only time he had phoned in, though, was to ask about how to clean a copper kettle!

In spite of this crucial difference in John's and Alfred's relations to the mediated public sphere, there are similarities when we consider, finally, the links between talk and action. It is worth noting first, with Putnam in mind, that both were in clubs or networks that were in decline. There is no evidence however that this decline was of any consequence for these diarists' opportunities for or likelihood of political or civic action. In any case any thoughts of public action were *for both* cut across by a broader lack of political efficacy:

> there's really very little an individual can do. In fact, nothing that an individual can do. I could feel as strongly as I like about an issue and my wife's always complaining that I do feel strongly about an issue and do nothing about it because there's nothing you can do about it. Well I suppose I could do, I could stand in the middle of city square and spout but nobody's take a bit of notice, would they? (John, Northern suburb, focus group, January 2005)

> with the best will in the world sometimes you start to get an apathy about it, a weariness of it. A point where it comes to saying what more can you say, what more you know when you feel so, I think one of the troubles is that you feel so helpless as though you or I feel I could do something about it and I know damn well I can't and so as a result I can do nothing, whatever I think or say or do to anybody or write about is not going to make a scrap of difference and then you start, oh, what the hell. (Alfred, second interview)

What should we conclude from this diarist pairing? First, that media may to some degree provide opportunities for remote connection to debate that may compensate for a lack of opportunities to engage in face-to-face discussion; second, people may differ sharply in whether their public world exists independently of media, or emerges principally out of the practice of media consumption; third, regardless of the opportunities for engagement provided directly by certain roles or networks or virtually by media, any link to action about public issues may be cut across by an independent lack of efficacy. The habit of regularly consuming the news may, of course, still remain, provided it has been learnt in the first place; but that is much more likely among our older diarists than those younger.

## Second case study

How much does public connection draw on a socially privileged position, in terms of age, gender or socioeconomic advantage? Let us consider a very different pairing, that of two working class women. Although from different generations, Kylie and Jane both have rather few material or social resources. Kylie is 24, unemployed since having her baby, though she does occasional office work nearby her home in a large South London council block. Jane, who lives in a small, relatively poor town in the South East of England, is 52, a part-time customer services assistant with adult children, one still at home, and a grandchild whom she cares for on a regular basis.

Jane's life is a reminder of the once-strong working class roots of the Labour movement in Britain, and her present disillusion with politics matches the wider decline in local labour and trade union participation. But, as her own reflections suggest, it would be unfair to label this 'apathy', for the origins of her disillusion lie in an informed critique of the changing practices of party politics. When we ask if she belongs to any groups, her answer starts with the past:

> No, I used to do a lot of political, local political work. . . . Um, I came from a really working class family. Brought up to believe in working class values and just basically went from there. And I think somebody, at one point, knocked on my mum's door, knowing that she was a [party name] voter and asked her, could they have the committee rooms in her house. And it went from there basically.

Being among the most politically active of our diarists, Jane recounts a life of strong political commitment, enacted locally but connected to the national. By contrast, Kylie seems, at first, typical of today's supposedly apathetic youth, especially when she tells us:

> I just don't really understand it and therefore it just doesn't interest me. I haven't really got an opinion on anything to do with politics.

As we get to know her better, this turns out to be far from the case. Rather, she illustrates those young people for whom what counts as 'politics' is itself changing (Barnhurst, 1998; van Zoonen, 2001). For Jane, politics means traditional party politics. But though this is just what Kylie rejects, she does care, passionately, about the politics of global justice, while Jane expresses relatively little interest in the global.

Thus Kylie, sitting in her flat all day with her baby, consciously feels herself part of a suffering world, and her public connection is strongly emotional, framed by the 'global compassion' narrative of international news (Hoijer, 2004; Michalski *et al.*, 2002). As she sees it, she has a responsibility,

> . . . to *know*, yeah, to be aware of it and it's just all the children in Africa starving and the story I read ages ago, I think I actually mentioned it in there when he [her son] was first born about a little girl who was left on the roadside, yeah that really, even now, I always think about that. That really, really, really upsets me.

Similarly, talking about reading about the war in the *Mirror*, she breaks in –

> Yeah, the one where they was raping, was it the soldiers or the prisons, the soldiers were raping the prisoners, that was in the paper and that really upset me.

A young women, spending a lot of time on her own, perhaps feeling vulnerable, and with a baby – one can see the personal roots of her sense of connection. But for Kylie, this emotional experience is how she connects to a wider world, and she does so through the media (Lunt & Stenner, 2005). Without the media, she says, 'we'd never know anything of what's going on around us'.

As Lance Bennett has argued (1998; see also Coleman, 2005), this new conception of politics bears a different relation to the media from that of traditional politics. Consider the different ways Jane and Kylie discuss their own relation to the media. For Jane, the media usefully report on politics, but politics itself is grounded in the daily conditions of working class life. For Kylie, the media are an essential *player* in a globally connected world: without the media, she has no public connection.

Jane reads the newspapers because 'I do like to know roughly what's going on in the world or going on around'. She likes the soaps, because through them, she feels her own problems to be shared – 'it's not nice to know that other people have got problems, but you do know that you're not totally alone that way'. But they are just one part of her life. By contrast, the media form a constant backdrop, and focus, for Kylie's life: 'I've got the radio on most of the time I'm in the house' and, as a matter of choice, 'I watch a lot of documentaries and go through the paper in the morning'. If there's 'nothing much on' in the evening, she'll watch the ten o'clock news and then she'll read the newspaper. Thus it emerges that the news and documentaries enable Kylie to enact what she sees as her duty – to *know* what is happening in the world beyond her flat, indeed, to enact her duty to *care*:

> I remember watching a programme about racism. That really, really upset me. Made me very angry when I watched that programme and just really made me realise how lucky I am even, you know it's not easy but compared to how some people have it.

One of Kylie's primary frames is that of luck. Though not obviously living in fortunate circumstances, she reminds herself daily, through her use of media, that she is lucky:

> Yeah, I think it is important they [the media] make us aware of what's going on otherwise no one's gonna change. If you read the happy things everyday it doesn't make you feel, that you know it doesn't make you realise how lucky you are. You need, there's no point in putting all nice things in the paper if it's not the truth you know you need to know the truth and that's it.

She explains her sense of the imperative, the duty, to know what's going on in the world, in a striking sentence:

> Even if it's hurting and it's horrible you need to know. It's just, I mean it's also if there are crimes I mean you put them in the paper. That's how you get people coming forward and things like that, don't ya?

Her added comment is also interesting, for it suggests that by informing us about the world, the media stimulate action from the public. This contrasts with Jane's sense that the media report what is happening but are not themselves agents in the public world. As agents in the world, Kylie sees the media, especially television and radio, as offering a first-person view of the world, allowing her to experience it 'directly':

> Maybe it's 'cos they're there, if there's a war they'll be there and you'll see it going on, you can actually see it live, it's not just written down with a still picture, it's more you really do see what's going on. Demonstrations, they're more likely to be there at the scene actually reporting it and they have you know if there's something on they've got witnesses, they've got the police on the television speaking to them whereas the paper is just a source, a source and that's all you really see.

Mediated public connection, on a global stage, is an emotional experience. Indeed, even taking part in our project was, for Kylie, an emotional experience: 'Yeah, yeah, it was upsetting. Sometimes it used to upset me a bit you know, reading the things and writing it all down it used to, sometimes I got angry about things'.

It is other things that make Jane angry. As with the origins of her sense of public connection, Jane's growing frustration with politics is unrelated to the media. Rather, she is concerned with changes in the organisation of local politics, in the loss of a direct, face-to-face connection between politicians and the public. She frames this as a betrayal of the local roots of political commitment, comparing the process of political activism in her youth – canvassing votes, politicians walking the streets and meeting the people, sharing opinions – with the highly managed process of today's electioneering. Difficulties in her personal life have encouraged her to retrench, sustaining her once-proud political identity only in small ways – looking out for her elderly neighbours in her neighbourhood, chatting to customers at work, doing her best for her children and grandchild. But even these activities for Jane have a civic flavour, they represent 'community': 'I mean the lady that lives next door was there when I was born. She's 94. She was a friend of my mum's'. And they are motivating: following the troubles her daughter has experienced, she hopes to volunteer for youth counselling – for 'kids when they come out of care'. In short, Jane knows what's happening around her because she lives in her street, in her neighbourhood:

> You know, if you're feeling really down I can just walk across the corner and find somebody to say hello to, and especially as I work in a supermarket I speak to so many people now, and it's not being alone, I suppose.

Kylie by contrast knows what is happening around her primarily because the media tell her (for example local radio alerting her to a childcare group of 'when they've got the blood donors coming dow', or 'what's going on in the cinema'. This is not to say that Kylie is disconnected from the local. Indeed, she has tried to become active in her neighbourhood association, initiating a petition to the local council for a play space for children in her block of flats. This gives her an insight into the apathy of others, frustrating the success of her petition: as she says, 'all they've got to do is sign a bit of paper, really'.

The contrast, however, goes to the heart of how the mediated public sphere works differently for different people. Jane's public connection is more routinely grounded in the local and the everyday, this providing the main route for her to connect with the wider world:

> I just, basically my philosophy on life is that you treat others how you want to be treated. You know, and you make your connections every day living that way.

Kylie, by contrast, sees the local as a bracketing off of the wider world, fearing the local as a trap that narrows your world view:

> I just think it's very important . . . in everybody's life that you are kept in touch and that you do read things and realise that it's not just about you know where you live and what goes on around you. It goes a lot deeper than that.

Asked to explain, she reveals how, for her, mediated public connection is all there is – without the intervention of the media, people would be uninformed and disconnected:

> If there wasn't the papers and the news you wouldn't be aware of anything really, you wouldn't be aware whatever's going on all over the world, you just wouldn't know. Your world would just really revolve around [name of local area], that would be it, that's all I'd know about and it does go a lot further than that. There's a lot of things going on all over the world that you need to know about.

On Kylie's global stage, it is hard to sustain a sense of political efficacy. As she puts it, 'I leave them to get on with it. Can't change anything, can I?'. It is others – the media, other people – who will take action. This lack of translation from knowledge and caring to action is most evident in Kylie's lack of commitment to voting: 'I won't, I won't vote. I won't want to follow it'. We ask her why. Her answer, typically for her – though also here expressing a common view – concerns an *international issue*:

> 'Cos I don't really trust, I don't like what Blair's done when he's gone into Iraq, I just feel that, I understand that it was terrible what happened in America and I do understand that but I feel that Bush's got a vendetta against Saddam, he's using that to the best he can and I just don't, that's not what he was put in that position for. He's using his power, I think he's used it totally, he's just using it in a totally wrong way and I don't feel that Blair's, Blair's only reasoned argument for getting involved is that if we ever need America they'll be there for us but that's not the answer, that's not the answer, that's not a good enough reason to do what he's doing out there.

Jane, however difficult her life, could not imagine *not* voting, indeed, 'I don't think I've ever missed voting in any election'. It is personal difficulties, combined with an informed critique of the political process, that keep her from political action. To her regret, her children – of similar ages to Kylie – do not vote, though she and they routinely discuss politics and that is, for Jane, an important part of her life and of her civic responsibility as a parent.

The foregoing has brought out some key differences between these two women. We have seen how, for Jane, public connection has roots grounded in working class, and her personal, history so that the media valuably report on, but do not fundamentally mediate, her sense of public connection, while for Kylie, public connection must be understood globally, with the media playing an essential role in making us transcend our local, personal spheres so as to recognise the common, emotional bonds that unite humanity. But they both share what Carol Gilligan has termed an *ethic of care* (1993; see also Livingstone, 1994; Stevenson 1997), namely a particular, typically gendered, approach to the public sphere which stresses empathetic and contextualised judgements of the actions of others, and which contrasts with the valorisation of principles – of judgement, and of rational–critical discourse. For Kylie, the ethic of care is *felt*, through an emotional identification with distant others; for Jane, the ethic of care is *lived*, through a face-to-face engagement with people living nearby; but for both, it provides a route to public connection. We note last, in this context, that both struggle to act in accordance with this ethic of care – Kylie is disempowered by the very scale of her commitment, for the media tell her about global suffering but hardly provide any means of taking action; Jane is disempowered by the loss of institutional mediation, for where once work, trade unions, and political parties offered a structure for translating talk into action, these have declined in power, and the media that take their place in informing and connecting us, provide the space for talk only.

## Conclusion

We have shown how the mediated public sphere, as it is embedded in daily practice, is shaped by a number of constraints which cut across the obvious and positive point that media circulate discourse about public issues that might not otherwise come into people's daily experience. Our survey data presents the broader picture (although that too is stratified to varying degrees by demographic factors, both in relation to media consumption and social expectations related to news consumption). The diary data by contrast takes us closer to some hidden faultlines in this general picture. We have been concerned throughout with structural constraints linked to the *organisation* of talk, rather than the particular contents of media discourse, although there are hints in our survey data that interest in celebrity and reality TV (sometimes celebrated as potentially a positive sign of engagement with a mediated public sphere: Coleman 2003) may operate at variance with interest in either traditional politics or broad public issues.

The mediated public sphere remains, as Habermas' revised model prescribes, a key element in any normative model of how participation in democracies might work. We must however study the contexts for public-related talk and media consumption that are actually available to citizens in their daily lives. Doing so, as we have begun to explore here, confirms that public-related talk is only one element in the more complex mix that, as Peter Dahlgren puts it, may build a 'civic culture' and that, even when talk is taken by itself, effective opportunities may be more unevenly distributed than first appears.

## Notes

1. We gratefully acknowledge support under the ESRC/AHRB Cultures of Consumption programme (project number RES-143-25-0011): for fuller discussion of the project see Couldry, Livingstone and Markham (forthcoming 2006/2007) and www.public-connection.org. There is a parallel US project based on similar methodology nearing completion directed by Bruce Williams and Andrea Press at the University of Illinois, Urbana-Champaign (funded by the National Science Foundation). We appreciate the support and stimulation they have provided us.
2. The word 'public' is, of course, notoriously difficult, since it has a range of conflicting meanings (Weintraub and Kumar, 1997), but we cannot debate this, or defend our particular usage, here: see Couldry *et al.* (forthcoming), and cf Geuss (2001) and Elshtain (1997).
3. For details of our diary and survey samples, see Couldry *et al.* (forthcoming).
4. The elderly have been neglected in accounts of media consumption and popular culture: see Couldry (2000: 59). That is why we aimed in our project for as even an age sample as possible.

# 4
# The Local Public Sphere as a Networked Space

*Lewis A. Friedland and Christopher C. Long, with Yong Jun Shin and Nakho Kim*

In the United States, the public sphere has traditionally been grounded in the local community, and there has always been a close association between public space and community space. In both theory and practice, local communities and the public networks within them have served as 'schools for democracy,' however partially at times.

In this chapter, we examine this claim through a discussion of the relationships between local social networks, public networks, and local media ecology. Specifically, we examine the case of a local school referendum in Madison, Wisconsin, for two purposes. First, we empirically sketch a model of these complex relationships. Second, we use this framework to examine the dynamics of public formation in local community life.

We begin with our working theory of the local public sphere. We then, briefly, establish what these relations among the local public sphere, social networks, and a media ecology are. Next, we present the case of the Madison school referenda, examining, in turn, its history, timeline, and key actors, including the impact of newspaper coverage on public networks and the emergence of a blog-based social network that radically altered the local public sphere on this issue. We conclude by considering the implications of this case for the model that we are proposing, and some reflections on the model itself.

## The local public sphere

The Habermasian ideal public is grounded in a historical account that sees the emergence of a sphere of public speech, grounded in the kind of inter-subjective communicative recognition that later forms the foundation of his *Theory of Communicative Action* (Habermas, 1981 (1987)). The public sphere is not constituted primarily by a *form* of speech, rational deliberation, contrary to some of his critics, nor as a place. Rather, it is a communicative *relation* between speakers and hearers that requires a very specific set of institutional settings to emerge.

Dewey's earlier Pragmatist theory of the public sphere, articulated most fully in *The Public and Its Problems* (1927), remains distinct from that of Habermas, despite some broad overlapping concerns. Publics, for Dewey, emerge from *joint action on common problems*. Further, community and democracy are mutually constitutive:

> Wherever there is conjoint activity whose consequences are appreciated as good by all singular persons who take part in it, and where the realization of the good is such as to effect an energetic desire and effort to sustain it in being just because it is a good shared by all, there is in so far a community. The clear consciousness of a communal life, in all its implications, constitutes the idea of democracy (p.149).

Dewey's theory points the way to a more rigorous, empirically grounded understanding of how contemporary publics emerge. His emphasis on conjoint activity allows us to examine networks of action, which are simultaneously also discursive networks. His concept of the good introduces an internal normative dimension, the good as set by actors in community themselves; indeed, this shared good (or value) is precisely what constitutes community. Finally, it is this consciousness of a shared good and the conjoint activity necessary to realize it that is, for Dewey, the core of democracy itself.

Dewey, like De Tocqueville (2004) before him, sees the public schools as paradigmatic in the formation of the local public sphere in the United States. In his account, the schools grew from the publics formed around the problem of providing education as new townships were built. They grew as associations in civil society, not as government institutions. But – and this is critical for Dewey – these educational associations congealed into a 'state,' a more permanent set of arrangements for building, paying for, and maintaining the schools that were necessary for both community and town to thrive. This description of state formation from below draws on a real pattern of governance in the US, that in a changed form, persists to this day. After enduring as habitual institutional arrangements, these 'states,' or publics institutionalized in government, will almost certainly fail to address the problems they were originally designed to solve, or new problems will arise that render the older solutions unworkable. When this happens, the process of a public forming around a transformed set of problems should begin to emerge anew.

This is a useful model for thinking about the local public sphere today, for a number of reasons. First, the Deweyan concept of the problem-solving public is, at its core, empirical. Publics are identifiable at various stages of their formation, so we can describe and analyze their position in local communities, and further understand their effect on the trajectory of public problem solving. This emphasis on empirically identifiable publics, bound together in a larger public sphere (whose boundaries, in turn, are shaped by geography, government, and the space of cultural imagination) allows us to shift attention from the debate over the nature of 'the' public sphere (and its double, multiple publics) to both the process and consequences of public formation. In short, it allows us to see public as a *form of action*, as distinct from a discourse or identity.

Second, as Emirbayer and Sheller (1999) argue, the structure of the public sphere today is best understood as a set of interconnected social networks. That is to say, the structure of social groups from which publics form, are network structures, and these remain, in part, rooted in local communities. This does not mean of course that larger structures – national, global, or virtual – are not sources of public formation. It simply suggests that many significant publics are rooted in networks of groups in civil society. These networks often, indeed most often, are at least partially rooted in local space. A workable, empirical concept of the public must be capable of grasping these social networks in their complexity if it is to move beyond metaphor. The Deweyan problem-solving public does meet this criterion. By moving to the problem-solving framework, we can see more clearly which networks are addressing which problems, and what are the dynamics of their formation, particularly at the local level. (Friedland, 2006b)

Third, the problem-solving framework recast in network terms allows us to begin to address aspects of the macro-micro problem as it relates to problems of the formation of publics. In grasping the structure of the contemporary public sphere in the US this is particularly important. Given that the US is a federal republic, with policy formation taking place at the local, state, and federal levels, then a method of grasping public formation at each level, the complex interrelationship and dependencies among and across each level, and the forms and degrees of dependency of lower on higher levels of public formation is critical. While structures of nations differ considerably, we believe some form of this problem of the vertical integration of multiple publics at different layers of the social and political structure persists in formulating any public sphere theory that is sufficiently attentive to both national differences and public formation in the modern nation state.

Fourth, the problem-centered approach to the public sphere offers a new way of conceptualizing the relationships between local media ecologies and public networks. While we cannot develop this theory of media ecology here, in general we argue that local media ecologies are structured environments with stratified levels of dependencies (building on Ball-Rokeach, 2001). Some dependencies lie within the local media subsystem, for example, the well known dependence of much local television news on the editorial activity of local newspapers, or in a newer vein, the dependence of local blogging on newspaper journalism. Less well articulated is the dependence of the local news ecology more generally on community and civic ecologies. That is to say, news gathering is bound and shaped by the structures of local social, civic, and public networks. It often reflects them somewhat straightforwardly (as we will see), but there are times in which shifts in these networks themselves can reshape the flow of local media. At the most general level, these are open systems that shape each other through a complex set of interactions. We hypothesize that, as Internet-based forms of *local* communication continue to emerge, the net will have a more profound effect on these interactions among civic, public, and media ecologies. The Madison case offers an example of this re-channeling through the emergence of the local blogosphere.

In this chapter, then, we develop a specific case of the formation of a local public sphere around the schools in the US by presenting a local school controversy in Madison, Wisconsin. The case offers us a lens on the contemporary dynamics of public formation that takes in both the complex, interlocking, social and governmental networks, and media ecologies that are simultaneously rooted in locality and transcend local scale. The case speaks to the heart of the classic argument in Tocqueville and Dewey on the centrality of local school politics in the formation of the local public sphere, illustrating how these politics are still very much alive in American life.

In particular, the case demonstrates how a new public formed in response to an older, congealed set of problem-solutions. This new counter public managed, by skillful uses of social networks and new communications technologies, to defeat a powerful political coalition with deep roots in local social networks and strong support in the local newspapers, the traditional media of local public discourse.

Finally, this case shows the limits of the local public sphere, even in a case in which there is formal local control. Because it is a case of a controversy over local resources and the direction of local schools, it illustrates how local public formation is subject to multiple and cross-cutting influences and restrictions, such as tax policy, interests in social and cultural capital, and racial coding. It also demonstrates how a powerful opinion minority can come to dominate an issue of apparent wide local public interest using social networks and new technology.

## The Madison School referendum

The specific case that we are using to demonstrate these interrelationships is simple enough on its surface. Three interlinked school referenda were held in Madison, Wisconsin, during the spring of 2005 to determine whether to (1) significantly expand a school on Madison's South side that is attended predominantly by minorities; (2) to expand the overall operating budget of the school board, in part to pay for the new school; and (3) to expand the maintenance budget of the school board, also in part for the new school. While these referenda were formally separate, they were in fact all interlinked.

The referendum conflict has a historical foundation growing from race, class, and patterns of residence. In 1979 the Madison Metropolitan School District (MMSD) was under threat of a lawsuit by African American residents who claimed that resources for predominantly minority schools, concentrated on the South side, were inadequate. This pressure led to a 'school-pairing' plan, which linked a predominantly black, Southside elementary school and a predominantly white middle school, and involved busing. This pairing has continued for more than 20 years, largely accepted by the parents of both neighborhoods.

Kang (2000) found that the process of forming the pairing had left *four* major sub-publics, not all of equal size or power: a pro-pairing African-American sub-public; a smaller anti-pairing African-American group; a pro-pairing white sub-public; and an anti-pairing white sub-public. Each of these sub-publics formed a dominant set of arguments that entered the larger public discourse as frames, and each of these frames had a differential career in the local media. The pro-pairing African-American faction argued that while pairing was not the best possible outcome for their children, it was something that could be done immediately to improve their children's lives and education. The pro-pairing white parents largely made more generalized arguments, based on racial justice and equity, but also on the benefits of a diverse, multi-cultural education system for all children. The significant, but non-majority group of anti-pairing whites argued that the high quality of Madison schools would be compromised, that they had worked hard to buy homes in neighborhoods with good schools, and that this 'contract' would be breached if their children were bused. The anti-pairing African American group argued that pairing was a diversion. Their children did not need, necessarily, to be schooled with white children, as much as they needed a fair share of educational resources, and pairing would divert attention from this ultimate goal of equitable distribution. Each of these frames would, in its own way, become part of the background to the formation of the sub-publics around the 2005 referenda, forming a deeper context for the politics of schools, housing, neighborhood, property values, and race.

By 2005, an influx of minority children into the schools had significantly changed their composition, with 38 per cent coming from low-income families. Further, these low-income students remain concentrated in five disproportionately minority schools of the Madison Metropolitan School District's (MMSD) thirty-one elementary schools. More resources were being 'diverted' to educate this newer, less affluent group of students. The problem was exacerbated by a complex, state-imposed revenue cap on school spending. While the number of low-income and minority children was almost doubling, school expenditures were being slashed by US $46 million from 1993 to 2005. This split the public into two broad factions, those who wished to concentrate on low-income children and those who were concerned with the overall quality of the schools.

These broader issue frames were of course, built up through the detailed nitty gritty of local school politics. To establish a framework for understanding this detail, we turn to a brief timeline of events surrounding the referendum.

## Timeline

In January 2005, the Madison Metropolitan School District (MMSD) held the first public hearing on whether to hold referenda on the distribution of students in Madison schools and related budget issues. The MMSD board voted to place both issues on a ballot: whether to build a new Leopold School on the South side and whether to expand the maintenance budget to cover it. A third referendum, to expand the district's overall operating budget, was discussed but tabled.

In February, a proposal was put forward to close a number of Madison neighborhood schools in the context of building the new South side Leopold School, which generated widespread community controversy. Although subsequently withdrawn, this debate created the first public splits, which led to sub-publics forming on the referenda.

A March MMSD Board vote to eliminate 130 school positions intensified the controversy. In late March, the vote for the referenda was set for 24 May and the third question that would expand the overall operating budget of the school district was added.

A election on 5 April for two new school board members gave the issue a clear public focus. In the April election, one strong supporter of the referenda was re-elected and one strong opponent was elected. This was widely seen as giving the referenda opponents a public political victory, a second ally on the school board, a focus of their campaign, and political momentum.

On 24 May, the vote was held. As the result, the question on the new school in Leopold was narrowly turned down (Yes 46.7 per cent, No: 53.3 per cent), as well as the question on operational funding (Yes: 44.15 per cent, No: 55.95 per cent). Only question number three on the maintenance budget passed (Yes: 53.2 per cent, No: 46.85 per cent). Turnout was 20 per cent of all registered voters. This low-turnout was critical in allowing what was arguably a minority position, the defeat of the two referenda, to prevail with just over 10 per cent of the electorate.

## Public networks and campaigns

The scheduling of the referenda along with Spring school board elections activated (and reactivated) local publics. The anti-referenda group coalesced around a school board member, Ruth Robarts, who had been an original supporter of the Leopold School but switched her position after the January board meeting in which the decision to hold the referenda had been made. As early as April 2004, the previous year, Robarts had been involved in starting a local blog on school issues, SchoolInfoSystem.org (SIS) in conjunction with Jim Zellmer, a local high-tech entrepreneur. Robarts announced her shift of position on the blog which, as we will see, was the first public indication that school publics and media issues were becoming closely intertwined. SIS was also instrumental in supporting the successful election of a new candidate, Lawrie Kobza, to the school board. This nascent public against the referenda had been forming below the surface for at least a year, since the formation of SIS, but only broke into public awareness with Robarts use of SIS as a public medium for her announcement.

Still, in mid-April, even with Kobza's victory, most observers of local school publics assumed the referenda would easily pass. The coalition of networks supporting the referenda remained formidable. The MMSD itself supported the referenda, and could reach out to parents to mobilize their support. The majority of the School Board strongly favored the referenda. So did the editorial boards and, arguably, the newsrooms of each of the two daily newspapers (discussed below), as well as the leading local television station. Further, general business and city government interests supported the referenda (although the real estate group was split). In sum, a powerful local establishment lined up on the side of the referenda.

A series of publics formed and counter-formed, partly in response to each other. In March, Madison Citizens Acting Responsibly for Every Student (Madison CARES) was born as a formal organization to support the referenda, including the School Board President Bill Keyes and several members. In mid-April, Grandparents United for Madison Public Schools (GRUMPS), a pro-referenda group with high profile activists including a former School Board president, was organized.

Around the same time, Get Real, a group that opposed the previous Madison school referendum in 2003, announced its reactivation in an effort to defeat all three questions. Finally on 11 May, another anti-referendum group, Vote No For Change, was launched.

By the May referendum, then, the two sides were well set: the pro-referenda group encompassing much of the city's business and government establishment, state and local teachers' unions, the MMSD bureaucracy, the School Board, overlapping with Madison CARES and a broad citizen network, and GRUMPS, a cross section of Madison's liberal professional class. On the other side was the group centered around Robarts and Zellmer, and SchoolInfoSystem.org, an emergent alliance of (mostly) politically centrist, middle- and upper-middle class white professionals, and Get Real and Vote No for Change, more traditional and more conservative anti-tax groups. The pro-referendum coalition collected more than US $20,000 (of which more than US $15,000 came from teachers' unions), the anti-referendum coalition just over US $4,000, establishing a 4:1 overall advantage in funds (although in terms of grass roots contributions, they were almost evenly matched).

### News coverage of the referenda

The newspaper coverage of the referenda extended over five months in 2005. Here, we summarize only the most salient questions of that coverage: the newspapers' core coverage of local social networks; the overall semantic frames and their correspondence to those networks; and the emergence of an alternative public network, SIS.

The most notable element of the traditional newspaper coverage of the referenda was its almost perfect isomorphism with the network structure of the two major sub-publics, but particularly the pro-referenda network. Although the anti-referenda school board member was covered as part of the official story, it took a long time for the papers to catch up to the other layers of the anti-network, even though it had been publicly blogging for at least a year.

The two daily commercial newspapers in Madison, the *Wisconsin State Journal* (*WSJ*, circulation: 90,300 for 2005) and the *Capital Times* (*CT*, circulation: 19,357 for 2005), were the main traditional media outlets that covered the issues and positions of the school referendum in depth. Though there was some intensive coverage by local TV stations (the leading WISC-TV) and the alternative weekly paper *Isthmus* as well, the daily newspapers were the ones that printed the most articles and tracked the opinions of key players involved over the whole period. Though both dailies are owned by the same local media company (Capital Newspapers), their editorships are fully independent from each other. Despite its conservative editorial policies, the *State Journal* has been strongly supportive of the school system as a whole, even when it has acted as a friendly critic. As an institution, the pro-business interests of the paper lead it towards general support for quality schools.

The progressive *CT* the direct heir of the LaFollette Progressive tradition in Wisconsin, is almost the opposite of the *WSJ*. It has a left-liberal editorial policy and a formal commitment towards covering community issues in its pages. Its news staff and circulation are much smaller, however, and its reporters are more traditional professionally, generally eschewing innovations in reporting like public journalism.

These differences led to some complex sourcing and framing patterns on the referenda. The *CT* supported all three referenda (new school, expanded operating, and expanded maintenance budgets) explicitly through its editorials. The conservative *WSJ*, also carefully supported the referenda through its coverage, although one day before the vote, it editorialized against the question on permanent operational funding, although directly supporting the other two. The sourcing patterns of both papers did vary.

Both dailies covered the referenda extensively in the Spring of 2005 in both their news and editorial pages. The *CT'* editorials tended to rely more heavily on citizens' opinions, and the paper itself had a strong pro-referenda position. In the *WSJ* only three opinion pieces were by the editorial staff and most were from external writers, which included key actors. Though representing conservative and liberal positions on each editorial page, *WSJ* and *CT* both showed support for the referenda, differing only in the directness and fullness of support.

## Semantic networks on referenda

The two broad sub-public networks covered by each daily also yield a specific structure of frames. These are not simply a collection of frame heuristics, but are internally linked to each other in two semantic networks. Further, each semantic network is isomorphic with the sub-public that generates it. This is, of course, not surprising. We have understood that frames have sponsors and careers at least since the 1980s (Gamson, 1992; Snow *et al.*, 1986). The result here is not counterintuitive: strongly connected public networks are also aligned around similar frames; these frames themselves are semantically linked. What is interesting is the way that this powerful alignment of sub-public network and semantic network systematically occupies the issue space of local media. Cognitively, on any given issue, the media frame according to their networks of sources, as Tuchman demonstrated through the concept of the newsnet (Tuchman, 1978). But while she showed the dependence of the newsroom on the newsnet, she did not show its connection to the external structure of public networks. From another direction, Tichenor and colleagues (Tichenor *et al.*, 1980) have demonstrated how local elite networks shape the flow of news in local communities from above, but the connection to any specific network of networks is not specified. Our argument here is not systematic, but suggests how these levels of data might be connected and understood as interlocking and dependent networks of publics, frames, and coverage.

The major frames presented in support of the first referendum, the construction of Leopold elementary school, were supported by a variety of frames sponsored by the pro-referendum sub-public. Most were grounded in a stated desire for *maintaining quality public education* in Madison. This master frame of 'quality,' in turn, was supported by the subframes of (1) overcoming economic inequality, poverty, and housing problems; (2) improving the city environment for new business; and (3) training students to become engaged citizens. In contrast, the master frame for those opposing the construction of Leopold Elementary School centered around public disclosure of the school districts' budget information, concerns about the overcrowding on the one school site, and increased property taxes.

The discourses supporting the second referendum, the operating budget, were also organized by the *maintaining quality of public education* master frame. Major subframes included: (1) *public fiscal obligations*, including the willingness of citizens to pay high property taxes to maintain the schools, and fiscal responsibility; (2) *economic issues*, including maintaining the city's business climate and housing values, (3) *quality of life issues*, including the need to retain UW Madison faculty; (4) *citizenship issues*, including training a new generation of engaged citizens; and (5) *political issues*, including maintaining a progressive school board. The second referendum was also supported by (6) a *cultural capital* frame, specifically, the need to prevent planned cuts in the stringed music program. Finally, there was (7) a *quality of remedial education* frame, concerned with keeping bilingual and special education staffing levels high and maintaining current class sizes. In contrast, the opposition to the second referendum was mainly supported by (1) a *transparency* frame, a request for disclosure of school district budget information, a variant of (2) the *remedial frame*, saving cuts in bilingual education, and (3) a negative variant of the *public fiscal* frame, in this case, opposition to increased property taxes.

The frames of the third referendum, on the maintenance fund, ranged over a variety of issues. The *pro* frames drew on all of the frames discussed above in referendum one, adding the need to improve maintenance. In contrast, the opposition to the referendum was again, centered around *transparency* and *opposition to property tax increases*.

In general, the pro-referenda sub-issues were varied in scope, with a significant public master frame, linked to the theme of *quality of education*. On the other hand, the opposing frames were concentrated on one specific budget issue: too much spending unaccounted for, and the *need for greater transparency*. This rallying cry fueled the main opposition network, Schoolinfosystem.org.

## Schoolinfosystem.org

During the public debate about the 2005 school referenda, the website schoolinfosystem.org (SIS) operated as an informal social network for community activists from the both the left and right of the local ideological spectrum. While pursuing various and sometimes conflicting public policy agendas, members of the SIS network were united in their dissatisfaction with the quality of public discussion fostered by the school administration and school board majority, with the quality of coverage of school administration and policy by the local mainstream media, and in their total or partial opposition to the school referenda. As an open-access online forum for information, communication, debate (and rehearsal of debate) by individuals and organizations seeking to influence public opinion and deliberation on the schools, SIS functioned as a relatively specialized and dedicated discourse space in comparison to the local mainstream media's conventionally episodic and rhetorically formulaic coverage of the school referenda process and community debate. In this social role, the website was functionally aligned with the comparatively more analytical coverage of the referenda provided by Madison's alternative community weekly, *The Isthmus*, and also several local talk radio hosts, who also provided another alternative public platform for activists and MMSD critics associated with SIS.

Although the website first gained broad community attention and formal notice from the local mainstream media during the 2005 referenda debate, SIS was formed a year previous by school board dissident Ruth Robarts, a former teacher, alternative high school principal and University of Madison-Wisconsin Law School assistant dean then seeking a third term on the board, and Jim Zellmer, a local high-tech entrepreneur and principal in a firm producing computer-based 'virtual' tours of real estate for sale, and father of school-aged children. The two were not personally acquainted before Zellmer contacted Robarts early in the year and asked whether she would be interested in starting a website and online communication forum about the Madison schools. In April 2004, the two formed what was in effect a strategic political communication alliance with the goal of re-engineering the schools discourse.

From its inception, SIS was constituted as a complex social space consisting of two discrete but correlated communicative spaces – online and offline. Robarts recruited the early participants from among her network of community contacts developed during her years of involvement with the public schools as a teacher, administrator and elected official. This group consisted of individual community activists as well as representatives of local advocacy groups and represented a diverse range of views on both the social and economic issues facing the city's schools. This core group was invited to Zellmer's home, located in one of the city's most socially prestigious neighborhoods, for monthly salon like meetings where issues and ideas of common interest were discussed in the private space of his living room. Following the lead of Robarts and Zellmer, members of this group extended this discourse, or certain aspects of this discourse, to the SIS website, posting their opinions, observation, remarks, links to local and national news stories and other information of interest to the group, as well as responses to others' postings. The qualitative contrast between the character of the public discourse on schoolinfosystem.org and the private discussions at Zellmer's home exemplified the analytic distinction between frontstage and backstage social behaviors and the effect of the introduction of new media on those social considerations (Goffman, 1974; Meyerowitz, 1985).

From the outset, SIS had the strategic objective of influencing public opinion about schools by serving not only as a forum for expanding and enriching the public discourse but also more directly by seeking to become actively involved in the election of school board members who would, in the manner of Robarts (who watched election night coverage of her 2004 victory over a teachers union-backed opponent at Zellmer's home), challenge the administrative status quo. To achieve this goal, SIS regularly invited candidates and prospective candidates for the board to attend the monthly face-to-face sessions at Zellmer's home and talk with the group as well as to participate on the SIS website.

Both aspects of the SIS strategy reached fruition in the spring of 2005, first in the April school board elections and subsequently in the school referenda debate and balloting in May, as SIS emerged as a social force to be reckoned with. Lawrie Kobza, a first-time candidate for the board, had been an active SIS participant both online and offline and her candidacy was actively supported by Robarts and SIS, including Zellmer's endorsement on Kobza's campaign website, in a race in which she had decidedly underdog status against incumbent Bill Clingan, who was running with bipartisan political support from the local political establishment. In her public rhetoric on the SIS website and in interviews with other media, Kobza opposed the referenda and supported Robarts' oppositional stance to the board majority as well as the call by SIS and others for a broader public debate and improved communication about the public schools. Indeed, in reporting on both her campaign and her election-night victory 5 April, local mainstream media coverage emphasized both her alignment with Robarts and her ties to SIS.

In the public debate preceding the school referenda vote 24 May, SIS in both its online and offline dimensions functioned as a means of information exchange among members of the network and, for Robarts and others active in the schools discourse, as one component of a complex strategic communications strategy utilizing both mainstream and alternative community media channels. A decisive moment in the emergence of SIS as a key actor in the local public sphere occurred when Robarts, long a supporter of the Leopold Elementary School expansion proposed in referendum one, chose to publicly announce her change of mind in a 22 February posting to the SIS website. A lengthy *WSJ* story the next day on her change of position discussed her decision to make it public on the SIS website, which the article described as 'a Web site, which is run by private individuals and is often critical of the School Board and administration.' The article, which appeared on the front of the Local News section, quoted MMSD Superintendent Art Rainwater disputing factual claims made by Robarts in her SIS posting, and board member Juan Lopez's claim that Robarts on SIS was 'playing with the truth. I think this kind of forum is destructive.' Robarts was not quoted in the story and was said to have been unavailable for comment.

Given the story and the controversial role ascribed to SIS, it is reasonable to surmise that the story served to bring SIS to the attention of the broader Madison public and therefore had the effect, however unintentional by the newspaper, of markedly elevating the prominence and importance of SIS in the referenda discourse, and thereby significantly advancing the evaluative process by which SIS sought legitimacy as a new medium in the local public sphere. Indeed, in its coverage of the referenda vote, The *CT* in its May 25 editions on the results of the referenda vote included a sidebar story about the role of SIS under the headline, 'Web Blog a Growing Force in School Policy.' The story quoted Zellmer on the history and purpose of SIS and in the second and third paragraph included this assessment from local blogger and media critic Kristian Knutsen: 'With the April election of Lawrie Kobza, and today's defeat of two out of the three referenda, it is clear that there is an emerging property taxpayers' revolt in the city, one that is typified by many contributors to School Information System.'

The emergence of SIS decisively broke the fit between the coverage of the schools by the mainstream daily newspapers and the pro-school issue public. SIS was a medium of this break. Through the formation of the weblog, a counter public was able to form that had been largely ignored by the mainstream press, with the exception of the coverage of school board member Ruth Robarts in that particular individual role. Even during the spring, SIS was, as we have noted, rarely discussed. But it was gathering public affiliates, via the net and when the two referenda were finally defeated, it became clear that SIS had successfully worked as both a communication network and medium of public formation.

## The reconstruction of the local public sphere

Before SIS and the referendum, the structure of the public around the school issue was largely given by the prior existing community structure of social capital oriented to the schools: institutional actors, the mainstream media, organized community groups, unions and business. Before the emergence of SIS, we might say that we could have read the networks of publics engaged in the local schools from the pages of the papers, and seen an almost complete mapping of one on the other.

The coverage by the mainstream media largely reflected these existing institutional arrangements. The more central any given actor (individual or institutional) was in the network, the more likely he or she, or his or her organization, was to be covered by both newspapers. This was so regardless of the reporting philosophy of the newspaper (public versus traditional) or ideology (conservative v. progressive). Simply, the combined institutional and social capital structures of the community determined which aspects of the network were covered. This was also true for the semantic frames. Central actors were much more likely to have their frames entered into the public discourse in the newspapers.

We would have expected such a powerful coalition of actors, whose positions were centrally covered over the course of the referenda, to have prevailed politically. When business interests, the school board, the school administration, the teachers' union, and major segments of civil society coalesce around a position, it is reasonable to assume that they will prevail, other things being equal. Certainly, the preponderance of media power, both formal (editorial) and informal (news) was behind the three referenda.

But they did not prevail. Rather, a counter public, a rather clear minority, which opposed the referenda did, both in electing its candidates (two of seven) to the school board, and in defeating two of the three referenda, the two most directly related to expanding school services. Why?

First, we need to look to the network configurations of the opposition publics. They were situated in the heart of the middle- and upper-middle classes of the city, predominantly white, and connected, at least partially, to real estate interests. Although they were not conservative (per se) they were towards the center-right of a broader liberal consensus. They were highly motivated home owners, in wealthier parts of the city. Although we do not have hard evidence for this election, historically, such high SES citizens turn out and vote in higher numbers.

Second, they were able to mobilize and *extend* their existing social networks using a highly effective blog. Although the blog was a source of much opinion about the existing school board, it was also very effective in mobilizing and using statistics to perform a watchdog function. That is to say, it managed to establish itself, for some, as a legitimate alternative source of information and interpretation. Among its major public claims was that the school board was wasting money. It was able to demonstrate this claim effectively by publishing school budget data and analyzing it (something the papers did not do).

Third, because of historically low turnouts in 'off' elections, the total turnout for the referenda was just over 20 per cent. This allowed a highly organized group, *probably* a minority (although it may, in turn, have reflected the views of a 'silent majority') to dominate an election by capturing just over 10 per cent of all registered voters . So these elections may have been aberrations. However, school board elections being held in Spring 2006 and fought along the lines, offered new evidence of the power of the SIS group when two new candidates supported by the group were elected, and one narrowly defeated.

New technologies were used to solidify, mobilize, and extend newly forming social networks qua publics around the schools. They allowed a group that would likely have remained a minority to speak to a broader public, and mobilize sufficient support to defeat two referenda backed by both major media and an array of some of the most important public actors around schools issues.

On the one hand, this study suggests that local publics are still structured by the fault lines of social networks. On the other, the new technologies of the web, gave a conservative counter public a medium in which to form and mobilize. The core of that counter public pre-existed the web. But the web allowed it to grow, solidify internally, and extend its influence into the broader public realm. One irony, is that the blog emerged as a broader public force only after it was noted in the pages of the *WSJ*. The paper gave the blog both attention and, indirectly, legitimacy. This attention in the broader public sphere of the daily paper then allowed the blog to grow as an independent force.

This case raises many more questions than it answers. We have asserted that the prior structure of social capital strongly shapes the public networks that emerged on the schools issue, but we have certainly not proved that here. We also have asserted that there is a three-way mapping: issue publics map onto prior existing social networks; issue publics map onto news coverage; and news coverage maps the semantic frames raised by issue publics. Again, we recognize that this chapter has only outlined this argument with descriptive evidence, not proved this.

Finally, we have shown that a highly interconnected and stable complex–the networks of social capital, publics, and news coverage – was perturbed by a well organized counter public using blogging technology. But we still don't know whether the emergence of SchoolInfoSys.org a) independently changed the dynamic of a prior consensus; b) revealed the weakness of that consensus and the existence of a 'silent majority' that supported the SIS view; and/or c) represented the victory of a well-organized minority that was able to prevail because of a low-turnout and certain traditional electoral advantages because of its high SES. In fact, some combination of these factors could have been at work.

Still, this study begins to offer several new perspectives on the relationship between media and local public life. It links the Deweyan conception of the problem-solving public sphere to network methods. It demonstrates that there is a relationship between social networks and public networks, and that these, in turn, appear to shape the coverage of local issues. And it begins to show how the dynamics of social and public networks and new networked communication technology can combine to shift the balance on a complex local issue.

# 5
# Public Sphere and Publicness: Sport Audiences and Political Discourse

*Cornel Sandvoss*

Debates among political communication scholars and audiences of spectator sport often share a surprising consensus: while the first group has lamented the popularization and thus trivialisation of politics in which sport has played an important role, the latter has objected to the politicisation of sport. In this chapter I will explore the role the consumption of media sport plays in the contemporary public sphere and assess its consequences for forms of public discourse as well as patterns of sport consumption.

## Sports fandom as a public sphere?

As much as Habermasian scholars have envisioned political discourse as a truly public enterprise shielded from the private realm, sport audiences insist on sport as a private activity that should be performed and consumed in a sphere unsullied by other matters of public debate. However, the roots of the seemingly inescapable politicisation of sport lie in the core of modern spectator sport itself. While sports fandom is intrinsically private in its core motivations, the idiosyncratic bond between fan and object of fandom is inescapably public. As an 'interpretative' (Jenkins 1992) but also partisan community, sport fans – from soccer fans displaying their team colours to the self-proclaimed 'Red Sox nation' – tend to form a most visible audience group. At the same time, sports spectatorship has shifted from stadia designed for sport consumption to the same mass media – newspapers, radio, internet and, most prominently, television – in which scholars locate, for better or for worse, the public spaces that have succeeded the early bourgeois public sphere (cf. Dahlgren 1995, Curran 1997, McNair 2000).

However, the significance of spectator sport in the public sphere is not only the result of structural changes in the realm of spectator sport and its mediated representation, but also driven by agency. In the following dialogue two fans of the German club Bayer Leverkusen initially agree that football and politics should remain separate spheres:

> *Harald*: There are clubs that really insist that football and politics are linked such as St.Pauli or so. They can be a Nazi or ultra left-winged. I want to watch a football game, it is not a party conference.
> *Thomas*: But right winged slogans really upset me though . . .
> *Harald*: . . . yes, sure . . .
> *Thomas*: . . . if Bayer fans scream 'Uh, uh, uh' if a colored player has the ball, although we have got colored players ourselves – not to mention that it would be bigoted anyway – then this is really idiotic.
> *Harald*: Yes, also those people that do not cheer when Emerson [Brazilian international] scores, that is totally disrespectful.
> *Thomas*: It is the same when they go on about the Dutch who play for Schalke and Eric Meijer plays for us and everyone cheers for him. But the next moment they shout 'Scheiß Holländer' if one of Schalke's Dutch players has the ball.
> *Harald*: It's ridiculous. I don't like the Dutch particularly, but Eric plays here and all right then. (Sandvoss 2003: 51–2)

Contrary to their intentions, Harald and Thomas quickly engage in a debate which reflects their political beliefs through their fandom. Much like Tulloch's *Dr Who* fans 'it was not ("politics") as such which fans objected to, but "politics" attached to *another reading formation*' (Tulloch and Jenkins 1995: 172). The plea for spectator sport unsullied by politics is thus a reaction to opposing discourses: the liberal football fan who is appalled by rightwing supporters, the baseball traditionalist who opposes evident tendencies towards monopoly capitalism unsettling the game's competitive balance, or the sports fan opposed to immigration who finds him- or herself confronted with multiethnic teams reflecting the growing transnational mobility of professional athletes (Sandvoss 2003, cf. Lanfranchi and Taylor 2001).

Spectator sport, while still heavily gendered, thus forms a space of open and lively political debate that for television's domestic consumption context is less regulated and exclusive than the early bourgeois public sphere. It thus is part of a realm of popular media consumption that has been lauded by an increasing number of scholars, who are critical of Habermas' normative vision, as one of genuine social and cultural debate and progression. McKee (2005) has juxtaposed the opposing concepts of public discourse that follow by distinguishing between modern and post-modern conceptualizations of the public sphere:

> A 'postmodern', 'relativist' approach suggests that all . . . cultures may be as good as each other – the trivial, feminized culture is as worthy as serious, masculine culture; the vulgar working-class forms of communication should be respected as much as 'educated' modes of engagement . . . a 'modern', 'universalist' approach, by contrast, sees cultural difference as a problem to be overcome in order to guarantee quality. In order for all citizens to be equal

in society, they must all be informed about the really important issues in that society . . . and they must all discuss these issues using the form of communication that is best suited to equal public discussion (McKee, 2005: 27–28).

McKee's chosen terminology and his summary of these approaches are problematic as they simplify both sides of the argument, exemplified by the irony of McKee's construction of a uniform 'postmodern' position. However, the distinction McKee draws is nevertheless useful as it establishes the two poles between which I seek to assess whether the political discourses in the consumption of media sport mark the further decline of a free and rational public or constitutes an alternative public sphere in which significant cultural, social and political issues, which are neglected or insufficiently addressed in the official channels of parliamentary democracies, are negotiated and reflected upon. In developing a detailed and elaborate counter-conceptualisation of such a 'postmodern' public sphere, Hartley (1996, 1999) offers a useful starting point to explore the spaces of political discourse in sports fandom. To Hartley the liberal public sphere only constitutes one field of public discourse which is embedded within the broader spheres of all public communication described as 'media sphere' and 'semiosphere'. Within the semiosphere modes of 'DIY-citizenship' are formed (Hartley 1999), finding their historical point of reference rooted in contrast to Habermas' normative vision not in the rise of the bourgeoisie in early modern Europe, but the Hellenic city state 'where . . . democracy, drama and didactics were one and the same thing' (Hartley 1999: 7). Today, according to Hartley, the public space of the polis is reconstituted through a state of constant audienceship, or what Abercrombie and Longhurst (1998: 68–9) have described as 'diffused audiences', as now 'being a member of an audience . . . is constitutive of everyday life'. It is thus in the act of media consumption that Hartley (1999: 178–9) locates political discourse and citizenship: 'Citizenship is no longer simply a matter of a social contract between state and the subject, no longer even a matter of acculturation to the heritage of a given community; DIY citizenship is a choice people can make for themselves. . . . The places where you can find DIY citizens exercising their semiotic self-determination are on television and among its audience'. With television sport among television's most popular genres, the question is thus whether the political discourses among sport fans mark the decline of rational critical debate through their trivialisation and commercialisation or whether they can be described as forms of DIY-citizenship that in their inclusiveness and non-discriminatory nature supersede the achievements of the bourgeois public sphere.

## Sports fandom and DIY citizenship

All forms of discourse require a shared space. The above quoted debate between Bayer Leverkusen fans Thomas and Harald took place in the official

Bayer 'fan house', a meeting place for fans, which being jointly funded by the club and local government bears the hallmarks of the socially interventionist West German welfare state that Habermas (1962/1990) identifies as crucial factor in the decline of the public sphere. More recently, however, Leverkusen fans have resorted to an alternative sphere of discussion that is mirrored by fan communities across the spectrum of popular culture: the use of internet fora. *Werkself.de*, named after the phrase 'factory eleven' often used to describe the club owned by the pharmaceutical multinational Bayer, counts over 1,700 registered users in comparison to the approximately one-hundred fans who frequent the fan house.

A closer analysis of the structure of *werkself.de* reveals a space of discourse that indeed blurs the boundaries between democracy, drama and didactics as Hartley (1999) suggests. *Werkself* is divided into two thematic sections: the first is dedicated to users' shared object of fandom, including the most used thread entitled 'Bayer Leverkusen Stammtisch', deriving its name from the German for a table in a pub or bar at which participants, usually males, meet in regular intervals. The *Stammtisch*, while in folksiness appearing as the antithesis to the rational debate in early bourgeois salons Habermas describes, nevertheless constitutes a space that encourages forms of 'enunciative productivity' (Fiske 1992) in which discourses about the fan object and public as well as private life overlap. This quality of the *Stammtisch* as space of open and unrestricted discourse establishes important principles that inform the remaining threads in the forum. Despite its focus on the object of fandom, the participation of fans from different age, gender and socio-cultural groups in the *Stammtisch* fosters a dialogue in which questions of politics and identity inevitably return: following the draw of Leverkusen's Champions League match with Liverpool FC in December 2004, for instance, fans from both clubs initiated new threads in the respective online fora of the other club. On *werkself* a thread was started by a Liverpool fan with the following posting: 'hello I'm a liverpool fan. but i can only speak english. I am just interested in your thoughts on the champions league game with liverpool and leverkus' (*www.werkself.de*). While this post sought to initiate a discussion of the teams' chances of progressing to the quarter finals, the developing discourse quickly took another direction. After many regular users welcomed the Liverpool fan to the best of their abilities in English, a German posting by a Bayer fan the following day, stating his disapproval of the welcoming attitude of other Bayer fans towards Liverpool fans and expressing his dislike of the English through derogative terms such 'island monkeys' triggered a heated debate among users that continued over 159 posts for the next two months. While the discourse initially evolved around Leverkusen fans' experiences with English fan groups, the core of the debate quickly shifted to questions of local and national identity and the self-understanding of users as fans and citizens alike. While some fans insisted on the legitimacy of disliking and provoking those from other countries, the majority of users rejected such discourses in favour of a critical reflection on their own identity and notions of Germanness:

> Why is it so difficult for the Germans who live here to simply reach out sometimes? . . . This is 'only' about fans from another country and of another club who I for my part will definitely greet with hospitality and respect. However, the word respect, as so often, doesn't seem to be understood on this site (Thom 17, my translation, www.werkself.de).

Or in the words of a second fan:

> It is sad, how some people on here think. In principle always negative, unfriendly, uncourteous, and without humour. And probably terribly proud to be a German. They are exactly the clichés that exist about us. A good thing that not all of us are like that (Tommi, my translation, *www.werkself.de*).

As the debate unfolded, users failed to overcome their differences and no cathartic consensus emerged. In the days after the return leg was played, postings ceased. But this discourse is nevertheless evidence of the significance of the field of popular culture as a space for debates in which identities and citizenship are formed and exercised. It may be far from an ideal space; much of the discourses here and in sports fandom in general take place through the frames of national identity and nationalism, which as categories resulting out of the mercantile organisation of early modern Europe draw on the significance of the very state institutions that are so acutely underplayed in Habermas' account of the early bourgeois public sphere (cf. Eley 1992, Price 1995). Yet, the discourses we find on *werkself* are nevertheless meaningful debates between freely associating audience members in which boundaries between entertainment and politics, between identity and conviction, are crossed, giving further weight to Hartley's (1997: 182) claim that 'the major contemporary political issues, including environmental, ethnic, sexual and youth movements, were all generated *outside* the classic public sphere'.

## Publics and publicness

However, rather than supporting, in McKee's (2005) words, postmodern conceptualizations of public discourse, the study of sport audiences reveals two significant dimensions of the role of popular culture in the public sphere that are difficult to reconcile with such approaches. The first concerns the popular notion of alternative 'publics' or 'public spheres'. In addition to the first section of *werkself* dedicated to fans' favourite team, a second accommodates non-team based debates, ranging from threads dedicated to football and other sports to an open 'small talk' forum. Here postings cut across the spectrum of concerns and interests in modern everyday life. Threads dedicated to media events such as the reality TV programme *Big Brother*, the Eurovision Song Contest or the latest royal wedding, and everyday life advice regarding diets, speeding tickets or smoking here appear side by side with debates about the future of the Catholic Church in the wake of the death of John Paul II or discussions of Germany's recent political history marking the 75th birthday of the former chancellor Helmut Kohl. Others are dedicated to broad political themes such as the global anti-poverty movement or news topics such as the Asian Tsunami and the fight against racism in football and beyond (*www.werkself.de*). What the presence of all these topics illustrates is the interconnectivity and intertextuality of popular discourses. In this sense the use of the plural 'publics', upon which many recent studies of the public sphere highlighting the role of mass communication draw, is problematic. The root of the problem here is Habermas' (1962/1990) original analysis in which he carefully traces the formation of terms such as 'Öffentliche Meinung', 'public opinion' and 'opinion publique', yet condenses a historic ideal type as the basis of his normative vision in the concept of 'Öffentlichkeit'. Öffentlichkeit, it would follow, constituted a normative space, and consequently those who reject Habermas' normative ideals on the basis of its insufficient acknowledgement of differences along the lines of gender, sexual orientation, class or ethnicity could and did envision and describe alternative spaces: other public *spheres*. It is then, as Crossley (2004: 110) notes, 'because Habermas' conception of the ideal speech situation is based upon transcendental deductions from abstract and decontextualized models of communicative engagement, [that] these ideals seem impossible to realise in actual social contexts', and that notions of alternative normative and actual public spheres arise. The normative ideals and the empirical assessment of public discourses thus become interwoven in an unhelpful fashion. The public discourses taking place among sports fans highlight the need to separate these two levels of debate, in that they underline an inherent dimension of 'Öffentlichkeit' that has been conflated in its normative evaluation. 'Öffentlichkeit' does not, as its English translation 'public sphere' suggests, describe as space but literally translates as 'publicness'. It describes a *state or condition* that either exists or does not (as in the forms of autocratic rule found in much of medieval Europe preceding the rise of the bourgeois public sphere). However, as a state it has no plural in either a grammatical nor conceptual sense, and hence cannot be fragmented or divided. It is precisely this inherent and unavoidable interconnectivity of all communication that renders the notion of spheres of little value. It is therefore not, as so often assumed, the singular character of the public sphere on which its normative value hinges. Let us reconsider Garnham's (1992: 371) well-known claims in this context:

> the problem is to construct systems of democratic accountability integrated with media systems of matching scale that occupy the same social

space as that over which economic or political decision will impact. If the impact is universal, then both the political and media systems must be universal. In this sense, a series of autonomous public spheres is not sufficient. There must be a single public sphere.

The normative dimension of Garnham's account thus lies not in his insistence on a single public – which exists for the very reason that however heterogeneous a space of discourse may be, it only becomes public for its interconnectedness – but in his claims as to how this single public sphere should relate to legislative and executive decision-making processes. And it is on this level that Habermas still has much to contribute to an understanding of public discourse in contemporary popular culture.

## Citizens between self-determination and servo-mechanisms

The crucial question in assessing whether audiences of professional sports can indeed be described as DIY-citizens is to what extent their participation in the public sphere is based on 'semiotic self-determination' (Hartley 1999: 179) and how such semiotic self-determination is manifested in democratic processes. Semiotic self-determination presupposes both independence and reflexivity on behalf of the individual as *conditio sine qua non* of rational critical discourse. The above examples indicate that sport consumption and citizenship are not mutually exclusive spheres. Fans participate in discourses originating outside the realm of professional sport. By the same token, however, such discourses take place through the prism of fandom which in its psychological premises diverges from what is acknowledged as the basis of rational, critical and, not least, dispassionate discourses.

We therefore need to account for the social and psychological processes on which the relationship between fan and fan object (i.e. one's favorite sport, team or athlete) is based and thus how this relationship informs and shapes fans' participation in public discourses. Recent fan studies have increasingly focused on the psychological foundation of the interaction between fan and fan object (Stacey 1994, Elliott 1999, Hills 2002). Seeking to explore the psychological and social premises of sports fandom, I have previously identified a self-reflective relationship between fan and fan object in which the later functions as a mirror to the fans' self-image (Sandvoss 2003, 2004, 2005). The most obvious example of this self-reflective relationship on a rhetorical level is fans' regular use of the pronoun 'we' when describing their object of fandom. On the level of meaning construction the self-reflective quality of fans' favorite teams and athletes is illustrated by diverging and on occasion even opposing readings and meanings which fans derive from the very same fan object. Rather than a denotative core of the fan text such readings reflect fans' sense of self, beliefs and convictions (Sandvoss 2003). Sport audiences thus participate in the public sphere through the medium of the object of fandom.

Yet, this participation in discourses through the prism of the fan object would not impact on the substance of public discourse if the fan object functioned as a neutral medium. However, as McLuhan (1964) reminds us, we cannot separate such content from its form. Let's briefly return to Harald and Thomas's discussion. Harald claims that he doesn't 'like the Dutch particularly', but equally is prepared to subordinate his anti-Dutch feelings to the object of fandom ('Eric plays here and all right then'). Harald's quote illustrates a process in which not only the fan shapes the fan text in the act of reading, but the object of fandom shapes the substance of his convictions and beliefs. The fan serves an extension of his own reflection much as 'Narcissus mistook his own reflection in the water for another person. The extension of himself by mirror numbed his perceptions until he became the servo-mechanism of his own extended or repeated image' (McLuhan 1964: 41). Confronted with a changing object of fandom that no longer conforms to his previous convictions, Harald functions as servo-mechanism of his fan object and begins to alter his own beliefs and opinions. The political discourses among fans are thus embedded in the social and economic macro conditions that are woven into the textual nature of the fan object: consumer capitalism, intertextuality, and economic globalisation with their implications on migration and erosion of national and ethnic identities. Following the increasing migration of professional athletes and the resulting international makeup of professional teams, fans whose identities are built on categories of the national or ethnicity lose the basis for the participation in related discourses as they find it increasingly difficult to communicate such discourses through their changing object of fandom. While in the case of xenophobic, jingoistic or racist attitudes, most of us will consider the exclusion of such themes from public discourses hardly deplorable, the problem here is one of the principle by which participation in public discourses is limited though the prism of fandom.

This is further illustrated in the case of followers of American professional sports, such as baseball, outside North America. Major League Baseball (MLB) in Britain, for instance, attracts a young, professional and largely male audience. These audiences command comparatively high educational capital and displayed particular interest in politics and international relations.[1] In a study of this audience group I undertook in 2004 and 2005, interviewees' interest in non-domestic sports often correlated with a distinctly internationalist outlook and broadly centre-left political views. While these views did not appear in conflict with an interest in American sport when baseball first became a regular fixture of British television schedules during the Clinton administration in the early 1990s, the recent changes in US foreign policy have rendered such forms of fandom problematic: following the attacks of 11th September 2001, American sports media and the baseball industry have sought to celebrate baseball as quintessentially American in its mediated representation employing 'patriotic' signifiers such as adding the Stars and Stripes to franchise uniforms, while athletes, such as the Red Sox pitcher Curt Schilling, joined the campaign trail to support George W. Bush's re-election. Conversely, public shows of disagreement with baseball's new politics rarely featured in its mediated representations. The silent protests of Puerto Rican first baseman Carlos Delgado, against the US-led war in Iraq by remaining seated during the 7th inning renditions of 'God Bless America' was reported only by a small minority of liberal media outlets such as the *New York Times*.

While British–American relations dominated public discourses in Britain in the wake of the invasion of Iraq, the shifting textual substance of the sport of baseball and its franchise teams undermined potential spaces of political discourse in the realm of sport consumption for many British and other European fans critical of America's changing geopolitical role. Many interviews seemed acutely aware that their spaces for debate in baseball were eroded:

> There is too much American propaganda, especially in Canadian cities. When the [Toronto Blue] Jays decided not to sing God Bless America, Bud Selig [MLB commissioner] said all teams *must* play God Bless America. . . . Politics are getting too much involved, the congress getting involved. It's just, let's play the game, as far as I am concerned. Bud Selig is more about politics and more about money (Warren, 26, from London).

> I am political person so it definitely comes into it. It's funny. Even the Randy Johnson thing, I don't like Randy Johnson because of that redneck thing, but I don't really quite dislike Curt Schilling that much, even though he is equally redneck, cowboy type, *and* he campaigns for George W. Bush whom I can't stand (*laughs*), That definitely was a killer though – put me off Schilling. He can do up his ankle now. But you do put those things into it, because they are the players I shy away from. I do like more flamboyant players like Pedro (Chris, 33, London).

While these fans nevertheless find alternative points of identification through which they seek to articulate their counter-hegemonic views – Canadian teams or Latin players such as Pedro Martínez – both realize the unevenly stacked field of discourse in their favorite sport. To other fans a complete disengagement with the geopolitical aspects of baseball seemed the only feasible option. A number of interviews stressed their interest in British over American baseball, often avoiding the issue of politics altogether:

> I look at baseball on the field, and I don't really follow American politics. I do not deal with American politics.

> *Question*: Out of principle?

Pretty much. I mean, I really like the States, but politically they are a disaster. Absolute disaster. . . . I don't even have to argue about that. And I don't want the sport to mix in with politics (Daniel, 30, London).

Here, the fan object can no longer accommodate these fans' critical discourses, illustrating clear limits to the degree to which sport consumption offers a space of semiotics self-determination. Revising Hartley's concept of DIY citizenship I have thus suggested the notion of 'IKEA citizenship' in the consumption of popular culture (Sandvoss 2003): an engagement with public discourse that much like the assembly of flat-packed furniture is based upon the input of consumers, but in which our creativity is limited by what Habermas (1962/1990) has labeled the 'integration imperative' of the culture industry. As a space attracting consistently large audiences across different media, spectator sport is part of a public that is more encompassing than the early bourgeois public sphere ever was. However, in its inclusiveness it has tied consumers/ citizens to the agenda-setting power of media and sports industries even in areas of fandom where their own discursive productivity is most evident.

## Conclusion

The ambivalent semiotic processes in which fans on the one hand communicate through the fan object while it in turn structures the frames through which such discourses can be expressed does not quite warrant the distinction between 'public' and 'mass' that C.W. Mills (1956) suggests and which Habermas resorts to in the conclusion of *The Structural Transformation*. Neither, however, does it support the celebration of popular culture and mass media as means to broaden political engagement and participation. The analysis of the role of spectator sport in the public sphere documents not only the empirical and normative problems of Habermas' account but also the shortcomings of many of his critics.

From this study of the participation by sport audiences in public discourses three particular findings follow: Firstly, the wide range of topics and issues debated among fans, such as in the Bayer internet forum *werkself*, serves as a reminder that Öffentlichkeit constitutes a *state*, not a *space*. Publicness, as a state, may be in decline or under threat, but it cannot, by definition, be fragmented as its fragmentation would automatically equal its disappearance. The notion of publics or public spheres at first originated in studies of particular audience groups disenfranchised from the official spaces of political debate in liberal democracies to whom such spaces came to constitute 'arenas for the formation and enactment of social identities' (Fraser 1992: 125). While it is easy to see the appeal of the notion of 'publics' in this context, the example of spectator sport illustrates that it is precisely on the basis of mediated intertextuality and for the nexus between popular entertainment and political debate that the boundaries between fandom and citizenship are crossed.

Secondly, the vivid participation of sport fans in discourses from the narrowly political (such as anti-war protests) to broader questions of cultural and social life is further evidence of public debates of civic significance outside official spaces of political discourse in liberal, parliamentary democracies. The engagement of sport audiences in such discourses thus problematizes divisions between the private and the public realm. Habermas and most of his critics are of course in agreement in recording the erosion of such boundaries, yet evaluate such processes differently: while Habermas laments the collapse of the private sphere, to his critics it becomes the basis of its widened reach. The discourses among sport fans do not match Habermas' (1989: 160) description of a 'pseudo-public and sham private sphere of cultural consumption' in which 'so-called leisure behaviour, once it had become part of the cycle of production and consumption, was already apolitical, if for no other reason that its incapacity to constitute a world independent of immediate constraints of survival needs'. While the second part of Habermas' assessment is confirmed by a distinct lack of a true utopian potential in discourses among sports fans as they communicate through the frames of their object of fandom, this only renders debates in the realm of sport consumption apolitical in the most radical interpretation of the term in which no truly political discourse can exist in the condition of industrial modernity (cf. Marcuse 1964/1991) – which if we look at *The Structural Transformation* in isolation from his subsequent work (Habermas 1981) is of course part of Habermas' argument (cf. Holub 1991). Regardless of whether this may be true, it remains a conceptually unhelpful move in which we lose the ability to account for the very real issues of nationalism, ethnicity, religion or gender negotiated in acts of sport consumption. However, as much as the blurring of boundaries between the private and public realm is no evidence of the complete demise of the public, neither is it a sign of its vitality. When, for example, van Zoonen (2001: 671), drawing on another segment of popular contemporary television programming, proclaims that '*Big Brother*'s success . . . proves, with wider popularity than has feminism, that the bourgeois division between the public domain, with its concomitant regulations, and the private with its own code of conduct is not widely accepted or appreciated, and has moreover lost its social functionality', she fails to account for the hierarchies and regulations 'which the white male bourgeoisie created' seamlessly give way to new limits of discourse created through the industrial and commercial framing of the mass media texts through which they are eroded. If Habermas underestimates the substance of political discourses in mediated popular culture, interpreting it as the salvation of the public sphere would hover between political naivety and a collaborative stance towards the culture industry which not only Marxist scholars will regard to sit uneasily with concerns over open and equal discourse.

This leads us to a third and final consideration: popular culture is not a neutral medium. If we criticise Habermas for a lack of awareness as to how the physical and social context of the early bourgeois public sphere maintained boundaries of class and gender, we must not overlook that mediated texts as vehicles of audiences' engagement in the public sphere structure such engagement in similar ways. Among sport audiences rational discourses give way to participation in public debates through the prism of fandom. The intense psychological bond between fan and fan object shapes and constraints the nature of possible discourses. As macro political and economic conditions change, the basis of oppositional discourses among sport audiences is at risk of suffocation as the example of baseball fans in Britain illustrates. While as McKee (2005: 196) argues 'the consumption of culture is part of the political process', this does not mean that it makes an unproblematic contribution to this process.

It is precisely this point at which the crucial challenge – to and also the most acute shortcoming of – approaches to the public sphere in media and communication studies lies. Given the nature of the discipline many such approaches have seized upon the aspects of Habermas' work describing communication and interaction. Their case has often rested on documenting viable forms of political discourse taking place in public life and private consumption alike. However, Habermas' (1962/1990) argument, and herein lies its central normative dimension, is not about forms of political discourse or forms of rational–critical dialogue alone, but in its essence concerned with the structure of the entire political processes. It is an argument about the interplay of political discourses and executive and legislative decision-making processes. The question thus is not if forms of political discourse are part of the political process, which by definition they are as long as we understand the public sphere or 'publicness' as non-fragmentable entities. Instead, we need to ask exactly *how* discourses contribute to *which* political processes.

In the case of the consumption of spectator sport the answer, which I believe carries wider validity in light of the many parallels between the affective relationship between text and reader in sports fandom and in other realms of media consumption, is one that while documenting public discourses outside the liberal public sphere nevertheless validates some of Habermas' fundamental concerns. In the narrow terms of parliamentary democracies, discourses among sport fans can occasionally translate into changing voting patterns, or in rare cases even to the formation of political parties (Bale 1993).[2] In most cases, however, affiliations in sport consumption either follow from existing political beliefs, or are based on the same socio-demographic, ethnic and religious backgrounds forming such convictions. The political discourses in sport consumption strikingly coincide with a party political system in which public dialogue is marked by 'rigid habit' (Habermas 1989: 213). The media spectacle of a pseudo-dialogue between political parties that merely confirms party supporters' opinions bears hallmarks of fans' partisan identification with sport teams.

More commonly participation in the public sphere through sport consumption will impact on political processes outside the channels of parliamentary democracy through social movements as well as politics of identity, in other words, the ways in which we, as individuals and audiences, relate to and interact with others. It is here that the public discourses among sport audiences have an important role to play and where their greatest progressive potential lies, from anti-racism campaigns to critical reflections on fans' identities. Many will consider such issues as naturally outside the governance of the state. However, it is also evident that political discourses are most thriving in spectator sport where its audiences are otherwise excluded from public debate and political decision-making processes. The English working classes found in football one of the very spaces for the articulation of their political aspirations while they were excluded from positions of power. When US sprinters John Carlos and Tommie Smith raised their fists in support of the black civil rights movement during a medal ceremony at the 1968 Olympics in Mexico, their attempt to interject public discourse was witness of the far-reaching exclusion of black Americans from public life outside sport. During the decades of Franco's fascist dictatorship, the terraces of Barcelona's Nou Camp were the only remaining public space in which Catalan identity and separatism could be displayed in relative safety (Duke and Crolley 1996, 1995). Consequently the growing significance of seemingly private places of consumption in the public sphere is also an indication of the failure of the political system. The shift of public debate to spheres of media consumption signals the disintegration of rational dialogue and decision-making that is at the heart of Habermas' normative vision. The public discourses in sport consumption are a form of *ersatz* that fulfil an important need in sublimating for a lack of participatory spaces for debate elsewhere, but they do so at the cost of severing the link between these debates and legislative decision-making processes. In contrast to de Coubertin's Olympic motto – l'important, c'est de participer – in the public sphere taking part is far from all that matters.

## Notes

1. In my survey of 135 baseball fans in Britain, conducted from May to June 2004, 83.7 per cent of respondents declared to be 'interested' or 'very interested' in politics and current affairs.
2. Such as in the case of South London based football club Charlton Athletic, whose fans initiated a campaign to ensure the club's return to its former stadium after being refused planning permission by the local council. Eventually, Charlton fans formed their own political party successfully contesting many seats in the 1990 local elections.

# 6
# A Necessary Profession for the Modern Age?: Nineteenth Century News, Journalism and the Public Sphere

*Henrik Örnebring*

Habermas argues that the 'enemy' of rational–critical debate in the public sphere is not only the commodification of news but specifically the commodification of news as entertainment. In traditional Enlightenment fashion, Habermas is deeply suspicious of media content geared towards entertainment, emotional appeal and human interest (see for example Habermas 1992: 164ff, 171f, 175f). In contrast, this chapter argues that it is the genre of news itself, specifically with its focus on timely information about current events presented in an easily understandable fashion, which is incompatible with the rational–critical debate described by Habermas. The genre of news, as it emerged in the late 19th century, is incommensurable with rational–critical debate as defined by Habermas.

The emergence of news as a genre must in turn be viewed not only in relation to the commercialisation of the press (although this is an important factor, as I hope to show), but also to another, closely related development: the emergence of journalists as a distinctive professional group and journalism as a distinct field of practice. This relationship between news, journalism, the press and the public sphere has not been fully explored previously. One important reason for this is that the conceptual boundaries between news (as a form of text), journalism (as the practice of producing such texts), newspapers (the medium carrying news – and other forms of text) and the public sphere (as a virtual space of rational–critical debate) frequently are blurred or collapsed entirely, as when 'news' and 'journalism' are used as synonyms, for example. By going back to the time period that Habermas defines as the beginning of the decline of the public sphere, the latter half of the 19th century (Habermas 1989: 142f) and offer a historical analysis of a number of key developments, I wish to remedy this conceptual blurring and present an account of the decline of the public sphere that places news itself and journalism itself at the centre stage.

## The decline of the public sphere: Habermas revisited

The first and most important cause of the decline of the bourgeois public sphere (literary as well as political) is the commercialisation of the newspaper press (Habermas 1989: 168ff, 185ff) and later of mass media in general (Habermas 1989: 170), as this quote illustrates:

> The history of the big daily papers in the second half of the nineteenth century proves that the press itself became manipulable to the extent that it became commercialized. Ever since the marketing of the editorial section became interdependent with that of the advertising section (until then an institution of private people insofar as they constituted a public) became an institution of certain participants in the public sphere in their capacity as private individuals; that is, it became the gate through which privileged private interests invaded the public sphere. (Habermas 1989: 185)

When the press transforms from an institution driven by political interests into a business enterprise, this in turn makes 'debate' a good that can be consumed, just like any other (Habermas 1989: 164). It should be noted that though Habermas describes the earlier bourgeois press as 'primarily politically motivated' (Habermas 1989: 185), he does not view the party press that emerges in the 19th century very positively – rather, he refers to this type of newspaper as 'the party-bound press' and points out that the editor, and thereby implicitly the content, essentially was controlled by a politically appointed group of supervisors (Habermas 1989: 186).

Closely related to the transformation of the press into a business enterprise adapted to a mass market of readers is the rise of advertising, both as an activity and as a type of text. This is of course part of the commercialisation of the press – a mass-market press can reach mass audiences and thus advertising becomes an important revenue stream. But the rise of advertising has more insidious consequences than political debate-oriented content being replaced by advertising content:

> Private advertisements are always directed to other private people insofar as they are consumers; the addressee of public relations is 'public opinion,' or the private citizens as the public and not directly as consumers. The sender of the message hides his business intentions in the role of someone interested in public welfare. . . . The accepted functions of the public sphere are integrated into the competition of organized private interests. (Habermas 1989: 193)

Advertising subverts rational–critical debate and replaces it with a competition for audience attention through public relations. In the perhaps most often-quoted words of Habermas, the audience goes from debating about culture (*kulturräsonnierend*) to consuming culture – from citizens to consumers (Habermas 1989: 159ff).

Like his account of the emergence of the bourgeois public sphere, his analysis of its decline is clearly structuralist, as can be seen particularly in the sections that deal with the history of the press (the first quote in this section, (p. 185), is indicative in this regard). Media institutions are considered to have almost no agency of their own. Habermas consistently describes the press and other mass media as mostly reacting to or expressing other economic and political changes in society. There is no consideration of the fact that media institutions could be actors in their own right, with goals of their own that need not necessarily or consistently overlap with that of the 'privileged private interests'.

In the rest of this chapter, I will present an expanded version of Habermas' narrative of the decline of the public sphere. 'The media' should be understood not as an institution that simply transforms from being political to being a business, but as a complex field consisting of the interrelated phenomena of the medium itself (the particular form and structure of the *newspaper*), a set or type of texts (*news*) and a set of professional practices expressed in discourse (*journalism*).

## News as form and genre in the late nineteenth century

For Habermas and those who share his view of the decline of the public sphere, there is little doubt what the problem with news is:

> In addition, the share of political and politically relevant news changes. Public affairs, social problems, economic matters, education, and health . . . are not only pushed into the background by 'immediate reward news' (comics, corruption, accidents, disasters, sports, recreation, social events, and human interest) but, as the characteristic label already indicates, are also actually read more rarely. (Habermas 1989: 169–70).

> Depoliticization is a major discursive phenomenon and refers to a compound of discursive trends which can be observed in the British press from the 1850s onwards. To begin with, it designates the progressive de-selection of politics as a journalistic topic. During the second half of the 19th century, editors began to reduce the amount of political news and to fill newspaper columns with lighter topics. (Chalaby 1998: 76).

> The development of an entertainment-based working-class newspaper press is more than a century and a half old. The decline of the newspaper press relative to the magazine press is at least fifty years old. The shift in balance of journalism away from the production of serious material towards entertainment is certainly not a new phenomenon. (Sparks 1991: 69)

In other words, the decline of the public sphere is made manifest in the sub-ject selections of newspaper editors: politics as a subject area gets less fre-quent and less voluminous coverage.

There is nothing *prima facie* wrong with this argument – in fact, the decreasing volume of politics as a subject of news has solid empirical support (see Chalaby 1998: 77 and Berridge 1976, for example). However, I would suggest that the problem goes deeper than subject selection. I will argue that it is in fact *the genre of news itself*, as it is constituted in the late 19th century that precludes coverage of politics according to the ideals of rational–critical debate suggested by Habermas. To put it differently, the problem is perhaps not that there is less news about politics, but that news and politics in the Habermasian sense are to a great extent mutually exclusive.

What do I mean by 'news' in this context? Defining news is complicated by the fact that all genres, including news, change over time. What was con-sidered news in a 17th century periodical would probably not be recognised as news today. But there is at least a widespread consensus that 'news' in a form that would be recognised by a contemporary audience developed in the 19th century. For clarity's sake, I shall refer to this kind of news as *mass news*, for reasons that will hopefully become apparent. It is this kind of news that is incommensurable with rational–critical debate.

## Mass news and mass newspapers

A generic feature of both pre- and post-19th century news is obviously *time-liness* – news has to be new. News is the reporting of recent events and current facts not previously known to its audience. This holds true for the newslet-ters and corantos of the 17th century as well as for the 19th century news-paper. What is considered 'new' and 'current' is relative, of course. The 17th century corantos frequently contained 'news' about events months, some-times even years, in the past, but regardless of when they originated they were still new to their audience. Of course, industrial capitalism made time-liness on an entirely different scale possible, and the temporal space between an event and the reporting of it shrunk considerably.

We should note that timeliness has no necessary relation to *importance* or *intention*. Seventeenth century *fait divers* and the news ballads before them, focusing on sensational events and gruesome, titillating stories of crime were no less timely than the trade-oriented information in the corantos. One was produced with the intent to entertain and one with the intent to inform (this is one case where the simplistic information/entertainment duality is actually relevant), but they both contained 'news' in the sense of reports of recent events. This might seem like a trivial point, but I want to make clear from the outset that the difference between pre-19th century news and mass news is not that mass news is designed to entertain and pre-19th century news isn't, but that mass news is designed mainly to attract audience attention and satisfy a predicted audience interest (cf Williams 1977: 49, Seymour-Ure 2000: 17f) –

something that can be done with timely information as well as entertaining sensations, or indeed information presented in an entertaining fashion.

The development of mass news as a genre is intimately connected with the development of a new medium, the *mass-market daily newspaper*. Indeed, one can even say that mass news was developed to fit in the mass newspaper. The genius of the mass newspaper, from a marketing/financial perspective, is its unabashed diversity, its carefree intermingling of 'information' and 'entertainment', its mission to cover 'all walks of life'. Though Habermas frequently treats 'the press' as a coherent institution (see for example Habermas 1989: 59ff and 168ff), the periodicals concerned with rational–critical debate that formed the basis of the bourgeois public sphere in the 17th and 18th centuries were quite distinct from the mass-circulation newspapers of the 19th. Habermas describes the path from debate-oriented periodicals to a commercialised mass press as a more or less linear development, when he is in fact comparing two different mass mediums with related but different generic histories.

The periodicals that Habermas consider constitutive of the bourgeois public sphere (both literary and political) were not 'newspapers' in that they did not contain much 'news' in the sense of reports about recent events. Instead, their content mainly consisted of criticism (again, both literary and political), arguments, debates, statements and other kinds of writing, all with the intention to express and possibly influence opinion. The generic ancestor of the periodical devoted to rational–critical debate was the dialogue form and classical rhetoric, and its generic sibling was the Enlightenment book or pamphlet devoted to the moral and/or intellectual betterment of fellow men.

The mass-market newspaper, on the other hand, was born of industrial capitalism. It was influenced by the debate-oriented periodical but soon grew into a quite different beast. The major structural change in the press as a whole this time was the parallel and linked development of a mass audience and of advertising aimed at a mass audience.

In order to attract advertisers, a newspaper must attract a mass audience, and this was achieved through two related strategies. The first was *diversity*. Mass-market newspapers covered 'life as a whole' (in the words of Seymour-Ure 2000: 17) and within their pages were to be found an eclectic mix of classified ads, society news and gossip, and later comics and sport (a very different mix of content compared to the debate-oriented periodical). The second was the creation of *mass news*: a form of news designed in the main to attract audience attention and to satisfy perceived reader's interests.

In order to fit in the mass-market newspaper and the new production order of late industrial capitalism, mass news must then be (a) *timely*, (b) *easy to read and understand*, and (c) *entertaining*. The underlying strategy used to achieve these three goals was *factuality* – mass news is, first and foremost, reports about discrete events as facts (Stephens 1997: 244). These features of the genre remain the main characteristics of mass news into the present day. I will go through these criteria briefly here, and then go on to explain why each of these criteria are diametrically opposed to the ideal of rational–critical debate as presented by Habermas.

As I have hinted at previously, the industrially produced mass-market newspaper creates an entirely new frame of reference for the concept of timeliness. No longer is timeliness judged on a month-to-month basis but rather on a day-by-day-basis. Mass news becomes subject to a tyranny of the immediate. Rational–critical debate, on the other hand, requires time to gestate and take shape, as well as an awareness of the past. Chalaby, who has studied the importance of timeliness as a selection criterion in mass news extensively, puts it this way:

> With this new frame of reference, past events lost all newsworthiness. Journalists' focus on the last couple of hours could only undermine politics' old central position in the discourse of the press. . . . to report politics, the past needs to be constantly reactualized and this proved increasingly difficult for journalists whose time reference concentrates on the last 12 or 24 hours. Thus, with the advent of journalism press and politics ceased to revolve in the same time scale. (Chalaby 1998: 83)

Mass news must also be easily digestible – the characteristic generic features that relate to this are that they are *simplified* (both in terms of language and in terms of issue framing) and that they are *brief*. It is indicative in this regard that the word 'tabloid', first used to describe newspapers by Alfred Harmsworth (later Lord Northcliffe), originally refers to medicine in the form of a quick-acting, easily digested pill: consuming mass news should be like consuming patent medicine. Harmsworth's *The Daily Mail* was 'the daily time saver', the ideal medium for the quick-paced twentieth century (Tulloch 2000: 131f). With a heterogeneous mass audience, it is safest on the part of the publisher not to assume any extensive advance knowledge in its members. Again, this is difficult to reconcile with the frequent need for extensive explanation and intellectual demands placed on the audience by periodicals focusing on debate and traditional politics.

Finally, mass news are also designed to be entertaining, achieving this by the interlinking of form and content: any given subject area is much more likely to feature in mass news if it lends itself to narrative storytelling (like sports and society news, for example). Rational–critical debate on current issues of common concerns is often demanding and probably seldom viewed as immediately entertaining. For that reason, mass news is always ready to make politics entertaining, for example through personalisation and focus on political scandal.

But what about factuality, the strategy connecting timeliness, simplicity and entertainment value? Surely factuality is not a bad characteristic for texts in the public sphere? Intuitively this seems strange. But then, we must remember that 'fact' in journalistic discourse is opposed to 'opinion' – and the Habermasian public sphere is founded on the expression and exchange of opinions. I will return to the problematic nature of factuality in the next section, 'Journalism as practice and profession in the late 19th century'.

## Mass news as opposed to rational–critical debate

When Habermas, Chalaby, Sparks and others use human interest stories as a prime example of what it is that displaces politics as a subject of news, they treat human interest stories as a genre distinct from news (this distinction is incidentally also upheld by many journalists). From my viewpoint presented here, human interest is not a genre distinct from news but rather a different sub-genre of news, that still fulfils all the criteria of mass news: timeliness, simplicity and entertainment value.

In short, it is the genre of mass news itself that is incommensurable with rational–critical debate. The shift from one type of content (traditional politics) to others (gossip, sports, sensational crime) is predicated on that the sphere of politics is very difficult to render timely, easy to understand, brief and entertaining. Mass news as a genre is thus fundamentally opposed to rational–critical debate, which needs time to gestate and develop, often expects effort from its audience and participants, frequently requires lengthy, intellectually challenging arguments, and is not *a priori* entertaining.

Historians of the press would agree that all these developments in one way or other are consequences of an increasing commercialisation of the press as an institution (Lee 1976: 67ff, Cranfield 1978: 204ff, Koss 1981: 306ff and Curran & Seaton 2003: 24ff covers these developments in Britain, Emery & Emery 1978: 199f and Schudson 1978: 18ff the US, Johannesson 2001: 126ff, 149ff, and Petersson 2001: 302ff in Sweden, just to take an example from outside the English-speaking world). I want to expand this explanatory model to take the internal workings of media institutions into account and to present a view of media institutions as something more complex than just vehicles of capitalism without any agency of their own. The next step, then, is to examine a notion that gradually takes hold in the late 19th century: the notion that mass news is a type of content that can only be reliably produced by a specific class of professionals – journalists.

## Late nineteenth century journalism as practice and profession

Habermas himself actually hints at a link between a new kind of news and the growth of a new professional class:

> Editorial activity had, under the pressure of the technically, advanced transmission of news, in any event already become specialized; once a literary activity, it had become a journalistic one. The selection of material became more important than the lead article; the processing and evaluation of news and its screening and organization more urgent than the

advocacy of a "line" through an effective literary presentation. (Habermas 1989: 185–6)

His use of the word 'journalistic' in this context is somewhat problematic, however. 'Journalism' as we know it today is a relatively new phenomenon, born of the latter half of the 19th century (Chalaby 1998: 9). To apply 'journalism' as a term for the activities of the press in general is misguided, as journalism as an activity is deeply intertwined with the rise of mass news.

Much has been written about the professionalization of journalism. I cannot do this rich field of study justice here, so I will limit myself to a number of key issues that illuminate the relationship between the emergence of a new genre (mass news) and the emergence of a new profession (journalism). With mass news fast becoming the dominant type of news, journalism as a profession becomes focused on newsgathering and reporting – rather than offering analysis or opinion, for example. Michael Schudson puts it thus:

As news was more or less 'invented' in the 1830s, the reporter was a social invention of the 1880s and 1890s. Early newspapers had been one-man bands: one man acted as printer, advertising agent, editor, and reporter. (Schudson 1978: 65)

When mass news became the most important feature of the mass market newspaper, the newspaper had to rely increasingly on professionals trained in the gathering and assembly of the raw materials of these news: facts (again, rather than opinion). Schudson continues:

These accounts [of how beginner journalists learnt their profession, author's note] suggest that reporters may have developed their attachment to facts despite themselves, forced into it by the organizational pressures of daily journalism. (Schudson 1978: 81)

These two quotes clearly illustrate how journalism as a profession came into existence in order to satisfy an industry demand for a particular type of content. But these explanations are only half the story. The professional collective itself must also be considered as an actor in the professionalization process. The actions of many journalists in the late 19th century can be interpreted as part of an ongoing collective quest for *status* and *legitimacy*.

The profession of editor or publicist always carried with it some measure of status. For a long time the publishing of periodicals was not a commercial but an ideological venture, so editors could not be suspected of having motivations based on financial gain – highly suspect in a society where hereditary aristocracy was still alive and well! Being a writer for a periodical did not necessarily carry with it any special status, however. And if the specific writing task was the base gathering of facts and anecdotes, the status was low indeed (see Lee 1976: 106f, Brake 1988: 7f and Conboy 2004: 112f for examples of contemporary attitudes).

The professional hierarchy among men (for it was mostly men) of the press in the 19th century was slightly subtler than this, however (the following discussion of status differences builds on the research of Lee 1976: 108ff and Elliott 1978: 173ff). The editor was at the top, but within the editorial profession there were differences in status between centre and periphery (London and the provinces, in the case of Britain).

The leader writer came next in pay and status. On about the same level as the leader writer were the parliamentary reporters and foreign correspondents. Beneath them came the sub-editor, i.e. the person whose task it was to manage journalists and reporters directly and to edit particular sections or subject areas within the newspaper. At the lowest rank was the regular reporter, the person most directly involved in producing mass news. It is telling that the high-status echelons of the profession (editor, leader writer, parliamentary reporter) were those that were concerned with traditional public sphere activity in the Habermasian sense, i.e. the expression and discussion of opinions.

As writing-as-profession transformed in the 19th century, it became an important goal for professionals to raise its status and acquire social and cultural legitimacy (Elliott 1978: 176f, Jones 1996: 122f, also see Johannesson 2001: 221, 225ff). An important strategy for achieving this goal was the rhetorical positioning of journalism – and thereby journalists – as the Fourth Estate; of journalism as a necessity in modern mass democracy. Many scholars have studied this (among them Boyce 1978, Elliott 1978: 182f and Conboy 2004: 109ff). If we view this in relation to the professional hierarchy I have described, it is clear that the 'Fourth Estate' legitimization strategy largely was applied by those at the top of the profession, that is the editors, reviewers, commentators and those concerned with the shaping and expression of public opinion (Conboy 2004: 123ff, also see Brown 1985: 93).

The ones at the lower end of the professional hierarchy initially had to legitimate themselves and attempt to raise their status in a different way. Instead of focusing on their role in modern mass democracy, their way to professional identity lay in emphasising their ability as craftsmen. Lucy Brown describes this strategy in the following way:

> It can be shown that, apart from such people as drama critics or City editors, who needed particular kinds of experience or contacts, most journalists had begun their careers in their teens, or as soon as they left the University. Journalism was seen as a specialized craft. The discipline of writing, to a specified theme, at a fixed length, to a precise deadline, is probably one that can only be acquired when young. This early entry alone gave journalists a distinct identity, separating them from politicians on one hand and 'men of letters' on the other. (Brown 1985: 80)

In other words, journalists attempted to achieve legitimacy through the fact that they were trained in a specific set of skills that allowed them to produce the type of content characteristic of mass-market newspaper: mass news. Journalists made the ideals of this genre their own, and linked their own legitimacy to the fact that they could produce a type of content that was based on fact rather than opinion – news rather than debate.

The process of 'fact' being separated from 'opinion' in the minds of journalists and newspapermen and, consequently, in the newspaper press, has been well described by many scholars (Herd 1952, Schudson 1978, Wiener 1988: 53ff and Stephens 1997: 244ff, for example). Most of these authors also link the separation of fact and opinion to a gradual de-politicization or de-ideologization of the press. As mass news became the dominant genre of writing in the press, so did the overtly ideological content of newspapers become more and more marginalized, evident only on the editorial pages and sometimes not even there (as demonstrated by Chalaby 1998: 102ff).

The division between fact and opinion, and the concomitant process of de-politicization of the press, are well known and well researched. But the point I am making has so far not been made explicit by researchers: the fact that this de-politicization is a result of journalists adapting to a specific genre, and that the process is reciprocally linked to the rise of this specific genre as the central component of the modern newspaper.

The legitimacy of the editor or publicist was derived from his links to existing, organized, respectable political interests, and his membership of an educated upper middle or upper class. Following on from this, the legitimacy and status (and influence!) of periodical publications was decided mostly by how well they contributed to public discussion and public opinion formation (see Lee 1976: 121f, Berry 2002: 15ff).

During the late 19th century, a new way of constructing legitimacy gradually developed, mainly among the lower strata of the professional hierarchy of the newspaper press. There, claims to legitimacy were increasingly based on *not* being ideological and engaging in partisan debate but instead focusing on 'the reporting of facts'. Stephens links the 'inverted pyramid' format (which developed into the most important building block of mass news) to this new focus on 'fact'. Only with the arrival of the inverted pyramid, a format organized around the presentation of facts in order of importance (as judged by the journalist's professional sensibility), do facts find their 'true voice' (Stephens 1997: 246). Journalism is legitimate only insofar as it produces 'facts' and 'truth', not opinion.

From this point of view, engaging in open debate in a pluralist environment of attempts at partisan public opinion formation becomes suspect rather than desirable activity. Indeed, one of the most important rhetorical devices in the quest for legitimacy in the late 19th century was that journalists must be 'independent', i.e. independent from direct political patronage. The view advanced at the time was that the best way to guarantee this independence from party politics was a commercial press that focused on the reporting of facts rather than opinion (Conboy 2004: 111).

The rise of mass news is also related to the idea of the informed citizen (see Schudson 1998), that is to say that the citizen of a representative democracy above all needs access to unbiased, truthful information about current events in order to make informed political decisions. The ideal of the informed citizen does not place the same strong emphasis on *participation* in public affairs through debate and discussion as Habermas does. On the other hand, the ideal of the informed citizen fits very well with the new self-understanding that developed among journalists and newspapermen in the late 19th century. In the bourgeois public sphere described by Habermas, it was the *press as an institution* that is deemed necessary in a functioning democracy and public debate. In the late 19th century, as journalism became increasingly specialised, the foundation was laid for the notion that it is *journalists* rather than the press as an institution that are necessary for a functioning democracy.

## News as the negation of rational–critical debate

What, then, does all this tell us about the public sphere and its purported decline? First of all it must be pointed out that mass news does not become the dominant genre of press texts overnight, and neither do editorials, debate, political reporting and opinion-based writing disappear overnight. In fact, it is quite easy to see that the latter forms of writing still exist, though not to the same extent as they did before the second half of the 19th century. And in the late 19th century, mass news existed parallel with many other genres of writing in the press. What happened was rather that a process began where what I call mass news (but that we just as well could call modern news, or news as we know it today) rose to become the dominant genre of newspaper writing, edging out and marginalizing genres more closely associated with the Habermasian public sphere.

My contribution to the ongoing debate about the decline of the public sphere could best be described as a simultaneous critique and support of Habermas' original argument. On one hand, there is significant empirical support for the position that particular types of content (news about politics, openly partisan opinion-based writings) actually have declined in both volume and importance since the heyday of the bourgeois public sphere. And while it must be acknowledged that the rise of mass news also meant a *widening* of the bourgeois public sphere, in that new audiences actually got access to news and furthermore to news that they wanted to read (Örnebring & Jönsson 2004), the basic thrust of Habermas' decline argument seems to hold true.

On the other hand, Habermas and many of his followers are misguided on two counts. First, in their view that the decline consists of entertainment supplanting information, based in turn on the presupposition that information and entertainment are mutually exclusive characteristics in a text. Second, in their view that the media institutions themselves have a limited agency in this process of change.

In relation to the first point, I have argued throughout this chapter that the problem of journalism and its place in the public sphere in fact goes deeper than a supposedly blurred borderline between information and entertainment, or that 'serious news' have been replaced by 'non-serious', entertainment-oriented news. I have also argued previously that the information/entertainment dualism is highly problematic (Örnebring & Jönsson 2004). My suggestion is instead that it is *news* as a genre that is incommensurable with public sphere debate and public opinion formation in the Habermasian sense. News as we understand it today cannot in my view ever sustain a public sphere unless it transcends its generic limitations, in particular the limitations imposed by the focus on timeliness and the perceived need for simplicity.

In relation to the second point, my argument is not so much a refutation as an expansion of the viewpoints offered by Habermas and others. It is evident that most of the structural, professional and textual transformations in the press that take place in the second half of the 19th century can be explained by increased commercialisation, the birth of mass advertising, the related need to reach mass audiences, and so on. The problem with this explanatory model is that it views the press solely in its capacity as an economic actor, when the press in fact consists of a number of overlapping but distinct fields: *journalism*, or the field of practice, *news*, or the textual field, and the *medium* field (where daily newspapers form one part of the press as a whole alongside Sunday newspapers, periodicals, and so on) as well as the business field.

As I have shown, these fields interact in complex ways where the rise of the daily mass-market newspaper is linked to the rise of mass news as a genre, which is in turn linked to rise of journalism as a profession. The press is not just reacting to external changes in the economic structure of society. There is a constant negotiation between these external factors and the internal workings of the press as an institution, where the legitimization of journalism as a profession is perhaps the most important manifestation. This process of legitimization goes on to the present day, and the positioning of journalists as representatives of a necessary profession for the modern age is becoming ever stronger. There has been a shift from a Habermasian view of the press *as an institution* central to the proper functioning of the public sphere, to a media-centric view of *journalists* as the only true guardians of public discourse and debate. The collective of journalists must be assigned both agency and responsibility in order for us to properly assess and analyse the decline of the public sphere.

# 7

# 'They Just Make Sense': Tabloid Newspapers as an Alternative Public Sphere

*Sofia Johansson*

At the centre of media controversy, tabloids continue to be the best-read newspapers in the UK. But in spite of their popularity, these papers are often accused of debasing democratic communication. Indeed, tabloid journalism in the UK and elsewhere has been placed at the forefront of a 'dumbing down' of the media, whereby popular, commercial media fail to measure up to Habermas's seminal idea of the public sphere as a forum for debate on matters of public interest.

Underpinning the criticisms of tabloid newspapers are assumptions about their influence on readers. Yet, as empirical research on the subject is virtually non-existent, assertions about the relationship between tabloid journalism and public sphere discourse are, at best, educated guesses. This chapter seeks to provide some original insights into the functions of tabloid newspapers in the lives of readers. Can tabloid news contribute to a public sphere as derived from Habermas? To answer this question I have interviewed young adult readers of the *Sun* and the *Daily Mirror*, the two circulation leaders among the popular tabloids. Readers' responses to traditional public affairs news, and to tabloid focuses such as celebrity stories shed light on tabloid newspapers as possible grounds for a public sphere.

## Tabloids and 'tabliodization'

There is little doubt about the centrality of tabloid journalism to debates about media standards. While sometimes considered 'unworthy' of academic attention (Langer 1998: 8), tabloid newspapers and their historical predecessors, such as the 'penny dreadfuls', have always stirred controversy among those anxious about the impact of populist journalistic traditions (see e.g. Conboy, 2002: 1–30). A contributing reason for such concern is the sheer numbers these news forms often attract. In the UK, the tabloid press dominates the national newspaper market, with the popular tabloids (the so-called 'red-tops') holding a majority share of the total newspaper circulation. These have further developed a highly contentious brand of journalism characterised by the typically sensationalist news style and blurring of boundaries between private and public, politics and entertainment, as well as by a partisan political engagement, a celebrity-orientated and sexualised news agenda and the use of cheque-book journalism and paparazzi coverage.

The *Sun*, launched as a tabloid by Rupert Murdoch in 1969 and a best-seller since 1978, is often regarded the most hard-hitting in all of these respects. Dubbed the 'rottweiler of British journalism',[1] it has developed cut-throat competition with other tabloids, particularly for the same down-market readers as the *Daily Mirror* (launched in 1903). Today, these two publications share characteristics of format, style, content and readerships. It is however worth noting that the *Sun*, despite backing the Labour party in three consecutive elections, generally takes a conservative stance on social issues such as crime and immigration, whereas the *Mirror* has a history as a socialist newspaper and continues to place itself within a left-wing context. In 2003, the *Mirror* was re-branded the more 'serious' of the two, which meant increased attention to issues such as the Iraq war – although it subsequently went back to a tabloid focus on showbiz (see Engel, 1996, Chippendale and Horrie, 1999, Conboy, 2002 and Horrie, 2003 for histories of the tabloid press).

A main framework for the analysis of tabloid newspapers today is the much-discussed 'tabloidization': (news) media increasingly and generally turning to entertainment, sensationalism and the realm of private affairs (see Sparks, 2000, for a full discussion). Here, tabloid priorities are seen to have a devastating influence on public life, simplifying important issues and turning media audiences away from news of political relevance (e.g. Franklin, 1997). Tabloid newspapers, further, have themselves been observed to undergo changes which then would mean a greater than ever adverse effect on readers. An example is Dick Rooney's (2000) content analysis of the *Mirror* and the *Sun*, where he found a sharply decreasing percentage of editorial space devoted to 'public affairs', between 1968 and 1998. Rooney concludes:

> The *Mirror* and the *Sun* do not have a public-sphere editorial agenda. Their readers probably do not have any interest in the workings of the establishment or establishment organizations and do not wish to monitor them. (ibid.: 107)

Thus, tabloid content is claimed to be directly linked to the interests of readers, in a downward spiral of trivialisation and political apathy.

As is evident in Rooney's analysis, underpinning much of the critique of tabloids and tabloidization is the Habermasian notion of the public sphere. As pointed out by Martin Eide and Graham Knight, the public sphere as 'a normative ideal essential to a well-functioning democracy' (1999: 535) has had most currency among media scholars. Tabloid newspapers have been judged to fail this ideal, paralleling Habermas' (1989) own criticism of the commercial mass media as replacing rational–critical debate with individuated, apolitical consumption of culture. Strict Habermasian readings of tabloid newspapers, therefore, have left limited options for exploring their potentially progressive and democratic functions. Nevertheless, subsequent re-conceptualisations of the public sphere open doors for alternative takes on tabloid journalism.

## Alternative conceptions

Particularly relevant for thinking about the role of tabloid newspapers is the re-evaluation of the public sphere in terms of plurality and alternative publics (e.g. Fraser, 1992, Negt and Kluge, 1993, first published 1972), the boundaries of the political (e.g. Curran, 1991, Garnham, 1992, Livingstone and Lunt, 1994) and the way that affect, often a structuring agent of tabloid discourse, has recently been considered central to popular engagement in the public sphere, in providing emotional vehicles for debate (e.g. McGuigan, 2000, Macdonald, 2000, Lunt and Stenner, 2005, Lunt in this volume). These alternative conceptions of the public sphere have created room for examinations of diverse publics, as well as of how these can be reconciled under a normative dimension, even though they also open up the problem of how to reconcile pluralism with a common democratic polity (Calhoun, 1992: 38, Garnham, 1992: 369).

Broadening definitions of what constitutes democratic public communication are paralleled by more optimistic interpretations of tabloid journalism. The most vocal defender has been John Fiske (1989, 1992), who has argued that tabloid journalism is a site of resistance to dominating power structures, where parody and scepticism are used to interrogate disciplinary norms. More recently, Kevin Glynn deploys a similar outlook when asserting that the critique of tabloid formats 'seeks to control public life by delegitimating popular tastes and marginalizing those who possess them' (2000: 105). These understandings of tabloid journalism can be placed within the wider context of a shift in media studies towards an emphasis on audience activity, which has led to an increased interest in previously devalued popular formats.

However, pointing to alternative understandings of tabloid media and bringing attention to an element of elitism in the criticism, assumptions of resistive readings are based on scarce empirical evidence (see e.g. Gripsrud, 2000 for criticism of Fiske). A little noted aspect to this side of the debate is also that scholarly defences for tabloid media generally focus on the more 'benign' and playful formats (Turner, 1999), such as talk shows or supermarket tabloids, whereas it is harder to see inherent democratic capabilities in an arguably more reactionary form of populism such as the *Sun* (Turner, 1999). But, it is worth acknowledging the ideological tensions that do exist in this material, and to examine its use in specific circumstances. Henrik Örnebrink and Maria Jönsson (2004) for instance suggest that the tabloid press has historically functioned as an alternative to a mainstream public sphere (for example broadcast news and newspapers considered most 'important'): an idea that shall be elaborated in relation to this readership study.

For, while the dispute surrounding tabloid journalism stretches from one polar end, as the demise of an enlightened society, to another, where tabloid media are hailed as liberating, attention to audiences is scarce. Two previous qualitative, English-language studies of the experience of tabloid reading – Elisabeth Bird's (1992) study of US supermarket tabloids, and Mark Pursehouse's (1992) article on a small number of *Sun*-readers – have provided some insights, with both for instance finding that tabloid reading was related to an alienation from, as Bird puts it, 'dominant narrative forms and frames of reference' (1992: 109).[2] But these studies do not specifically tackle the issue of the public sphere, and the remaining part of this chapter will bring in the voices of readers to this discussion.

## Research method

To do this, I interviewed 55 London-based, regular readers of the *Sun* or the *Daily Mirror* either individually or in small focus groups between May and January 2004/05. The focus is not on the affluent, well-educated sections of readers, but on readers drawn from the social segments constituting the majority of the readerships. Participants were aged 18–35, a large and crucial age group for the competition between the two papers (Rooney, 2000: 94), and in the C1C2DE social category – such as clerical workers and skilled and unskilled manual labourers – which represents over three-quarters of both papers' readerships (National Readership Survey, 2005). To get access to 'naturally' occurring groups, such as groups of friends or colleagues, these were recruited through the use of contacts and 'snowball' sampling (see May, 2001:132). All in all, 35 male and 20 female readers participated. Most of these were white and British, with six participants of colour, two non-Western immigrant readers (from Jamaica and Nigeria) and four immigrant readers from countries in the West (Portugal, Greece, Poland, Australia).

In total, 11 groups of 3–6 readers were interviewed, with at least two groups of male/female for each paper and one group each of mixed gender. These were semi-structured and taped, taking place where participants were thought to feel comfortable, such as quiet pubs and cafés, and in several cases at workplaces. The individual interviews were arranged similarly to the focus groups, but provided more personal data.[3]

## Tabloid reading and the public sphere: some limitations

Talking to readers, it became clear that conceptualising tabloids as a basis for a public sphere is problematic, and it is worth bringing attention to difficulties with this proposition before developing it. To start with, readers did not describe the *Sun* and the *Mirror* as high-quality sources of information about public affairs. Within most of the discussions these were portrayed as of poor journalistic standards, evident in descriptions such as 'crappy papers' and 'rubbish', as well as in the use of defensive adverbs such as 'only', as in 'I only read it out of habit'.[4] Readers' descriptions, then, corresponded with the tabloid critics in terms of these papers' value to the public sphere. While such devaluation is likely to be shaped by negative images of tabloids in the 'mainstream' public sphere (see Ang, 1985: 110, for this phenomenon with relation to popular culture), it raises questions over their potential for forming a public sphere basis.

Instead of emphasising the quality of content, a primary reason given for reading the *Sun* and the *Mirror* was that they provided 'an easy read', explained in part by their absorption into routines such as commuting or breaks from work. 'It's not a paper you really read, it's a paper you flick through', as one female *Mirror*-reader put it. Although this casual style of reading does not preclude a role for tabloids in furthering knowledge about current affairs, many readers declared a limited interest in traditional public affairs news, particularly that outside of a direct sphere of experience. An example can be given from an interview with Daniel, a 34-year-old decorator, who preferred the *Sun* because he experienced abstract social issues irrelevant:

I mean, this [the *Sun*] is light reading, in general terms. And I think the broadsheets . . . for my life, I don't wanna know about stocks and shares, and I don't wanna know about Wall Street crises or . . . what's going on in Beijing or whatever. As I say, day-to-day things, I just wanna know about. A light read.

Such emphasis on 'day-to-day things', also exemplified in how readers stated they preferred their tabloid because it focused on 'London' or 'England', may support notions of tabloids as fostering a distancing from wider social structures.

Similarly, news about parliamentary politics overall emerged as a less favoured part of the content, and was only discussed after prompting. The majority of male readers, irrespective of social grade, stated they had some interest in politics, which gets an assigned space on page 2 in both papers. But, as opposed to news about celebrities and footballers, stories about parliamentary events did not seem easily remembered or talked about. The difficulty remembering these stories could be explained by the more conventional style of reporting (see Connell, 1998, for distinctions in tabloid reporting), or be related to the perception among some readers that politics was too contentious to discuss. However, it could also be seen as an expression of disinterest in political processes.

Certainly, female readers were vocal about their apprehension to politics, and did not like to read the page 2 news. As exemplified in this interview with Maria, a 20-year-old laundrette assistant, for many female readers 'politics' was a difficult subject to talk about:

**Interviewer:** When it comes to the way the *Sun* reports on politics, how would you describe it?

**Maria:** Erm . . . I think they tell you everything about politics, you know, they tell you what each party has said and they . . . (. . .) to be honest I haven't really got much to say about it, cause I don't . . . really take much notice of it. Of the . . . you know, polling and all the rest of it, and. . . . So I wouldn't really . . . I can't really tell you much about it.
**Interviewer:** Is there one particular story that you've read that you do remember or . . .?
**Maria:** Not at all.
**Interviewer:** No?
**Maria:** Not at all. I don't really read . . . na, I don't really read about that. It's not . . . for me [laughs].

Accentuated by Maria's nervous laughter in this conversation, the 'disinterest' appeared linked to a view politics as out of reach of one's competencies, 'way over my head' as a female *Mirror*-reader expressed it. Such lack of confidence in the ability to understand political processes is possibly furthered by newspapers that place a heavy emphasis on traditional conceptions of gender, where, for example, the political news on page 2 is juxtaposed with the infamous Page 3 pin-up in the *Sun*.

A distancing from politics as a subject, expressed especially by the female readers, was paralleled by the distrust in politicians articulated by readers across the board. Statements like 'politicians can't be true to their words' or 'they're all the same' highlighted readers' suspicion of political representatives. As shown by Frank Esser, a case could be made that press coverage which mixes frequent allegations of political misconduct with disreputable gossip and scandal (as is the case with the tabloids) may deepen public distrust for political institutions and governments (1999: 315–18). Although one should be careful with assertions of causality, readers' pessimistic attitudes to politicians could at times be placed in this context, as illustrated in this discussion with a construction worker (aged 33):

**Don:** When . . . [browsing through the *Sun* to describe the current political reporting] it used to be all the time, it seemed every other day there was a political issue. Now . . . here you are [reads headline]: 'MPs CASH IN'. But they [the *Sun*] don't seem to . . . they've not gone to either party, sort of glossed over it.
**Interviewer:** Do you think, if you are reading something like that, the story about the MPs, about them spending a lot of money, would it affect what you think about MPs?
**Don:** I don't . . . I don't need to read it in the newspapers. Cause . . . I mean, they're in a privileged position, and it's . . . What we know about the Euro MPs is: £350,000 a year and an expense account as long as your arm. They sell out! So . . . I've not got a lot of time for politicians.

Despite Don's assurance of not needing 'to read it in the newspapers', the connection between the typically accusatory *Sun*-headline and his view on

MPs, especially those working for the EU, which, with its anti-EU position, are one of the *Sun's* favoured targets, is striking. While there is a fine line between a critical outlook and cynicism, the harsh anti-establishment stance favoured by the popular tabloids can link in with distancing from mainstream political processes. Thus, some of the critical claims against tabloid newspapers are borne out in research with readers.

## Tabloid accessibility

However, to gain a more comprehensive understanding of the roles of these papers one should also take into account the ways in which they can further knowledge and competencies that enable participation in a public sphere. One of the crucial issues to consider is accessibility of information; an essential element to Habermas's public sphere and a basic requirement for citizenship in a democracy.

Accessibility was a strong theme in the conversations with readers. While mid-market tabloids, such as the *Daily Mail*, were seen as too text-heavy and conservative in their views, and the 'quality' broadsheets were often deemed out-of-bounds – 'for business-class people' – the *Sun* and the *Mirror* were appreciated for being 'down to earth', for keeping an affordable price, and for making ordinary people visible in news discourse. As illustrated in the following extract from a group of students in their late teens, this visibility provided an identificatory link between the news and the readers:

> **Interviewer:** Are there any other parts of the paper [the *Mirror*], apart from sport, celebrity and politics, that you read?
> **John:** Just the general, the general articles at the beginning of the paper, sort of thing. Just the everyday stuff that they report on.
> **Interviewer:** Do you like the way they report on everyday stuff?
> **John:** Yeah. Cause, they report about normal people as well. Not just famous people. So, it's just a bit more on your level. . . .
> **Tariq:** Yeah, like, that's when you can really reflect [sic] to it. Cause that's just like a normal person like us.

The tabloid attention to 'normal people', then, could facilitate understanding of news items, and contributed to an experience of inclusiveness. For some readers, as shown in the following extract from a group of bus drivers (aged 26–35), this experience was related to the notion of a proletarian forum unobtainable elsewhere in the press:

> **Ronnie:** I suppose the papers are structured for people in all walks of life, you know. And this [the *Sun*] is more or less for the working class than your middle class. And then you get your *Mail* for the middle class or the upper class, and . . .
> **Interviewer:** Right. So it's kind of different in aim . . .

**Ronnie:** Yeah. You know, they aim . . . this is really for *us*, you know. . . . We don't end up going out buying *The Times* or the *Financial Times* cause we don't really need to read that, do we?
**Jack:** The English . . . is different too . . . it's less grammatical, you know what I mean, it's got pictures, and kind of . . .
**Nick:** The lower class papers, they've got like . . . a little of life.
**Jack:** Yeah.
**Nick:** I mean, that's how you live. Some people don't admit it because they've got a few pounds in their pocket. . . . But at the end of the day, if you're gonna go and buy a paper, this is it.

As emphasised by Nick, a Greek immigrant, the *Sun* was in this group considered the only paper that reflected the experiences of ordinary working people; exemplifying how tabloids can provide an identifiable news forum lacking elsewhere.

The ability to reach readers alienated from other print news should also be linked to how comprehension of news is facilitated. Not unsurprisingly, the lively, humorous style contributed to the ease of reading, with the youngest readers in particular stressing their preference for catchy headlines and 'graphic pictures'. Likewise, the newspapers were appreciated for using a language close to everyday speech, with readers for example explaining that 'I'd rather read something I'd say myself' or 'they talk like us'. This conversation with a secretary at an accountancy firm (aged 34), shows how the informal vernacular contributed to an experience of 'making sense':

**Interviewer:** How would you describe the language of the *Mirror*?
**Victoria:** It's easy to read. It's easy to read.
**Interviewer:** In what way is it easy to read?
**Victoria:** It's just . . . it will put it plainly, kind of informal. . . . It just makes sense to me!

Crucial to this sense-making process is the role of literacy. Jack, in the previous extract, was not alone in perceiving other newspapers as too long, using too complicated language, and being too difficult to read – an obstacle that in this study seemed especially manifest for some of the blue-collar readers as well as some immigrants. Unprompted comments among these readers on own literacy, such as 'I read ok, but . . .', assumptions that 'you have to use a dictionary' to understand other papers, and the frequent praise of the tabloid language as easily understood, highlighted that literacy, even in a developed Western democracy, determines the 'choice' available to newspaper readers.

## Political knowledge

As tabloids provide accessibility to print news, a case can be made for their role in furthering political knowledge. This is especially imperative to consider given that studies have shown a correlation between exposure to print media and higher levels of political knowledge (Buckingham, 1997: 346). And, while a strong interest in politics for the most part was not directly articulated, both male and female readers were keen to get an overview of the daily round-up of current affairs, to 'know what's going on'. At times of explosive current affairs, this interest could turn into a pressing desire for information:

> When the war kicked off, and you know, it was in the whole paper [the *Sun*]. I mean, you read it, and you . . . you're engrossed in it for a good hour, aren't you, when you're reading the paper. Reading all about it. (Chris, 29, shop-fitter)

In these situations the newspaper seemed to take on an interpretive function, which complemented televised news and helped to clarify complex issues.

Thus, a certain amount of information necessary for public sphere discourse is distributed through the tabloids. As noted, there are likewise reasons to widen the parameters for what constitutes 'political' knowledge, acknowledging that this also will be formed outside of overtly rational discourse, only indirectly related to the practices of parliamentary democracy. Celebrity stories, for instance, presented opportunities to debate morality and social norms – matters that may well have their place in public sphere discourse. Tabloid celebrity exposés likewise contain an element of criticism of social privilege (Connell, 1992), which was appreciated by readers, who liked the way the newspapers 'pulled down' those with fame, money and success (see Johansson, 2006). Such 'personality politics' are not necessarily progressive (see Buckingham, 1997: 358), in that using celebrity stories as an outlet for social frustration may work against societal change as much as it cultivates a critical stance towards privilege, but it is important to recognise content outside of traditional current affairs as contributing to public sphere competencies.

It could be claimed, finally, that in a media-saturated society, a vital skill for participation in a public sphere is the ability to critically evaluate media texts, and that on one level tabloids equip readers with this skill through a self-reflexive relation to the news production. Readers were certainly highly sceptical of their reading material, and showed a clear understanding of the effect of commercial pressures on tabloid news output. Taking tabloids 'with a pinch of salt' appeared the norm. Indeed, readers were using various strategies to evaluate journalistic techniques, for instance by deeming political news more 'true' than the reporting of celebrities, by thinking of quotes as more important than the reporters' comments, and by not believing a story until it was widely reported or 'on TV'. A comparison can be made to viewers of reality TV formats, which have been shown to learn about production strategies from watching the shows (Hill, 2005: 106).

Yet, the same reader could appear sophisticated in some areas of decoding, for example a female *Sun*-reader who provided an in-depth critique of the sensationalist headlines, but less so in others, as when this reader showed little awareness of the *Sun*'s political allegiances or its place in a larger media corporation. Caution should therefore be applied in terms of how far such critical media literacy skills puts the reader in a position to 'see through' the newspaper, as this hinges on more wide-ranging knowledge about media and society.

## Talk and participation

Yet, these newspapers are able to communicate with groups alienated from other sources of print news, and contribute to competencies necessary for forming opinions on issues of public interest. Further, the sociable and participatory nature of the reading should be examined, as equal participation and interaction are guiding principles to a public sphere. As Peter Dahlgren has pointed out: 'without discussion among citizens, the label 'public' becomes meaningless' (1995: 151). Although such discussion can take many forms, informal talk between members of social groups is arguably a vital part of this, and one where tabloid newspapers, among the readers in this study, played a crucial role.

To understand the role of the *Sun* and the *Mirror* in such talk, their public use must be noted. 'On the train', 'in the pub' and 'at work' were some of the places mentioned for the reading, with the papers piled up in corners of some workspaces I visited during the fieldwork. Their contribution to social activity was further exemplified in how some participants would read the papers together, with an important use of the reading to strengthen social bonds with other individuals:

> **Charlotte:** They give you, like, enough to . . . basically understand what has happened, and maybe even, kind of, discuss it with other people, kind of thing. It's like a social thing.
> **Interviewer:** Do you talk about what you read [in the *Sun*]? . . .
> **Nicole:** I think newspapers and even the news on the telly are conversation points anyway. They can lead to. . . . Like, my boyfriend works and I'll. . . . If I've read the newspaper today. . . . If he phones me, I go, 'have you read the newspaper today?' We generally read the same thing or we watch the same news, if we haven't seen each other. And, he'll say 'yeah, I heard about so-and-so.' And we might discuss it for a couple of minutes. But it's something . . . I don't know. It's like it's something to talk about. It generates conversation between people.

As observed in this group of friends (aged 18–21), such sociability can be seen as a major use of news in general (see e.g. Jensen, 1992: 230 and Gauntlett and Hill, 1999: 55–57); and tabloids here served a bridge to shared cultural grounds.

Partly, social interaction was facilitated precisely through the 'soft' tabloid focuses criticised in the tabloidization debate – celebrity stories, sports, agony aunt columns, horoscopes and bizarre human interest. As Schudson (1997) has suggested, there might be a difference between 'political discussion' and social chitchats stemming from such subjects, yet most readers did not distinguish sharply between different kinds of subjects, with group discussions moving freely between the 'main stories' of current affairs, such as immigration and the Iraq war, to Britney Spears' love life. As Dahlgren reminds us, 'the permeability of contexts, the messiness and unpredictability of everyday talk' means that that ' "the political" is never *a priori* given, but can emerge in various ways' (2003: 160). The everyday conversations stimulated by these papers can, at least, have potential to open up into political discussion.

This communicative aspect should also be placed in relation to the sense of participation in a wider forum for public discussion. Readers experienced dialogic tabloid textual devices such as phone-ins, calls for stories and pullout posters as furthering a sense of a *community*, with the *Sun* and the *Mirror* successfully having established an overall feeling of connectedness. As exemplified in the following discussion with a 27-year-old Portuguese catering assistant, reading the daily newspaper meant feeling that 'your say really counts':

> **Interviewer:** Do you think that what you read about politics in the *Mirror* would contribute to how you feel about politics in any way?
> **Luigi:** I think so. Most of the people who read it are just ordinary people so. . . . And they [the *Mirror*] do things quite good, like, surveys and stuff, which is good.
> **Interviewer:** What, surveys of . . .?
> **Luigi:** Something like, what people think. It gives you the opinion, like, that your say really counts. So that's nice as well.

Perceived as giving a voice to 'ordinary people', this community-building characteristic to tabloid newspapers must be seen as crucial to their appeal, and underlines the ability of popular journalism to mobilise a sense of collectivism.

At times, this collectivism can purport to affect social change. A difference here emerged between *Sun*- and *Mirror*-readers, where a number of male *Mirror*-readers had embraced an overtly political approach, in the discussions taking a standpoint against for example racial discrimination, sexism and warfare. Buying the *Mirror*, for these readers, signalled active support for the paper's radical stance on issues such as the Iraq was, as well as an appreciation for its broader left-wing agenda. Shown in this discussion about football coverage, it was also interpreted as a rejection of what was seen as the *Sun*'s extremism:

> **Interviewer:** Do they [the Mirror] cover a particular team more than other papers?
> **Michael:** Erm . . . No, they're quite . . . actually, they're not biased to one team, which is good. . . . You know, it's interesting to see what's gonna happen now, with, you know, this tournament [the European Cup].
> **Interviewer:** Oh yeah?

**Michael:** . . . I'm interested in seeing how they, how they are with the issues regarding foreign teams. When England play foreign teams. If they get really patriotic. The *Sun* gets really, really [raises his voice] 'let's get them!' The *Mirror* aren't usually as bad as that, you know. Cause the *Sun* and the *Star* go really, like, bulldog British. And it's a bit intimidating, you know. It's kind of like a bit too . . . too, kind of patriotic British thing, yeah.

Then, a final point to emerge out of this study is that while tabloid newspapers are generally treated as a singular phenomenon, readers make important distinctions between them. These distinctions may have a bearing on the way the reading relates to public sphere discourse, and are worthy of further research.

## Conclusion: tabloid newpapers as a public sphere?

In this chapter, I have attempted to add a layer to the debate about how tabloid newspaper reading relates to the public sphere. The overall perspective is that the public sphere concept is at its most useful when developed and problematised in terms of a variety of real audiences and media forms.

It is clear some tabloid readers do feel distanced from mainstream political processes, with a common distrust of both politicians and journalists. In particular, female readers in this study experienced politics as outside of their experience and competence. It is likely that these newspapers, in drawing on anti-establishment sentiments and emphasising traditional conceptions of gender, play a part in maintaining this experience. Overall, likewise, it appeared the newspapers had an agenda-setting function as to what kind of news was discussed, and I am convinced they can contribute to determine conceptual frameworks for understandings of society.

Yet, it would be inaccurate to describe the reading as apolitical. Although an interest in politics may not be directly articulated, current affairs news is valued as part of the overall content. For some, tabloids are the only *accessible* forum for printed current affairs analysis, and can help clarify complex issues. The major function of the newspapers to provide 'talking points', around which readers make judgements through interaction with others, further corresponds with a communicative public sphere ethos. Such discussions do not necessarily confine to public affairs in a strict sense, but, as in the case of talk about celebrity stories, covering morality and social privilege, they raise questions of what is deemed to be in the public interest.

A strong theme emerging from the readership research is that tabloid reading can contribute to an experience of participation in a wider collective, which, again, is contrary to ideas of tabloid readers as engrossed in the individuated consumption of culture. This will to collectivism can be juxtaposed against social fragmentation elsewhere, for example in the erosion of trade unions, and it highlights the potential of popular journalism in encouraging participation in a public forum. However, in this study, it was only in the discussions with a number of male *Mirror*-readers that such participation had taken a more overtly political and socially progressive form, indicating a possible difference in the role of the two newspapers, and highlighting the need for a more differentiated outlook on tabloid media. There is a suggestion here that ideological roles of individual media outlets are more important than the stylistic features of tabloid journalism *per se* for contributing to a progression of the public sphere. Likewise, such a contribution is clearly dependent on a wider socio-economic context where issues of general education and media literacy are vital to developing the skills necessary for an equal participation in public sphere discourse.

The findings, then, call for a re-evaluation of simplistic perceptions of tabloid newspapers. On the one hand, tabloids appeal to and may advance experiences of alienation from mainstream political developments, on the other they provide what are in many senses the foundations for a public sphere as derived from Habermas, as accessible and participatory forums. In spite of a problematic relationship between the papers and progressive social efforts, it is suggested tabloids can provide the basis for an alternative public sphere for readers alienated from dominant perspectives. Rather than leading to a naive defence for tabloid newspapers, this conclusion should point to a more nuanced outlook on their analysis, and the need for a better understanding of when and how the potential of tabloid journalism can be harnessed for common good.

## Notes

1. A quote from *The Economist*, on the cover of Chippindale and Horrie, (1999).
2. The tabloid newspaper and the US supermarket tabloids are different for instance in that the weekly supermarket tabloids do not run editorials about politics.
3. All names are pseudonymous to protect respondents' privacy.
4. Age and type of occupation determined how far readers would distance themselves from the newspapers, with younger readers more likely to exclaim affinity to their tabloid, and white-collar readers more distancing.

# 8
# Rethinking Public Service Broadcasting: The Historical Limits to Publicness

*Michael Bailey*

It is widely known that the history of British broadcasting is inextricably inter-twined with the concept of public service. The main justifications for public service broadcasting are its commitment to due impartiality, to maintaining cultural standards over and above the pursuit of profit, and to representing a diversity of competing social interests and ordinary everyday experiences. Moreover, the principle of public service continues to inform contemporary debates about how best to organise and regulate not only broadcasting but the media generally. In contrast to free market liberals who define the media as a private commodity, promoting deregulation, market competition, and the sovereignty of the individual consumer, advocates of public service communications argue the media ought to be managed as a public good available to all, and that the public be treated as social citizens with universal needs and wants.

In recent years, some communication and media studies scholars have turned to the work of Jürgen Habermas, particularly his concepts of the 'public sphere' and 'communicative rationality', in an effort to defend and reinvigorate the ideal and institutional embodiment of public service broadcasting (see Collins, 1993; Garnham, 1993; Keane, 1996; Scannell, 1989; Thompson, 1995, among others). Whilst such authors acknowledge the shortcomings of Habermas's conceptual framework, and differ considerably in their appropriation of what is generally thought of as critical theory, they nevertheless continue to argue for the continuing relevance of a Habermasian approach to the study of the interrelationships between the mass media, political economy and democratic politics. Furthermore, unlike that strand of media studies that is largely concerned with the ideological effect of mediated representations, neo-Habermasians are more interested in the institutional allocation of cultural resources and the necessary material conditions for ensuring rational debate, public accountability, social equality, citizens rights, cultural democracy, and so forth.

Whilst there is much to support and recommend such analyses, the analysis I present here is one concerned with contextualising the emergence and institutionalisation of early public service broadcasting as one of many instruments whose function was to govern through processes detached from the formal apparatuses of political authority, thus overcoming the paradoxical concern of liberal governmentality, the danger of 'over-governing'. More specifically, I mean to demonstrate that the formation of public service broadcasting is better reconsidered as a civilising mission whose political rationality was to render the listening public more amenable to techniques of cultural governance and particular regimes of citizenship. As such this chapter represents an attempt to provide an articulation between the rich empiricism of the extant histories of broadcasting on the one hand and cultural theory on the other, in particular Foucauldian governmentality theory.

## Governmentality and cultural regulation

The originality and relevance of Foucault's (1991) research into what he called 'governmentality' is its attempt to explain the emergence and subsequent development of a practical political rationality that concerns itself with the art of government, how to best govern a group of human beings constituted as a population, the basis of any modern state's wealth and power. Historically, this became especially important during the eighteenth and nineteenth centuries, when most Western nation-states experienced extraordinary increases in the size of urban populations, a phenomenon that represented all kinds of new economic and socio-political probabilities and uncertainties. Henceforth, government is less to do with the government of a province or a territory, as proposed in Machiavelli's *The Prince*, and more to do with the government of people, their relations with other things internal to the state, and how to best dispose of things for a plurality of ends that are politically and economically expedient at a given moment in time: how to increase a nation's wealth, how to maintain a healthy and prosperous populace, how to stimulate birth-rates, how to effect certain ways of behaving and thinking, and so on.

A further characteristic of modern government is how to introduce 'economy' into political practice, that is maximising the political and economic efficacy of government whilst reducing its cost. Unlike traditional political theories of government, which tend to focus on juridical-state sovereignty, Foucault proposed an historical thesis whereby the rationality of 'government' is expanded beyond the traditional practices of the state to include an ensemble of voluntary, statutory, and professional agencies (e.g. the 'psy' disciplines, social welfare, education, medicine, religion, recreational organisations, etc.), the result of which is the growth of more complex discursive forms of power organised through multifarious non-coercive disciplinary social practices and bodies of knowledge. Rose and Miller (1992) argue this pluralisation of modern government, and the accompanying relativisation of the commonly attributed boundaries between state and civil society, becomes a form of 'acting at a distance'. Government takes place as much in everyday practices as it does in and through state and quasi-state institutions. Understood thus, government does not simply refer to that sphere of political activity normally thought of as government in the constitutional sense, but as an activity that consists in governing human conduct by means of what Foucault called 'governmental technologies', the instruments and practices for actualising political rationalities.

An analysis of government is thus concerned with the ways in which certain social relations and the conduct of populations come to be problematised and objectified as sites for political intervention. One of the most significant and enduring concerns for modern government has been the regulation of social activities and fields of knowledge which have come to be described as 'cultural'. The historicity of modern cultural governance can be traced back to the emergence of Victorian rational recreation – museums, parks, libraries, art galleries, etc. – at a time when anxiety over the quality of British culture and civic life became increasingly centred on the use of leisure. Concomitant with the development of more public and accessible forms of leisure we see the emergence of a cultural apparatus that was aimed at rendering the popular masses more visible and, it was supposed, more governable by making them subjects of civilising influences previously available to the social elites only. As pointed out by Tony Bennett (1992), culture becomes both an object and instrument of a governmental programme aimed at social management and, when expedient to do so, social reform. Hence the assimilation of rational recreation with the various institutionalised movements for temperance, educational reform and other reformist organisations whose core rationale was the general drive for social and moral improvement.

The relevance of this broader historical argument is that the positive role assigned to rational recreations as civilising technologies of government was carried through into the early twentieth century. This was especially significant in the context of Britain in the 1920s and 1930s, which, like most industrial nations during this period, was experiencing varying degrees of social unrest and economic depression, prompting widespread fears among political and cultural elites that the moral and intellectual leadership once exercised over the general populace had greatly diminished (see LeMahieu, 1988). That this perceived crisis in social hegemony coincided with early twentieth century extensions of the franchise represented a further problem for those in authority; if representative democracy and parliamentary sovereignty were to function in a way that served the interests of the state, it was imperative that the newly enlarged electorate be taught how to exercise their democratic rights and duties not as members of a social class but as social citizens. Needed was a cultural technology of government which could mediate the demands of a conservative cultural minority on the one hand and the demands of a newly created mass democracy in need of an educated and informed citizenry on the other, while maintaining an appearance of neutrality and universality. It is to these governmental apparatuses to which I now turn, in particular the formation of public service broadcasting under the aegis of the BBC.

## The birth of broadcasting

In order to fully understand the BBCs rationality as a technology of cultural governance it is necessary to know something about its constitutional origins. Formed in 1922, the BBC started life not as a public corporation but as a private cartel, consisting of several wireless manufacturers. Though to all intents and purposes a private enterprise, broadcasting was characterised by a significant peculiarity: unlike the press, licence to broadcast was regulated by the state. Moreover, just as broadcasters required permission to broadcast, so too were the listening public required to obtain an official licence for listening-in. Whilst this conferred certain economic benefits upon the consortium of wireless manufactures, not least an exclusive monopoly to broadcast and an entitlement to half of the ten shilling licence fee, the industry was subject to what was then an unusual degree of public control and officialdom by comparison with other media.

The transformation of the BBC into a public corporation was signalled by the Crawford parliamentary committee (HMSO, 1925), called into being to specifically consider the future of broadcasting. Of the many recommendations, the most significant proposal was that 'broadcasting be conducted by a public corporation acting as a Trustee for the national interest, and that its status and duties should correspond with those of a public service'. Hence it came to be on 1 January 1927 the BBC was effectively nationalised under Royal Charter, and as such became one of the earliest examples of a national public utility. However, it is important to note that the BBC was not an overtly state controlled public body. Rather, it was and remains a quasi autonomous public body effectively run by a state-appointed executive Board of Governors. More crucially, it epitomised the contradictory tendencies in a shift to collectivist public services whilst maintaining a element of *laissez-faire* in terms of being independent of direct state interference. In short, the BBC was indicative of the way in which new forms of governance were being created, neither state nor commercially run but what we now call quangos. Thus though the BBC has come to be regarded as unique in its actual constitution, the institutional form was quite compatible with what was happening elsewhere, whereby governmental aims and objectives were enacted from a distance within and without state apparatuses.

One of the earliest and clearest articulations of the idealisation of public service broadcasting was expressed by John Reith, the first General-Manager and Director-General of the BBC. Born a Scotsman, and a lifelong devout Christian, Reith's part in shaping the policy of the BBC, not least its public service ethos, was distinct. He more than anybody championed the BBCs civilising mission. Reith's concern for a particular vision of public service broadcasting was unmistakable, not least his emphatic belief that, 'to have exploited so great a scientific invention for the purpose and pursuit of 'entertainment' alone would have been a prostitution of [broadcasting's] powers and an insult to the character and intelligence of the people' (Reith, 1924: 17). For

Reith, the ordinarily accepted meaning of the word 'entertainment', that is simply to 'occupy agreeably', was 'incomplete' in the sense that it amounted to a mere 'passing of the time, and therefore of wasting it'. If there was to be entertainment, it should be 'part of a systematic and sustained endeavour to re-create, to build up knowledge, experience and character . . .'. Like rational recreationalists before him, what was important was to show the public 'how time may be occupied not only agreeably, but well'.

Not surprisingly, Reith was not at all prepared for the BBC to be content with 'mediocrity' nor for it to engage in any activity that detracted from 'high moral standard', as evidenced in his highly unpopular Sabbath policy whereby only religious broadcasts were permitted. However, Reith's disdain for popular culture was not the contempt espoused by many of his contemporaries. Their dislike of mass culture was in defence of their own minority culture and its elitist exclusivity. Reith, on the other hand, was a 'progressive' (LeMahieu, 1988). Not only was he altogether optimistic about the emergence of new technologies of mass communication, if managed properly; following Matthew Arnold, he also genuinely wanted to make available as widely as possible the best 'in every department of human knowledge, endeavour and achievement' (Reith, 1924: 34). However, and more crucially, Reith did not trust the public to reach out for the 'sweetness and light' he and Arnold so desired. His lofty idealism and high-mindessness bore all the hallmarks of nineteenth-century conservative paternalism. Reith's own inflection of conservative paternalism was best encapsulated in what was undoubtedly his most infamous remark about the public not knowing what they want or what they need.[1] Though in charge of what was undoubtedly the mass media *par excellence*, Reith was in no doubt whatsoever that broadcasting was 'a servant of culture' and that culture was 'the study of perfection' (ibid.: 217). Of course, this strategy was part of a broader deontology whereby everybody had a responsibility not only to cultivate one's best self, but more importantly, to cultivate others for the good of the whole. In other words, broadcasting was first and foremost about self-improvement and self-discipline; moreover, it could act as a possible corrective to the irrational tendencies of popular recreation.

## Uniting the nation: broadcasting and monopoly

The BBCs institutional base, particularly its exclusive right to broadcasting, was crucial to its civilising mission. Reith thought unity of control essential not only on technical grounds but also to maintain high standards. Without the 'brute force of monopoly', a phrase he was to use later when writing his autobiography, Reith (1949: 100) doubted whether a public service broadcasting ethos would have even been possible.

> Almost everything might have been different. The BBC might have had to play for safety; prosecute the obviously popular lines; count its clients; study

and meet their reactions; curry favour; subordinate itself to the vote. *Might* have had to; probably would not; but its road would have been far harder.

An earlier articulation of this argument was expressed by Reith whilst giving evidence before the Sykes Committee, where he made abundantly clear the advantages of maintaining broadcasting under unified control (PO Archives, Post 89/21). Apart from 'there being a very good economy in having one Broadcasting authority', Reith was even more emphatic about the 'very great advantage in having one uniform policy of what can or cannot be done in broadcasting', with all regional broadcasting stations and their Directors 'under a very definite continuous control'. Hence the priority given to centring policy-making and production on London and to favouring the National Programme over local and regional broadcasting. The policy would be further guaranteed by recruiting only those of the very highest calibre to a newly emerging class of managerial professionals and by a network of advisory committees providing expert guidance from outside, more or less negating provincial amateur efforts to pioneer early wireless technology and programmes that encouraged genuine audience participation.[2]

Reith's insistence on unified control was not only aimed at managing provincial cultural differences. An even more interesting feature of the discourse about the BBCs monopoly was that it nearly always invoked the American experience of broadcasting regulation, whose chaos of the ether and excessive commercialism was often held up as an inferior alternative to the highly regulated public service model adopted by the BBC. If the British nation provided a positive definition of the BBC's purpose, America provided a negative definition (see Camporesi, 1994). The prevailing opinion among many BBC staff and British politicians was that the values embodied by the BBC were vastly superior.[3] By contrast, American popularism was both exploitative and immoral. American civilisation failed to inspire confidence amongst Britain's cultivated elites, particularly its crass democratic appeal and valorising of egalitarian values. Many British critics during this period were of the opinion that effective political leadership could not be expected of the newly enfranchised public. America's advocacy of rule for and by the people had resulted in a dictatorship of the masses. Others objected to the way in which American populism played upon the common, baser instincts. They particularly loathed America's commodifying of culture and the consequent undermining of their own cultural ascendancy. The BBC embodied this anxiety, hence its *raison d'être* as custodian of the nation's cultural heritage.

## BBC English

The BBCs civilising mission and idealisation of cultural enlightenment not only pertained to the dissemination of the right ideas and knowledge, but also to wider cultural practices. In this cultural struggle, the preservation of the English language took centre stage. Extolling the virtues of 'King's English', or what has since come to be known as 'BBC English', Reith thought that 'broadcasting may be of immense assistance' in correcting 'the most appalling travesties of vowel pronunciation' (Reith, 1924: 161). This idea was affirmed in the practice 'to secure . . . men who, in the presentation of programme items, the reading of news bulletins and so on, can be relied upon to employ the correct pronunciation of the English tongue'. Consequently, announcers were subject to rigorous preliminary tests, in addition to regular instruction in the technique of broadcasting the spoken word, and had to be free of regional dialect and personal idiom. Similarly, much on-air debate and discussion was restricted to people of suitable calibre and decorum.

The BBC was assisted in its mission to disseminate standard English by the Advisory Committee on Spoken English, formed in April 1926. Its body of eminent persons included: A. Lloyd James, Professor of Phonetics at London University, the Poet Laureate, Robert Bridges, George Bernard Shaw, Logan Pearsall-Smith, and Rudyard Kipling. The Committee was responsible for making decisions on how best to pronounce 'debatable words'. More than this, the Committee endorsed the BBC's general policy of only employing announcers who spoke standard English. Like Reith, Lloyd-James (1935: 27) was insistent that broadcasters be 'educated' and maintain 'high standards of clarity and intelligibility', since broadcasters 'are in the process of determining the future form of our spoken language as surely as the printer and type designer determined the form of our printed language'.

Underlying this insistence that all broadcasters, announcers in particular, speak standard English was a deep-rooted concern that spoken English was disintegrating into 'a series of mutually unintelligible dialects', which, in Lloyd James' opinion (1935: 27), were 'fed by local prejudice, parochial patriotism, and petty nationalisms'; 'a menace not only to the unity of the language but to the unity of the English-speaking peoples'. Broadcasting's dissemination of the spoken word was a means of arresting these disintegrating influences. More crucially, Lloyd James' prioritising of speech in the general order of things and social practices, and his obsession for effecting a state of universal cultural enlightenment, became a prescription for the standardised citizen.

> When we have turned out standard citizens, all on one plan, all of one character and temperament, all educated along the same lines, brought up in standard homes by standard parents, and when we have furnished them all with standardised opportunities for the acquisition of a standardised culture, and the attainment of a standardised career, then we shall have a standardised speech, for speech is the reflection of all those things. (Lloyd-James, 1935: 109)

Yet again, we can see how the BBC was an instrument with which to unite the nation around a universal, common standard. In this particular instance,

Englishness was defined by the primacy of correct English. Standard English was thought to be the language of the educated and cultured. Such standard-isation was the key-stone for ensuring cultural citizenship, the measure of any-thing and everything of socio-cultural significance, and the quintessence of middle-class respectability. Many BBC employees thought that the improve-ment of the English language would facilitate the general uplift of the English nation. It is with this in mind that Stuart Hall (1986: 43–4) notes that the fun-damental task facing the BBC was how to reconcile the many regional – but nonetheless English – voices into its 'Voice'; a voice which was in turn reflected back to the nation as the 'Standard Voice'. Anything that detracted from this unity, in this case divergent pronunciations, were thought to be yet another aberration, that may tend towards chaos.

## Learning over the air

Whilst broadcasting's core rationale was to unite the public around a nucleus of cultural values and practices that helped foster a sense of national citizen-ship, identity and sense of belonging, Reith also saw broadcasting as a solu-tion to yet another potential crisis in liberal democracy: the problem of an uninformed electorate, something he thought to be 'a serious menace to the country' (Reith, 1924: 113). Like many of his middle-class contemporaries who had a deeply-rooted sense of civic duty, Reith feared that the ever increasing massification of popular culture would detract from the pursuit of cultural enlightenment. The crucial difference, however, was that Reith was optimistic about broadcasting's capabilities to bring about 'a more intelligent and enlight-ened electorate'. The way in which the BBC went about this was to inculcate its listening public in the art of 'civil prudence', that is to say, a series of self-governing, ethical obligations that aimed to actualise a regime of 'educated citizenship'.

Thus a major activity of the BBC from its inception was educational broad-casting. As well as general educative programmes, the BBC inaugurated spe-cific educational broadcasts both for children and adults. Of these, the BBC regarded adult education as especially crucial to the post-war reconstruction effort, particularly in terms of creating an enlightened democracy. The first systematic provision for broadcast adult education started in October 1924, shortly after educational broadcasting had been established as an adminis-trative department in July 1924. The appointment of its first Director, J. C. Stobart, seconded from His Majesty's Inspectorate for Education, was reported on the front page on the *Radio Times* (13 June 1924) under the heading 'A Broadcasting University'. The peculiarity and significance of a civil servant being loaned to what was still then a business organisation did not go unnoticed and was 'taken as evidence of the Government's realisation of the national importance of broadcasting'. The administrative work of the education department was greatly aided by the appointment of the Central

Educational Advisory Committee in August 1924. Each regional station had its own Local Educational Advisory Committee, thus ensuring the co-operation of Local Education Authorities (see Briggs, 1961: 242). Furthermore, the BBC stressed co-operation and mutual goal-sharing with existing adult education agencies, particularly government approved ones, such as the British Institute for Adult Education and the Workers' Educational Association.

One of the earliest collaborations between these different agencies was the publishing of what was by far the most significant of the various inter-war reports directly concerned with broadcast adult education, *New Ventures in Broadcasting* (BBC, 1928), otherwise know as the Hadow Report. The tone of the report was overwhelmingly optimistic. 'The educational possibilities of [wireless] are almost incalculable. Even if no single item labelled educational ever appeared in the programmes, broadcasting would still be a great educational influence.' The report also considered the bureaucratic advantages afforded by wireless: 'Unlike the lecturer, it can be everywhere at once. It is the perfect method by which to conduct what has been described as "insidious education".' In other words, the technology of broadcasting was comparatively cheap and ubiquitous.

Among the report's main recommendations were: (1) the establishing of wireless listening groups; (2) and the setting up of a Central Council for Broadcast Adult Education comprised of representatives from important national bodies concerned with adult education and Area Councils representing local educational interests. The Central Council for Broadcast Adult Education was formally brought into existence in November 1928. The Council based its policy on its belief 'in the unique and decisive influence of wireless on the future of civilisation' (WAC R14/124). Two key objectives were identified. First, it aimed 'at inducing among listeners a high standard of intellectual curiosity, of critical ability and of tolerance to all views held and expressed with a sincerity and a regard for truth'. This required 'a respect, even a reverence for truth in all its aspects and a desire for knowledge unfettered by dogmas of any kind'. Second came 'the more particular and tangible objective': to educate listeners in 'an appreciation of the forces of transformation and change in the world about them', especially 'the developments of science, the enlargement of knowledge and the evolution of social custom and practices'. Here we see the general goals of culture, civilisation, and democracy being translated into educational principles: the reverence for 'truth' (as opposed to 'dogma') and the understanding of 'science', 'knowledge' and 'custom'. Note the neutrality of the discourse: not a single truth we can tell them but a respect for truth; not a subservience to the natural order but an understanding of scientific and social change. It verges on advocacy of a kind of sociology but one clearly oriented to a dispassionate understanding which might well produce an urge to reform but not to revolution.

Of even greater significance was the BBCs heeding of the report's other recommendation, the organisation and development of wireless listening groups. The stated object of listening groups was to develop 'the capacity to listen to other people's ideas even when they are unpalatable, and to follow up by discussion and calm analysis' (*The Listener*, 23 January 1929). Not unlike the tutorial class system operated by most approved adult education providers, each group had a designated leader whose role was to 'guide and shape the discussion and know sufficient about the subject to take a lead with confidence'. That said, group leaders were not necessarily required to have specialist knowledge but should be 'educated' and 'respectable' persons from business and the professions. What mattered, as noted by Robert Peers (1934: 86), the first university Professor in Adult Education, was that the person chosen as leader should not only 'be competent to guide the discussion' but also 'have the ability to restrain his own and others' garrulity'. The rationale for listening groups was less concerned with the dissemination of knowledge than it was with endowing individuals with new capacities for self-development and self-regulation. And the role of group leaders was to inculcate listeners in self-regulatory practices that were concurrent with the art of self-governance, that is rational discussion, tolerance, restraint and impartiality. It was important that the listening public be taught not what to think but how to think and how to imitate exemplary conduct. Understood thus, listening groups were as much to do with contact between conduct and conduct as they were with contact between mind and mind.[4] Of course, they were also an expedient way of de-politicising the discussion of social issues likely to cause conflict of public opinion. Such differences were to be suppressed in the interests of the community at large, the nation.

## The art of listening

A further characteristic of broadcast adult education was the way in which the listening public was constituted according to a hierarchy of listening subjectivities. By the 1930s the BBC began to differentiate between the casual and the serious listener.[5] That is to say, one can discern an order of discourse in which the serious listener was deemed to be culturally superior and something the casual listener should therefore aspire to. Casual listeners, that is listeners who lay outside the scope of discussion groups, presented a special difficulty inasmuch as their cultural habits and comportment were unknowable. Consequently, they were not as easily subjectable to techniques of individualisation and normalisation. This was problematic from a governmentality point of view since it presented an affront to the order of proper conduct necessary for ensuring social solidarity and civility. Converting casual listeners into serious listeners was thus crucial to the construction of an informed and ordered listening public, as the Central Council for Broadcast Adult Education Executive Committee recognised:

> The welfare of our nation depends upon a rapid increase in the number of those who were ready to think for themselves and ready to exercise individual judgement, ready to enter into a real relationship pooling their

own mental resources with others in order that all together, as each gained some glimpse of the whole variety of truth, they might shape their policy as a people with reference to the whole of it. (WAC R14/120/4)

Crucial to this project was that broadcast adult education was constructed as a self-acting imperative which the listening public voluntarily followed in pursuing the abstract rhetoric of 'educated-democracy'. If broadcasting was to function effectively as a technology of government, it was essential that the audience be active and not passive in its listening; better altogether that the listening public actively participate in the regulation of its freedom, thus forming the necessary habits to conduct its own behaviour. Consider for example the following paragraph from a BBC publication on how to organise discussion groups and what they were for:

> . . . if democracy is to be a real democracy, it must be an educated democracy . . . Broadcasting, breaking down the barriers of space, destroying distinctions of class, placing its resources at the service of all men, whether rich or poor, can do more to ensure an educational democracy than any other single agent. Whether it does do all that it can do, depends mainly on the listener. (BBC, 1932: 39)

Similarly, an article to appear in *The Listener* (8 August 1934) reiterated: '. . . if we are gradually to develop a finer and nobler civilisation, our citizens must care more and know more'. Again, the discourse of educated-citizenship was as much about disciplining citizens in the art of self-government so as to have a deeper sense 'of social responsibility, of sympathy and of the willingness to help in working for a common purpose' as it was with equipping them with abstract rights and freedom. In order to secure governance from a distance it was necessary for individuals to translate the values of a higher and distant authority into their own terms, such that they provide both totalising and individualising normative standards for conduct. It was essential that the listening public both in its entirety and as individuals cared more about its civil responsibilities. This was particularly so in the early twentieth-century when governmental attempts to reconstruct a new social order and reinvigorate national efficiency greatly depended upon a politically obedient citizenry.

## Conclusion

What I have sought to demonstrate in this article is how one might understand the formation of public service broadcasting and the subsequent development of BBC culture as a technology of cultural governance whose *raison d'être* was to create and maintain an educated citizenship unified around a corporate national culture comprised of traditional English cultural values, and thereby counterpoising the perceived excesses and degenerative effects of mass culture. Whilst this vision of the nation drew on old and new ideas about culture and democracy, what was new about broadcasting was that the transmitter represented not merely the single voice of the BBC but the collective voice of the nation; while the receiver was the collective populace, the nation, but each addressed individually, personally. More crucially, the disembodied voice of radio expressed the perfect ideal of the nation, of which the collective bodies of the various listening publics were but imperfect material embodiments, thus allowing the BBC to construct itself as the central cultural legislator for the nation.

More often than not, this resulted in the exclusion of any cultural practices that were neither national nor centralised. Of course, this was a fundamental paradox for the BBC: in seeking to 'include' all in what is a narrow version of the nation it must perforce exclude those who do not 'belong' in its version. In other words, the problem facing the BBC, was that the national character of radio was not inherent in the medium *per se*; rather, it had to be constructed. As with all forms of nationalism, the BBC had to construct what it was not, as well as what it was. Thus the BBC went out its way to diffuse an image of itself that was distinctly un-American in an effort to maintain an outward display of Britishness. The BBCs mission was to unify the nation, not just around what was best, but, and perhaps more importantly, around the best of British. However, such national unification required the dissemination and policing of common norms. Hence the reason why broadcasting sought to represent the perfect ideal, 'the best that has been written and said'. BBC English was perhaps the most salient feature of this idea of 'the proper'. Correct pronunciation was a major effort of social unification and standardisation, a means of policing of a geographically dispersed and socially fragmented national population.

Uniting the nation in this way was undoubtedly the core rationale underpinning the BBCs wider civilising mission, especially its commitment to cultural forms and activities that had an educative function. It was widely assumed among cultural and political elites that mass entertainment coupled with education would result in good citizenship. In other words, the rationalities of public service broadcasting and citizenship were intertwined. Both sought to effect discursive practices that addressed the public as ethically incomplete subjects in need of cultural training. It is with this in mind that one can begin to understand how taken for granted public service practices, become problematic, not least because these practices are bound up with the production of politically expedient subjectivities and modes of conduct. The formation of good and cultured citizens on the one hand, and the docile and useful subject on the other, amount to the same thing – there is an interdependence between citizenship rights and disciplinary power. In the case of the BBC, it functioned as a benign instrument of educative entertainment. Its role was to instruct the public in useful cultural values and practices that would serve both to inform and educate but also to discipline and regulate.

## Notes

1. Reith expressed this belief even more candidly in a speech at Cambridge in July 1930: 'The best way to give the public what it wants is to reject the express policy of giving the public what it wants' (cited in LeMahieu, 1988: 145).

2. In 1936, Charles Siepmann, by now Director of Regional Radio, published the first comprehensive *Report on Regions*, in which he concluded that 'centralisation represents a short sighted policy', not least its effecting of 'a uniform pattern of thought' and 'standardising of taste and values'. So concerned was Siepmann for securing a better position for the provinces, he suggested 'some sort of charter of rights for the regions' be considered (see Harvey & Robins, 1994: 42).

3. Camporesi (1990: 269) warns that the degree of opposition to American broadcasting 'materialised in, and lived on, a discourse on America which should be handled cautiously', since US broadcasting was falsely conceptualised 'as a synecdoche of American society', exaggerating the polarity between American commercialism and British public service. Indeed, there is evidence to suggest that the commercialisation of American broadcasting was not the inevitable, natural process as is often assumed, but was the result of much uncertainty and resistance on the part of the broadcasters, advertisers, and listeners (Smulyan, 1994).

4. Not surprisingly, public libraries were particularly favoured as venues for wireless discussion groups. They were ideal as disciplinary public spaces as they were supervised by highly skilled cultural technicians in the form of librarians.

5. For example, A. C. Cameron, then Secretary of the Central Committee for Group Listening, described those listeners that did not wish to commit to being members of approved adult education agencies as 'the Second XI of adult education' (*The Highway*, November 1937).

# 9
# Digital Radio and the Diminution of the Public Sphere

*Stephen Lax*

It is more than 70 years since Bertolt Brecht lamented that radio was 'one-sided when it should be two-sided', urging instead that it should 'let the listener speak as well as hear . . . radio should step out of the supply business and organise its listeners as suppliers' (Brecht 2000 [1932]: 42). While short on detail, Brecht argued that more citizens could be involved in the transmission side of radio. Instead, governments and broadcasters around the world have sought effectively to restrict access to radio in favour of the ubiquitous one-way model of broadcaster and listener. 'Radio' for most people means the reception of sounds of various natures, the creation and selection of which are made by someone else.

Nevertheless, radio remains one of the more accessible platforms for those who believe in a more open, participatory and accountable media. While, in common with the press and television, radio tends to be dominated around the world by commercial interest (increasingly concentrated in the hands of larger, transnational media corporations) in combination with some level of public interest (public service broadcasting for example), there are a number of different ways in which it can be argued that radio allows for greater public participation. For instance, talkback radio or the phone-in has been a feature for several decades – the first phone-in in the UK was heard in Nottingham in 1968 (Crisell 2002: 147) – and is now established as a staple part of the radio diet. Here, we hear, however briefly, the voices and views of sections of the audience rarely represented amongst regular presenters and programme makers. Douglas suggests phone-ins act as 'electronic surrogates for the town common, the village square, the meeting hall, the coffeehouse . . .' (2004: 285). To some extent, then, this addresses Brecht's goal of 'turning listeners into suppliers', but editorial control clearly remains with the radio station and Hendy cites evidence for the various ways in which the phone-in falls short of democratic ideals (Hendy 2000: 205–9). A more explicit form of participation is in the direct production of radio. At its simplest, this might be the individual (and friends) broadcasting on an ad-hoc basis, either illegally as a pirate station or legally like some of the low-power FM (LPFM) stations in the US. On a larger scale, however, it also includes small radio stations run by groups of people with little or no commercial interest but with some broad aim of fostering inclusivity and social gain – usually designated community radio, these stations operate to varying extents in many countries. Here we might approach more closely a public sphere in radio. While commercial stations are inevitably compromised by their need to attract advertisers and generate profits, and public service broadcasters in receipt of substantial public funding must similarly compete for substantial audience share, small community stations can operate with greater freedom from these constraints. By deliberately aiming to include a wide range of citizens' views, and involving them directly in production and editorial decisions, this sector of radio has been shown to give voice to groups frequently marginalised by 'mainstream' radio (Lewis and Booth 1989; Jankowski *et al.* 1992). O'Connor's account of the miners' radio stations in Bolivia, for example, demonstrates the vital political role of these small stations (O'Connor 2004).

However, community radio has generally operated at the margins of broadcasting. In the United States, the LPFM movement has found itself squeezed by the commercial interests of the National Association of Broadcasters (Riismandel 2002; Opel 2004). In the UK, radio broadcasting remained dominated for the first five decades of its existence by a commitment to concepts of public and universal service, with little space (including frequency space) allocated for alternative voices. By the 1970s however, following campaigning by a number of activists, community radio plans were at an advanced stage, but a change in political climate resulted in commercial radio interests being prioritised. Once again, proponents of a more accessible radio found themselves squeezed out by the insatiable appetites of the more powerful commercial and public service lobbies.

The launch of digital radio in the 1990s presented new possibilities. The transmission of digital signals to carry the audio content made much more efficient use of the available spectrum and meant that there would be space for a vastly increased number of stations. One barrier to the development of greater diversity in radio, the unequal distribution of scarce spectrum, had thus been lowered. It would seem then that the coming of digital radio would have the potential to open up the airwaves and enhance radio's contribution to the public sphere. However, this emerges at a time when governments around the world are pursuing neoliberal economic agendas, and the idea that new radio spectrum should be seen as a public good rather than a commercial resource is seen as out-of-date. The experience in the UK, the country where digital radio is most developed, suggests that any opportunity to develop radio's contribution to a digital public sphere is being neglected in favour of commercial interest.

## Digital radio technology

Radio production has taken advantage of digital technologies for many years now, but it is only recently that the transmission and reception of radio signals have begun to move from analogue to digital. This slow progress is in marked contrast to the relatively widespread adoption of, or certainly awareness of, digital television. A further contrast with digital television is the development of a number of different standards for the digital radio system. A brief description of the different forms is essential to an understanding of the development of digital radio policy in different parts of the world.

As with television, digital radio can be delivered over any mass media platform: through cable systems, via satellite or over the air using terrestrial transmissions. In the analogue world, the latter is the most familiar and universally-available means of listening to radio. A simple technology, it works with cheap receivers and functions on the move with portable equipment, yet can also deliver high quality audio to state-of-the-art receivers as part of a hi-fi system. For digital technology to replace analogue, it must deliver similar audio quality or better, and it must also include the key radio attribute of portability and mobility, and so *terrestrial* digital radio systems have received most attention and development. In contrast, cable and satellite radio are generally received on fixed systems, usually part of a cable or satellite television set up.[1] It is thus the terrestrial digital radio services that the industry anticipates will most precisely replace analogue radio.

Terrestrial digital radio is currently dominated by one format, known generally as DAB (for Digital Audio Broadcasting). Developed in Europe from the mid-1980s, DAB was intended as a replacement for analogue FM radio, and domestic broadcasts began in a number of countries in 1995. While initial geographical coverage was low and receivers expensive and limited in availability (in much the same way as the launch of any new broadcasting system), ten years later DAB radio services were operating in 28 countries within and outside Europe (World DAB 2005). However, the level of development is uneven: in some of these countries services are advanced, while in others early developments have stalled. For example, in the UK over 85 per cent of the population can receive DAB, including new digital-only public and commercial stations. Meanwhile, neighbouring Ireland has not progressed services beyond Dublin-based trials. The adoption of digital radio receivers shows a corresponding variability: the UK is again the leader, with over two million receivers sold by the end of 2005, while in many other countries (including some with significant DAB coverage), take up has been minimal.

The relatively slow adoption of DAB (even in the UK the receivers sold account for barely three per cent of all radio receivers) is complicated by two further developments: the adoption by the US of a different digital radio standard, the in-band on channel (IBOC) system branded as HD radio, and the introduction of an international digital radio system, Digital Radio Mondiale (DRM). Both are completely different from the DAB system and can be seen as competing formats. While there remain doubts about IBOC's technical quality in comparison with DAB, others claim its adoption is opportunistic, consolidating the position of large radio groups in, effectively, forcing smaller stations including LPFM stations off the air (Ala-Fossi and Stavitsky 2003: 71); and although both the DRM Consortium and the World DAB Forum describe their two systems as complementary (DRM 2005), the emergence of alternatives means the future direction of digital radio's development remains uncertain.

Nevertheless, the DAB system is demonstrably operational while others are still emerging from the trial stage and, of all the countries operating DAB services, the UK has the highest levels of broadcasting and listenership. It serves therefore as a useful illustration of the ways in which the adoption of digital radio reflects media policy and has implications for radio's role in the development of a public sphere.

## Digital radio in the UK

DAB transmissions began in 1995 in the UK when the BBC broadcast its five existing domestic services from a small number of DAB transmitters across the country. Commercial radio stations began digital transmissions in 1999. DAB digital radio works differently from analogue in transmitting signals in wide frequency bands known as multiplexes. A multiplex carries digitally coded audio data for a number of radio stations simultaneously, typically between five and ten. The data is tagged so that a radio receiver, 'tuned' to a station, extracts and reassembles the data for the audio stream of that particular station. Thus, whereas with analogue radio the broadcaster is responsible for the organisation of its station's transmission, with the introduction of DAB the radio station became separated from the transmission of its service, and transmission of a collection of radio services became the responsibility of the operators of the DAB multiplex. In fact, the first UK multiplex was awarded to the BBC for transmission of its own services, so the relationship between broadcaster and transmission remained, but in the commercial radio sector, individual radio stations have had to make arrangements with the multiplex operator for the carriage of their services. With the exception of the BBC multiplex, all licences to operate DAB multiplexes were awarded to commercial companies. These licences were advertised by the regulator at that time, the Radio Authority, and a competitive bidding process determined the outcome of the award. The first award, for a national commercial multiplex, was awarded in 1998 to the sole applicant, Digital One, which in turn contracted with the three existing national analogue commercial stations to transmit their services, and carried an additional seven new services (later reduced to five). Subsequently a series of 46 local and regional multiplex licences have been awarded to other commercial companies, in most cases comprising consortia of the existing large analogue radio groups. The arrangement of these local and regional multiplexes means that in more than half of the UK, a typical DAB listener is within range of two local multiplexes in addition to the two national multiplexes, giving access to 35 or more radio stations (Thomas 2002). Elsewhere, the number of multiplexes received might be fewer, and by the end of 2004 there remained 14 per cent of the population which was unable to receive any DAB signals at all (Ofcom 2004a: 102–3).

The consequence of these developments is that many radio listeners in the UK now have access to a number of new radio services, twice as many or more compared with analogue, provided of course they are within range of the full complement of national and local multiplexes. A number of these new stations are available only on digital radio – three BBC services began in 2002, and by the end of 2004 there were also 32 digital-only commercial stations (though most of these are available only in certain areas). There are also a number of existing local analogue stations which are broadcast on digital multiplexes in new areas – two BBC services (the World Service and Asian Network) available regionally on analogue are transmitted nationally on digital, while 14 commercial local stations broadcast beyond their analogue locales (Ofcom 2004a: 102). To give these numbers some context, the 35 digital-only stations comprise a small proportion of the total of 177 different radio stations on the DAB system. Hence, although the introduction of the DAB digital radio system has brought with it a substantial increase in capacity, that extra capacity is predominantly filled with existing commercial stations and a smaller number of additional public service stations. To date then, there is little sign of radical innovation following the introduction of digital radio and instead a listener is likely to notice two significant changes: the reception of 'local' radio stations from another part of the country (for instance, London-based stations such as XFM are carried on numerous local multiplexes across the UK); and a small number of new stations solely available on digital radio.

The first of these developments represents the transformation of existing local commercial stations into 'quasi-national' stations and, while much advertising on these stations is not geographically-specific, it can be a little disconcerting to hear notices of events such as concerts taking place hundreds of miles away. This dislocation is further compounded by the absence of a number of existing, genuinely-local *analogue* stations from their local DAB multiplex. Fewer than half, 45 per cent, of existing local analogue commercial stations were being carried on their local DAB service by the end of 2004, principally because of the high costs of carriage charged by the multiplex operators (Ofcom 2004a: 101, 116). In particular, the smaller commercial stations are least likely to be carried on DAB. Hence, the 'most local' of a listener's local commercial services generally remain available only on analogue radio. In this way, the introduction of DAB brings with it a tendency away from local and towards regional or (quasi-) national radio.

What of the new, digital-only stations? Of the eight new stations available nationally, three are provided by the BBC and five by commercial operator Digital One. Five of the eight are familiar, mainstream formats (chart, adult, easy listening music); two are spoken word (audio books, drama serials, archive comedy programmes), and the last is an urban/black music station. Among the new 'local' digital-only stations, there are a number of specialist or niche stations, such as a country music station or stations for minority ethnic groups. Nevertheless there is still a high degree of mainstream formatting, and almost all digital-only stations are in fact networked across a number of local multiplexes and so do not in fact pretend towards serving any particular locale. In many cases there is also a high degree of computer-automated production and the often lifeless, programmed output has caused one production company director to describe them as 'juke-box automatons whose pre-recorded presenters make Smashie and Nicie sound genuine' (Ackerman 2005).[2] Hence, while the digital-only stations alone suggest some movement towards specialist programming, given their small numbers in comparison with simulcasts of existing analogue stations, there is little extra diversity to be found on digital radio. Indeed, as the new UK radio regulator the Office of Communications, or Ofcom, points out, the expansion of capacity has not encouraged new entrants to the radio market: of the 167 commercial stations on DAB at the end of 2004, 'only 12 of these are owned by companies which do not have analogue radio interests. And of those 12 brands, many are hospital, community or student services which were already broadcasting prior to the advent of DAB.' The report adds that a number of independently-owned, specialist DAB stations have gone out of business or moved off the DAB platform (Ofcom 2004a: 116).

It seems clear that there is no easy or automatic connection between an expansion in supply of spectrum and an enhanced public sphere. Even without insisting upon Brecht's demand that the audience should be more involved with the production of radio, it is not possible to argue that digital radio offers its audience a significantly wider range of voices than before. If digitisation is to enhance radio's role in the public sphere, we should expect to see a number of developments. The additional capacity for stations should at the least allow a greater diversity of radio formats where maximising audience size would not be the principal determining factor in programme planning, as radio would seek an expanded role independent from commercial interest. In fact the introduction of digital radio does make it possible to approach more closely Brecht's ideal: digital production is relatively cheap and easy to use, and communications networks permit material to be readily shared; digital transmission arrangements within a DAB multiplex are far more flexible than analogue, allowing different numbers of stations to be carried at different times of the day, so that stations need not commit to full-time broadcasting. It would be straightforward to insist that small community stations should have a right of access on a non-commercial basis to their local multiplex in the same way that 'must carry' rules insist that the commercial multiplex operators carry their local public BBC service. Thus radio could become more accessible to a wider range of citizens, who would be able to contribute to debates within their communities. The capacity and flexibility of digital radio would in this way present a flourishing of diverse voices, from very small communities to larger groups of citizens. In fact, with the difficulties of transition for smaller, very local and community stations onto DAB, and the tendency to network hitherto local stations into quasi-national stations, it would be more accurate to argue that digital radio offers a less local, more networked and centralised service – if anything, then, a diminution of the public sphere.

## Commercial radio and DAB

The UK is unusual in having strong involvement from the commercial radio sector in its development of DAB from the outset. The 1996 Broadcasting Act set out how the regulator, then the Radio Authority, would advertise and license multiplex frequencies, following allocations of frequency blocks at the Wiesbaden conference in 1995. The government decision, as we have seen, was that all but one of the seven frequency blocks available in the UK would be used for commercial radio, and that licences to operate those multiplexes would themselves be allocated to commercial companies. Thus, the Act introduced a new tier in the structure of UK radio regulation, the multiplex operators. Described by the Radio Authority itself as 'gatekeepers' (Radio Authority 2002: 19), the multiplex operators would contract with radio stations to carry their services.

The level of interest in DAB shown by commercial radio reflects the rapid development of that sector in the UK. While commercial radio began in the late 1970s with a number of local stations around the UK, their licences carried a significant level of public service responsibility (in a similar way to the regulations on commercial television). Consequently, many stations struggled financially and it wasn't until the passage of the 1990 Broadcasting Act, which sought to deregulate commercial radio and expand the number of stations, that commercial radio became a significant part of the national radio landscape. While the number of commercial stations had only reached 50 by the mid-1980s, it had reached 150 ten years later; that growth has not slackened since and by the end of 2004 there were 275 commercial stations, including three national networks (Hendy 2000: 25; Ofcom 2004a: 26). In 1995 commercial radio took a larger share of the audience than the BBC for the first time and has continued to compete at around that level since (Crisell 2002: 249). Hence, the emergence of a new digital system of radio broadcasting, with the potential for a dramatic expansion in capacity, came at a time which was auspicious for commercial radio companies. Further deregulation followed in the 1996 Broadcasting Act and the 2003 Communications Act. Commenting on the plans before the passage of the 2003 Act, the chief executive of the Commercial Radio Companies Association (CRCA) commented: 'This is good news for local radio. The government has done much to ensure an environment in which commercial radio can prosper' (Brown 2002); and after the act was passed, he spelt out the commercial companies' role: 'CRCA successfully argued for consolidation of local radio to be permitted within the Communications Act and the government agreed that consolidation would be good for listeners' (Brown 2004). In truth, consolidation has been underway for many years: four or five large companies have come to dominate commercial radio – and in 2005, two of those, Capital and GWR, merged to form the largest single UK radio group, while Emap acquired Scottish Radio Holdings later in the same year.[3] The tendency is for smaller independently-owned radio stations to be bought up by the larger groups within a few years of their being awarded a licence. Consolidation on this scale, increasingly permitted under successive legislative acts, leads to what Habermas refers to as the refeudalisation of the public sphere (Habermas 2001 [1974]), large organisations increasing their control of, in this case, broadcast media. This process is not unique to the UK: the increasing dominance of commercial radio in many countries' broadcasting landscapes has been widely noted and, usually, lamented. Commenting on US commercial radio since the 1996 Telecommunications Act, McChesney states (2000: 76):

> Relative to television and other media technologies, radio is inexpensive for both broadcasters and consumers. It is also ideally suited for local control and community service. Yet radio has been transformed into an engine for superprofits – with greater returns than any other media sector – for a small handful of firms so that they can convert radio broadcasting into the most efficient conduit possible for advertising. . . . On Wall Street, the corporate consolidation of radio is praised as a smash success, but by any other standard this brave new world is an abject failure.

McChesney explains that in the years following the Act, over half of the 11,000 US stations changed hands, and there were over 1,000 mergers within the industry (2000: 75). Owning a large number of radio stations means costs can be cut by increased networking of programmes and sharing of presenters, and the local nature of the station is diminished. Instead we hear increasingly familiar formats wherever in the country we happen to be listening, and frequently very similar music selections. A significant benefit of this amassing of local stations from the owners' point of view is that they can present themselves to advertisers as *de facto* national broadcasters, and thus become much more attractive. The share of UK radio's advertising revenue that comes from national rather than local advertising has almost doubled since 1992, and now makes up 70 per cent of all radio advertising revenue (Indepen 2004: 13–14).

The pressure to concentrate ownership has the effect of commercial stations leaving out entire segments of the audience. Even when the licensing bodies strive for an element of pluralism and diversity in the awarding process, once bought up by the big radio groups, many stations' formats change so that what is broadcast often bears little resemblance to the proposals that won the licence in the first place (a noted example is the UK's Jazz FM: it played less and less jazz over the years in favour of mainstream music until in 2005 it gave up the pretence and rebranded as Smooth FM). Thus, despite an obligation on the regulator to encourage the provision of diversity, the experience of commercial analogue radio in the UK is a concentration on mainstream formats (Barnard 2000: 56–65; Hendy 2000: 28–41).

The tendency towards less regulation of the analogue commercial sector has been extended in digital radio. The clearest and most significant change, noted above, was the creation of a *commercial* gatekeeping role on the part of the multiplex operators, whereas in analogue radio the gatekeeper is the government radio regulator itself. In its interpretation of the 1996 Broadcasting Act, the Radio Authority illustrated how its role had diminished (Radio Authority 2001: 21):

> . . . the Authority is not empowered to specify the types or numbers of digital sound programme or additional services which it expects to be provided on a multiplex. . . . decisions about the choice and nature of sound programme and additional service providers are for the multiplex licence applicant to make.

These new gatekeepers are in fact the same companies which already dominate analogue radio. All 47 commercial digital multiplex licences have been awarded to one of the big five (now four) commercial radio companies, or consortia in which one or more of the four have a controlling interest. To illustrate the degree of concentration, the merger of Capital Radio and GWR left the resulting GCap Media in control of 26 of the 47 multiplexes across the UK.

Hence we sense, again, that commercial radio appears to have flourished in a deregulating market, a deregulation process which has been accelerated in the digital sector. There is little evidence of an increase in diversity and access to the digital airwaves on the part of the smaller broadcasters that usually seek to reflect the views and concerns of their locality and are thus often more accountable to their immediate community. Instead we see a clear indication that the additional capacity delivered by digital radio is seen principally as a commercial resource rather than a public good. If we examine the content of the DAB multiplexes in a little more detail, we find further evidence for the dominance of commercial interest. Two examples illustrate the trend.

Firstly, one of the many claims made for digital radio has been that it would deliver superior, 'CD-like' sound quality and indeed there is some justification for this (Lax 2003: 338–40). But there is a direct relationship between the quality of the sound of a digital station and the 'bit-rate' allocated to it: the more bits of audio data used per second in transmitting a particular station, the better the quality of the sound. However the capacity of the multiplex is finite, and giving one station a higher bit rate means there is less capacity for additional stations. Hence there is a tension between quality and quantity (number of stations). The consensus amongst DAB technicians has been that a rate of 256 kilobits per second (kbit/s) would provide best quality audio for stereo music (allowing for five or six stations per multiplex), while 192 kbit/s would be better than FM-quality (Hunter & Norfolk 1995; Ambikairajah *et al.* 1997). The Radio Authority in fact specified a minimum of 128 kbit/s, but with a caveat: 'It is stressed, however, that these are minima. The Authority expects that applicants will wish to balance the benefits of the high audio quality of digital radio at high bit rates against the capacity to include a larger number of programme services' (Radio Authority 2001: 25). In other words, while some programmes would be transmitted at minimum rates, higher rates for some kinds of programming would bring the benefits of higher audio quality to the listener. However, now the multiplexes have begun transmission we find most stations operating at the minimum, 128 kbit/s for stereo music, while only one operates at higher than 160 kbit/s, thereby reaching the 'better than FM' threshold. The multiplex operators have gone against the Radio Authority's recommendation and have prioritised maximising the number of stations over sound quality.

A second example is the use of digital radio capacity for delivery of non-audio data. Just as the digital data carried on a radio multiplex can deliver audio information, it can also deliver other kinds of data. So DAB receivers can display text such as station and programme names, scrolling messages describing programme content and so on; they can also display images (music CD covers for instance). This non-audio data need not of course be related at all to the radio content, but could include a teletext-like service such as news, sport or business information. The DAB multiplexes then have the capacity for delivery of both conventional radio and also potentially revenue-earning data services. Once again, there is a possible tension between using the multiplex capacity for the 1996 Broadcasting Act imposed a limit of ten per cent of multiplex capacity to be used for this type of data service. This limit was doubled by the Secretary of State in 1998, so that one fifth of the multiplex capacity can now be used for data unrelated to radio.

Hence we see that commercial rather than public service priorities are evident in the use of the new digital radio spectrum: the use of minimal bit rates in order to maximise the number of stations carried (and maximise the consequent appeal to advertisers); and the potential use of a significant proportion of the capacity for non-radio data services. More recently, Ofcom proposed relaxing both of these limits on how a multiplex operator might use its capacity (Ofcom 2004a: 141–4). In particular, Ofcom suggests that the specification of minimum bit rates for radio services should be replaced by a more subjective code of practice on quality statements, a relaxation which would allow further increase in the number of stations carried on each multiplex. The second change considered by Ofcom is to increase the current 20 per cent limit on the amount of the multiplex capacity which may be allocated to non-radio data services. Ofcom's position on digital radio is one which stresses the importance of the market in deciding how radio spectrum should be used. Indeed, it states this explicitly: in considering the best way of licensing any future radio spectrum, it states, 'Given Ofcom's preference for allowing the market to decide upon the best use of the spectrum, we are minded to allocate the frequency blocks . . . under the Wireless Telegraphy Act, without the need for a [more restrictive] Broadcasting Act licence' (Ofcom 2004a: 142). Elsewhere in the same document, it explains how an increase in supply of spectrum means the market can more readily be relied upon: 'The general principle . . . is that as spectrum constraints lessen, the need for regulation decreases, as the market provides ever wider choice. It could be argued that, as digital take-up grows, the need for regulation on analogue platforms will decrease, as listeners can experience the wider choice available on all platforms' (Ofcom 2004a: 57).

## Access to digital radio

Digital radio is not a free market as the entry costs are high. The digital carriage costs charged by the multiplex operators are significantly greater than a station's comparable analogue transmission costs, while for new entrants there are also the additional station start up costs. Ofcom does recognise this level of 'market failure' and acknowledges a need therefore for some degree of regulation, but the pattern of services available on DAB, and in particular the absence of a significant number of new, independent and innovative programming services suggests that the 'market plus minimal regulation' formula currently operating is not working. Ofcom itself has no proposals as to how to find space on DAB for small commercial and community stations (Ofcom 2004a: 141). While costs remain the biggest hurdle facing such stations (and there is no regulatory mechanism for subsidising the costs to these stations), they face the additional difficulty of the design of the DAB transmission structure. In the initial planning of DAB multiplexes, the regulators did not consider the increasing number of *smaller* commercial stations in the UK, and certainly did not acknowledge the representations made by the community radio lobby (Buckley 1995; Olon 2002). The geographical size of the multiplex coverage areas, modelled on the existing larger commercial and public service analogue stations, far exceeds that of the existing and planned smaller analogue stations, which would find themselves broadcasting in regions beyond their area of interest. For example, in Holland, proposed digital coverage areas for that country's almost 300 analogue community radio stations mean that each municipality's station, intended to serve just that locality (as it does on analogue radio) would be extended to cover perhaps another two areas. Putting this the other way round, with DAB each municipality would be served by two or three community stations, which would therefore compete with each other for revenue (de Witt 2005). Further, the development of the multiplex system favours broadcasting groups which own or run a number of stations, whether public sector (like the BBC) or commercial in nature. For independent, single station organisations, negotiations with the multiplex operating gatekeepers can raise issues of fair access, with some concern that as owners of radio stations themselves, multiplex operators might create difficulties in making space for what they see as competing services (Trefgarne 2001; Ofcom 2004b).

These difficulties are brought to the fore by the emergence in UK *analogue* radio, after many decades, of a new tier of community radio stations. Following pilot licences granted to twelve stations in 2002, Ofcom invited applications for new licences across the UK and by the closing date in December 2004 had received 192 applications, prompting its chief executive to note that this demonstrated 'considerable enthusiasm for community radio in this country' (Carter 2004). Covering a diverse range of communities of interest and a similarly wide range of geographical areas, and with limits on the amount of advertising revenue allowed, 84 stations had been licensed by February 2006 representing a significant new feature of the radio landscape. Here, with licences requiring these stations to generate social gain, we may expect some contribution to a radio public sphere. Yet for these new radio players digital radio is of little interest – since the announcement of the community radio application process, the Community Media Association, to which most community radio applicants are affiliated, has received almost no queries about digital radio (Reid 2005).

The evidence from the development of radio in the UK over the past decade suggests that there is no strong link between the technology of radio and its contribution to the public interest. While the UK has traditionally divided its limited radio capacity between the competing and powerful interests of public service and commercial broadcasters, the emergence of a significant amount of new digital capacity has created space neither for new entrants from hitherto marginalised constituencies nor indeed for little else that might be heralded as particularly innovative. Where we might look for a new public sphere in radio (and we must wait and see whether funding and other challenges mean we will later have to qualify this description) is in old fashioned analogue radio. While many argue that there is an inevitability about the eventual transfer of all radio to digital platforms, few suggest that such a transformation is imminent (for all that the UK is the world leader in digital radio, ten years after its launch fewer than three per cent of its radio receivers were digital). Meanwhile, other digital radio technologies, perhaps most likely the DRM system, are likely to become more suited to small-scale radio, and the development of hybrid receivers capable of switching between the different digital systems might begin to make the migration possible. However, the evidence suggests there is no guarantee that new digital systems will allow the emergent forms of radio successfully to contribute to the public sphere. If the experience of the DAB system's development serves as an example, it would seem that commercial interests are likely to predominate in any consideration of allocating new capacity. The pattern of development of radio policy in the UK since the 1970s mirrors the rise of neoliberal economics in this country and elsewhere. If we wish to safeguard the future of digital radio for the public good, then just as we are witnessing a growing political and popular opposition to neoliberalism generally, a similar resistance must be raised to any diminution of the new radio public sphere.

# Notes

1. There are two exceptions: first, two digital satellite subscription services operate in the US, Sirius and XM, generally received on in-car sets; secondly, World Space transmits subscription radio services from satellites across Africa, Europe and Asia to portable radio sets. Currently, both of these satellite radio systems remain niche services, remain unprofitable and do not compare in numbers with terrestrial radio as mass media.
2. Smashie and Nicie were two radio DJ caricatures noted for their contrived sincerity, first performed by comedians Harry Enfield and Paul Whitehouse on BBC TV in 1994 and now part of radio folklore.
3. The big four are the newly merged GCap Media, Emap and Chrysalis, followed by The Wireless Group (itself acquired in 2005 by Ulster TV). Between them, these own stations comprising three-quarters of total commercial radio listening, and a similar share of total radio advertising revenue (data from Ofcom 2004a: 29).

# 10
## On Becoming the Media: Low Power FM and the Alternative Public Sphere

*J. Zach Schiller*

KGRR,[1] Grand Ridge's new Low Power FM community radio station, is in a poor, conservative small town in northern California. Many station volunteers, however, dress in tie-dye and a few sport dreadlocks – a visual reminder of the alternative culture and politics they broadcast on KGRR's airwaves. This case of an 'alternative' community radio station illustrates the dilemmas of making and defining alternative public spheres.

In the classic formulation, the public sphere is an ideal forum or space in which theoretically equal participants formulate general societal interests through rational debate (Habermas 1989, 1992). Critics of the classic conception argue Habermas' bourgeois public sphere is exclusionary, thereby limiting the scope of any general interests derived therein to the specific 'horizons of experience' of its participants (Fraser 1992; Negt and Kluge 1993). The durability of the latter critiques, and the attractiveness of the democratic potentials that Habermas's public sphere embodies create an ongoing tension over how to understand the concept or its relevance.

When explicitly counterhegemonic political discourse is considered, a tendency remains to define the public sphere as exclusively political (Downing 2001; Atton 2002). While Fraser (1992) highlights the salience of the role of identity in informing counterpublic discourse, the discourse she theorizes is an explicitly political one. In contrast, Warner (2002) conceives of counterpublics as inclusive of the cultural as well as the political.

Further, debating whether Habermas's initial definition of the public sphere was accurate or relevant is perhaps today less productive than simply recognizing that exclusions of a wide range of perspectives, cultures, and ideas are the norm rather than the exception in contemporary media. Against such a backdrop, it is understandable why there remains scholarly preoccupation with conceiving of *counterpublics* whose participants articulate and defend the political interests relevant to their particular identity community (Fraser 1992). However, if multiple identities are to be accented and embraced rather than bracketed in the (counter)public sphere, as Fraser (rightly) suggests, the question arises of how multiple identity-specific public spheres may transcend their own boundedness to include multiple counterpublics.

In this essay, I develop a concept of the *alternative* public sphere, drawing on the work of Carey (1989) and Warner (2002) to analyze in the case of KGRR how distinct but overlapping counterpublics struggle to create an alternative public sphere in their local community. My purpose is to articulate the concept in such a way as to give attention to the political and cultural discourses that circulate within counterpublics, and to specify the relationship (and distinctions) between subaltern groups, counterpublics, and the alternative public sphere.

## Ritual and transmission models of communication

Carey (1989) makes a useful distinction between the ritual and transmission models of communication. As the means of communication in modern societies developed capacities to reach far-away audiences, so did their capacity to be centralized for purposes of control and/or domination. Thus did they also become vital stakes for contending forces in society to capture for the purposes of transmitting information meant to influence attitudes or change minds. It is chiefly this sort of communications model that Habermas assumes of the public sphere when detailing its origins and subsequent structural transformation. Habermas's critics, for different reasons, also assume the transmission model when suggesting that various 'others' be granted access to and representation in society through counterpublic spheres (Downing 2001; Fraser 1992). However, any conception of the power of public spheres that rests exclusively on a transmission assumption of what circulates within them remains limited, because it ignores how people and communities *use* and *interact with* modes of communication.

Carey also reminds us of the *ritual* model of communications, rooted in concepts such as sharing, participation, association, and fellowship (1989: 18):

> If the archetypal case of communication under a transmission view is the extension of messages across geography for the purposes of control, the archetypal case under a ritual view is the sacred ceremony that draws persons together in fellowship and commonality.

Communication, under a ritual model, 'operates to provide not information but confirmation, not to alter attitudes or change minds but to represent an underlying order of things, not to perform functions but to manifest an *ongoing* and fragile social process' (ibid.). Carey stresses communication that is also about the projection, sharing and maintenance of cultural forms and identities. Building on Fraser's assertion that identity matters in the formation of public spheres, I use Carey's notion of ritual communication to explore collective identity formation in KGRR.

Research in the 'active audience' tradition embraces the idea of communication as ritual, highlighting the agency of (usually marginalized) audiences to appropriate and reconstruct the images and information transmitted to them through the media (Dahlgren 1987, 1988, 1991; Frazer 1987; Hebdige, 1979; Jensen 1990; Nightingale, 2004; Radway 1984). However, this tradition largely examines such rituals of media *consumption*. Following Grindstaff (2002), the present study shifts empirical focus to the agency of producers of media, exploring the rituals of media *production*. Where Grindstaff is concerned with the rituals of producers in mainstream media however, my focus is on alternative media that, theoretically, are less restrictive of producers' agency.

## Alternative media, alternative public sphere

The initial concentration of the means of communication into the hands of the bourgeoisie – celebrated by Habermas, lamented by Brecht (1927, 1932) – led to their development along commercial principles. Later, the same commercialism that gave rise to the bourgeois public sphere also created the modern mass media and their search for the broadest audiences. The contemporary result is the largest concentration of power in the history of the media industry (Bagdikian 2004; McChesney 2004). Consequently, there have been progressively fewer opportunities for 'alternative' discourses and subordinate identities to find greater public circulation, leaving 'mass' audiences under the powerful influence of commercial broadcasters. Fortunately, recent reactions from within civil society to continued media consolidation create new opportunities both for 'ordinary people' to exercise their communicative agency as producers of media, and for empirical research on their cultures of production.

After the 1996 Telecommunications Act further deregulated American commercial media the ownership concentration in radio became especially high. Many independent community media projects emerged in response to a consequent decline of localism in radio. Assisted by the rise of the internet, community radio stations responded by networking to raise awareness about the importance of resisting further deregulation, and to promote group-consciousness as a grassroots network of community radio stations (Durlin and Melio 2003). The Internet has also given rise to a vibrant network of Independent Media Centers which facilitate the circulation of information relevant for anti-globalization and anti-war mobilizations (Coyer 2005). 'Pirate' radio activists also took to the airwaves by the hundreds in the late 1990s, creating an enforcement nightmare for the FCC, leading the regulatory agency to create a new class of Low Power FM license for community broadcasting (Sakolsky and Dunifer 1998; Schiller 2006; Tridish and Coyer 2005; Walker 2001). Many of these alternative media projects provide opportunities for marginalized groups to 'become the media,' and highlight the enormous pent-up demand for localism in the media.

Does the spread of alternative media constitute an alternative public sphere? Similar to Fraser's notion of counterpublics, Downing conceives of a set of alternative media institutions that together represent a kind of alternative public sphere (2001). He argues that radical media help define and keep alive a vibrant movement culture among their constituent radical social movement groups and organizations. Thus, these media help project, validate, and promote the collective identities of the movement groups whose interests they advance.

Research on producers of 'radical' media suggests that participants see them as important organizing tools, and view their involvement as helping give voice to oppositional politics and cultures (Coyer 2005). In other words, the immediate function of radical media for participants is to provide a flow of information and analysis necessary for creating and sustaining certain levels of movement mobilization. However, the parallel but more latent capacity of alternative media to create and sustain collective identities reveals the ritual dimension of communication, even when the manifest objectives for participants in radical media suggest a transmission model of communication – in this case to supply information relevant to create or sustain mobilization, and to effect social change.

To recruit new members and/or to change the minds of more people, however, the challenge for these media is to find audiences outside the proverbial 'choir' to which they tend to preach. Atton (2002), responding to the common tendency to view alternative media as self-enclosed 'alternative ghettos,' suggests a shift of perspective from alternative media to the alternative public sphere. He stresses the overall *field* of alternative media as the proper level of analysis, defining the alternative public sphere as a nexus of institutions independent of parliamentary influence that 'enable a public to address and debate political and social issues' (ibid.). For Atton, alternative media are only a part of the alternative public sphere; their audiences must also be considered as integral to the media themselves. 'The alternative public sphere treats its media and the constituencies they serve and inform (and are in turn informed by) as inseparable' (ibid.). In his case of the anarchist press, the alternative public sphere is seen a field of relations between members of a particular social movement organization and the alternative media they create to enhance levels of group communication. While a step in the right direction, this approach still defines the alternative public sphere in exclusive terms of specific movement media, even if we include the constituencies these media serve.

However, Atton does contribute a useful discussion of certain ritual dimensions of communication in the anarchist press. Specifically, he identifies the alternative values participants hold concerning production, distribution, and content, demonstrating how these values and aesthetics are actualized in alternative organizational practices. I find useful in Atton's formulation the shift of focus from individual movement media to the larger networks in which they are embedded, and, the emphasis on the specifically alternative values that inform participants' alternative organizational practices.

Further, both Downing and Atton *do* identify the collective-identity construction and maintenance roles that alternative media play, but only for the specific movements in which they are embedded. Remaining underspecified is how the social change orientation and the collective-identity producing aspects of alternative media interrelate, both within and between specific instances of them. The relationship of the ritual and transmission dimensions of alternative media, in other words, needs further elaboration. Despite Atton's interest in theorizing beyond the 'alternative ghetto' critiques, there is nevertheless always the danger of a certain insularity setting into such organizations in practice. I suggest this tendency can be explained by reference to the power of alternative media to affirm and validate a particular movement identity, *even when the primary objective of participants is transmission of information*. Participation in alternative media can yield powerful affirmation of subaltern or marginalized identities, but this affirmation can also impede transmission goals.

Participants of alternative media projects are typically motivated by frustration over mainstream media and culture. They resent how the dominant public sphere excludes their perspectives or cultures, turning to alternative media production to gain greater control over their representation. That they have built up such a vibrant alternative communications network is itself a vital infrastructural component of a larger alternative public sphere (Atton 2002). That they serve as important links for a global network of anti-globalization and anti-war activists (Coyer 2005), furthermore, is testimony to the power of a broader alternative public sphere in contemporary political landscapes. However, if participants only reach others in the 'choir,' empowering as that may be, they are not addressing a *public* (Warner 2002: 108). Instead of creating a counterpublic discourse within a broader alternative public sphere, the array of alternative media present today will instead remain a series of (vibrant) subaltern groups.

Expanding the circulation of ideas and culture outside of a particular subaltern group, though, risks the dilution of the identities or ideas making them subaltern in the first place. In other words a subaltern group is by definition in a subordinate position to mainstream ideas and culture, but crafting counterpublic discourse that resonates with the mainstream risks compromising what is uniquely subaltern. Too much emphasis on preserving the collective identities of the group, in contrast, limits the possibilities of broader political and/or cultural influence.

This is the paradox of subaltern groups aspiring to craft robust alternative public spheres, a tension that Warner calls the public sphere's 'fruitful perversity' (2002: 113). Creating counterpublics requires striking a balance between the identity-preservation and social change goals of subaltern groups within any given alternative media project. Moreover, considering the alternative public sphere as a *field* of alternative media and their attendant publics requires a careful empirical agenda exploring relations *between* the multiple counterpublics of Independent Media Centers, community radios, and other types of alternative media. How do specific counterpublic nodes of the alternative public sphere self-organize to achieve this sort of balance, and, how does the broader network of these specific, locally embedded counterpublics craft a workable balance of the public sphere's 'fruitful perversity' at a mezzo level? These are important questions needing careful empirical research, the result of which will help refine a theory of alternative public spheres.[2]

Community radio, I argue, is a phenomenon containing important lessons for understanding the coalitional challenges of forging alternative public spheres. *Within* many community radio stations are often found a collection of liberal, progressive, and activist/radical volunteers united under a common agenda to provide 'voice to the voiceless.' However the large variety of groups without voice has created a history of conflict within many community radio stations over defining the means for achieving their missions of providing a space for multicultural representations.[3]

Whether a community radio volunteer is driven by activist goals, wishes to engage in political discourse unavailable in the mainstream media, or is of a particular ethnic or cultural group seeking greater control over their means of representation, motivating them all is a desire to wield the *power* (transmission and ritual) of broadcast media. However, characterizing the activist/political vs. the ethnic/cultural tension as one between those seeking a transmission vs. ritual model of communication would be to miss the larger point at hand: to recognize each kind of group desires the power of community radio as *both* a means of transmission for purposes of influence and social change, *and* as a ritual of collective identity formation, validation, and reproduction. The case of KGRR illustrates how both models of communications are present for *each* of the two broad groups I identify.

## Grand Ridge Radio

Grand Ridge Radio was founded in early 2002 in a small, poverty-stricken town in northern California known for its conservative culture. Historically, Grand Ridge was a logging town and had been an important source of timber products. The mill was closed after a contentious strike in the early 1980s, devastating the local economy. Today, county welfare and social services workers comprise the largest segment of the labor force. As is often characteristic of poor communities, Grand Ridge has a bad reputation and a history of racial violence. When asked about how they think people conceive of Grand Ridge as a community, many volunteers cited the same stereotype as Chuck, a volunteer programmer and Board Member of KGRR: '*Grand Ridge?*' '*The armpit of the county!*' '*It's the – that's what this is called, the armpit!*' Importantly, prior to KGRR there were no local media serving the town. Against this backdrop, KGRR emerged as a 'voice for the voiceless' in Grand Ridge (Schiller 2006).

KGRR was one of the first LPFM stations to be created in California as a result of federal legislation creating the Low Power FM class of radio broadcast license in 2000 (Riismandel 2002; US Report and Order 2000). The new service was born of pressure from liberal Christian organizations with long standing in the communications rights movement (Horwitz 1997), and a diffuse yet powerful social movement of microradio activists organizing in response to the Telecommunications Act of 1996. However, lobbying from the National Association of Broadcasters and National Public Radio led to a limitation of LPFM to areas with uncongested radio spectrum (Schiller 2006; Tridish and Coyer 2005). Most of the roughly 773 LPFM stations on the air as of this writing exist in small rural communities, making KGRR more likely to share similarities with other LPFMs than with full power community stations in urban areas and college towns.

The all-volunteer, nonprofit station is comprised of two broad groups of active members I term the *consciousness raisers* and the *inclusivists*. On the whole, relations between the two groups are civil and most have become close friends (many use the word 'family' to describe their relationships). However, they pull from two-chambers of a larger progressive cultural 'toolkit' (Swidler 1986) to inform their approaches to crafting a progressive community in Grand Ridge. Ultimately, the two groups share more than they may sometimes recognize. Most notably, they all relish the 'found community' KGRR has created and they are embarrassed by and alienated from the conservative culture of their town. None had ever known other 'progressives' to exist in the area, let alone enough to put together an alternative radio station. KGRR has helped forge a distinct *progressive identity community* within Grand Ridge. Within this broad 'family' lies the underlying source of group solidarity at KGRR, but it is also from this solidarity that approaches to defining and building 'alternative' community diverge.

### The consciousness raisers

The consciousness raisers model KGRR on well-known community stations such as KPFA in Berkeley, KGNU in Boulder, or a host of others that have achieved staying power in their communities. Such stations are known for their progressive political programming and as a 'voice for the voiceless.' However, many of these flagship community stations exist in larger cities or college towns, with higher levels of economic and (alternative) cultural capital than are contained in Grand Ridge. Compared to such stations, KGRR struggles with fewer available dollars and volunteers, let alone volunteers experienced in alternative political cultures or organizations. Consequently, a hierarchical and somewhat heavy-handed management approach has developed as a pragmatic response to these resource limitations.

The consciousness raisers – chief among them the station manager, Ruth and her father and general manager, Simon – are motivated explicitly by a social change agenda. They feel strongly that Grand Ridge needs 'waking up,' and that KGRR can play a role by providing alternative news and progressive public affairs programming, in addition to airing alternative music and local entertainment. When considering the communications landscape as a whole, and politics more generally, they see an America kept in the dark about progressive alternatives to problems of domestic and foreign policy. They are passionate that KGRR remains a safe-haven for local progressives and hope the programming can contribute to forging a more vibrant, active, and engaged progressive community.

The consciousness-raisers fear that letting people into the station to do programs that are too 'mainstream' would reproduce problems they associate with the commercial media. Ruth explains:

> I don't think we'll ever represent the whole community, and I don't think that's really our goal. It would be a totally different station if we did it that way, if we thought that this station should be representative of what the population is. I make a distinction between representations *of* the community as opposed to information *for* the community. If 75% of the population is right wing, I wouldn't feel the need to have 75% of my programming based on that. But if 75% of the population is poor, I would think it would be very important to have a lot of information on how to deal with that. That's a real important part of the alternative press . . . anything that lives off of the mainstream is important and we'll include it.

Ruth makes clear that KGRR programming should be consistent with the 'alternative press' tradition or, more specifically, with the community radio tradition represented by Pacifica Radio. For example, KGRR airs syndicated Pacifica programming such as *Democracy Now!* and *Free Speech Radio News* (a program produced by former Pacifica stringers) that offer left-wing perspectives on contemporary politics. With these and other similar programs, KGRR provides 'information *for* the community,' in the classic transmission model of communications.

KGRR also creates for its volunteers a palpable sense of validation and inspiration for their alternative sensibilities, highlighting the power of the station as a ritual of collective identity production. Most of the active volunteers described how important the 'new family' they discovered at KGRR was to them, and how amazed they were at finding it in Grand Ridge. For some, the validation and sense of connection extends beyond the station walls. Ruth, for example, now feels connected to a national sphere of progressives. 'One of the best things about doing all this has been the sense of connection to folks across the nation who are doing this. How inspiring it is to feel a part of such a committed group of people. You really get a sense of being part of a movement.' Ruth's daily connection to this diffuse network is through both the syndicated programs she airs and the listservs offering daily communication between the members of the grassroots radio and Independent Media Center communities.

## The inclusivists

The station's inclusivists import an orientation to community radio that borrows from past experiences either with some variety of community radio, or an earlier era of 'freeform' FM rock radio. They tend to carry a noble yet somewhat unreflexive notion of the value of broadcasting the widest range of views and perspectives on KGRR; diversity and inclusivity are ideals to strive for, independent of the consequences that may result from implementing them in a place like Grand Ridge. Ironically, each group's overly rigid notions of 'alternative' clash in such a way as to threaten the shared goal of forging an alternative community in Grand Ridge.

Like the consciousness raisers, the inclusivists feel uncomfortable in the dominant conservative climate of Grand Ridge, but before KGRR they had no idea there were others like them in their community. While not overtly political, the inclusivists are no less passionate about using KGRR to promote a new image for the town, a more organic representation of its 'ordinary' people.

Lisa's programming ideas illustrate a basic function that community radio can perform:

> It just drove me crazy how the word just didn't get out around here. You didn't hear about it through the schools, you didn't hear about it, period. And I found out I wasn't the only one who felt this way. I worked with about 200 people in the welfare building so I would hear so many people saying the same things. So . . . I thought it would be really cool to have a community thing, where people could hear about stuff – our own little community station where [we] didn't have to cater to the whole county . . . just our community.

Lisa laments how little 'word gets around' in Grand Ridge about community events or services available to its residents, so she started a community events program. At noon every weekday, she reads (over background music) calls for help organizing parades, announcements of services and classes provided by the YMCA and library, updates on upcoming Frisbee Golf tournaments, promotions for plays at the community theatre and for local concerts, and a variety of other community events. The program is very popular and has helped enliven the civic and cultural institutions of the town by bringing them greater visibility.

Chuck considers KGRR an alternative to commercial media, and a way to alter the perceptions of Grand Ridge as a conservative, 'backwards' place. Unlike the alternative community envisioned by the consciousness raisers, however, Chuck instead defines it in terms of an *organic localism*, something he thinks is missing in commercial media. Where else but community radio can you hear genuinely local cultural expression or viewpoints on local matters? For Chuck, community radio is:

> Not presenting all the different kinds of music like reggae, blues and rock, Grateful Dead. . . . That's all wonderful, it needs to be there [and all these

are, in fact, aired on KGRR]. We all need that. But it needs the gift of community to make it thrive really . . . like the *old tavern*. Where's our tavern?! Maybe Jim's Coffee Shop is it. I know a guy who drives from twenty miles up in the hills every morning at 8 to get coffee and solve the problems of the world. That's what we could be doing.

The key here is how Chuck characterizes the importance of the 'gift of community,' illustrating what he means by reference to the 'old tavern.' The politics that might occur in the old tavern are less important to Chuck than the need to have one, so the 'gift of community' can make KGRR thrive.

Chuck later began a program called *Around Town*, featuring a local guest each week for a one-hour conversation. The guests may have an especially striking history or accomplished something noteworthy, but most often the program is simply an opportunity to introduce community members to each other and share with KGRR listeners what makes them tick. Guests have included local teachers, artists, and members of area environmental groups working to protect regional rivers, streams, forests, and wildlife. The conversations are casual, and reveal Chuck's own gift for getting people talking about what they do and why, nudging the conversation along to elicit a rich sense of who the guests are beyond their accomplishments or current interests.

Where Lisa uses the airwaves to stimulate local civic culture, and Chuck seeks an 'old tavern' localism, Henry's idea of alternative offers a 'super-inclusivist' perspective:

> I perceive alternative to be truly where everything is presented. If you're only presenting one side, you're not doing anything different from what that box is doing right there [pointing to his TV set in the living room in which the interview took place] because they mostly only present one side. So if you're only presenting one side, though it might be a *different* side, it's no different from presenting any other single side. When you're presenting both sides, or ALL of it, is when you're truly representing "the voice of the people." You're truly educating people then.

Henry is concerned that the consciousness raisers' strategy of using KGRR to build progressive community may backfire. If locals are upset with the commercial media, and likely to give KGRR a chance, he questions the logic behind KGRR being just another station presenting only 'one side' of things. Henry does not disagree with the politics or activism of the consciousness raisers. The larger issue for him is more strategic or pedagogical; changing minds in a conservative community is difficult, and *Democracy Now!* might not be the most pragmatic approach to building alternative community.

Other programs that reflect the culture in Grand Ridge include three Hmong-language shows, Native American music programs, world music, radio theatre, children's shows (some by children programmers), Veteran's shows, and an array of folk, blues, rock, and punk shows. There are even a few country music shows, one of which often plays tapes from recent karaoke nights at a local bar. While Ruth, Simon and a few other core volunteers are motivated by the consciousness-raising traditions and cultures of community radio, others are more interested in building KGRR as a place that reflects and promotes the diversity of perspectives and talent contained in Grand Ridge that defy the town's conservative, 'redneck' stereotype. This means among other things, children's programs, music programs that are reminiscent of early FM-era 'freeform' radio, talk shows that invoke an 'old tavern' feel, or a community events calendar that enhances the circulation of information about local community events and attractions.

## Internal conflicts

The inclusivists' sense of alternative identity is informed by general values of diversity, open-mindedness, and tolerance. In this they share more in common with the consciousness raisers than do many of their other peers in the community. However, they fear that the consciousness raisers' approach to alternative community-building may make KGRR seem intolerant towards the bulk of Grand Ridge listeners and are concerned that the very people the consciousness raisers want to 'wake up' will be driven away or view the station as irrelevant. Two brief examples illustrate this point.

The consciousness raisers have at times used their positions as station management to erect entry barriers against what they perceive to be fundamentalist or conservative programmers. Shortly after the Iraq war began, a popular programmer felt compelled to use his program to voice patriotic sentiments during what was supposed to be a music program. When station management suggested the programmer was deviating from his program proposal, the programmer became upset and defensive, and quit. On another occasion a woman seeking a slot for her son, who 'writes beautiful songs about Jesus,' was also turned away and pointed to 'all the other religious stations already out there.' Some inclusivists worry about these episodes, speculating that in a small town of 15,000 the thick grapevine can easily choke KGRR's 'grassroots.'

The consciousness raisers maintain that allowing mainstream (conservative) programmers could potentially open the door to KGRR drifting from a voice for the voiceless to another voice for the dominant groups and culture in (local) society. As progressives, they feel marginalized and outnumbered – characteristics of a subaltern group – and KGRR has become a mechanism for both validating and incubating their progressive identity community. Thus, even the consciousness-raisers, whose participation is explicitly motivated by a transmission model of communications, nevertheless experience a powerful sense of social cohesion, testimony to the power of the ritual dimensions of media production.

Further, the case also reveals the challenges volunteers face in striking an optimal balance between ritual and transmission dimensions of alternative media. To effect social change, the consciousness raisers *transmit* critical, radical, progressive perspectives aimed primarily at activist audiences for the purposes of informing but also of reproducing their collective identity as activists. However, too strong a focus on their own interests can prevent the reach of their counterpublic communications (Warner 2002), creating a pressure to provide more ideological diversity on the airwaves. The inclusivists advocate more open-mindedness, seeking to create programming that includes a broad array of local Grand Ridge citizens. Too strong a focus on attracting multiple perspectives though, in a town like Grand Ridge, can easily lead to the entry and possible dominance of the station by Grand Ridge's dominant conservative culture, making KGRR into just another mainstream voice.

## Conclusion

Ironically, in a local media outlet committed to 'undistorting' communication in their local public sphere, internal, organizational-level communication is distorted by an unreflexive adherence by both groups to overlapping yet distinct repertoires of alternative culture. The consciousness raisers draw upon an activist repertoire of 'alternativity,' and the inclusivists a more classically liberal rerpertoire. In the post 9/11 American political climate, the consciousness raisers find justification for exclusionary practices, preventing KGRR from becoming an ideal typical Habermasian public sphere. They point also to the rigid access boundaries progressives and other marginalized groups face in the heavily consolidated commercial media landscape to defend their maintenance of KGRR as a sanctuary for marginalized perspectives. The consciousness raisers also see KGRR as part of a broader network of community media projects and in this way feel connected to an *imagined progressive community*.

The inclusivists feel similarly alienated from the general conservative climate in post 9/11 America. However, they respond by simply reflecting and promoting in a more organic way the vibrant local culture already present in Grand Ridge. Some inclusivists frown upon KGRR reproducing the same 'one-sidedness' they perceive in mainstream media, even if the perspectives offered are 'alternative.' In a sense, the inclusivists seek the ideal public sphere, where everyone is welcome and can participate in the transmission and ritual dimensions of their local public sphere. The differences between the two groups of progressives at KGRR reflect a more general tension in the progressive cultural toolkit between 'radicals' and 'liberals.'

The alternative public sphere sought by KGRR inclusivists and consciousness raisers can emerge through adequately protecting the station's identity-nurturing capacity while also finding ways to create programming that may reach more 'average' Grand Ridge listeners; the transmission model certainly does not preclude innovative and nuanced programs that might better resonate with local listeners. Otherwise, instead of KGRR enabling an alternative public sphere rich with counterpublic discourse it risks remaining a subaltern group of local progressives, and their goals of creating a more progressive Grand Ridge will remain unattainable. Moreover, ureflexively embracing an 'open microphone' approach to programming can easily distort the subaltern mission of the station and turn KGRR instead into another mainstream media outlet.

KGRR, the 773 other LPFM stations now on the air, and the vast array of other alternative media projects emerging across America (and beyond) in the last decade represent an important advance for subaltern groups to circulate counterpublic discourse that, at minimum, validates their various marginalized statuses. Together, these alternative media are an important infrastructure for building counterhegemonic[4] political and cultural projects. 'Becoming the media,' however, is a necessary but insufficient condition for building a robust alternative public sphere. Within and among these new media, many different groups of 'ordinary' people now possess the agency to control the terms of their political and cultural representation. As important as this may be for validating and promoting various subaltern identities and agendas, a broader question remains regarding whether a truly counterhegemonic discourse can begin to circulate throughout civil society outside these specific groups. Effective counterpublic discourse requires recognizing and embracing the 'fruitful perversity' (Warner 2002: 113) of the alternative public sphere.

## Notes

1. KGRR, Grand Ridge, CA, or any other names appearing in this essay are pseudonyms.
2. Many fundamentalist conservatives who consider themselves marginalized within American political culture have constructed an 'alternative' radio and television presence and might be researched as alternative public spheres. A key difference, however, lies in the *organizational structures* marginalized groups choose to govern their media. Community radio tends towards a 'double alternative' model, in which collective identities and organizational structures are *both* 'alternative.' Some conservative groups self-identify as 'alternative' but adopt traditional, hierarchical organizational models. Similarly, KGRR is a progressive station with a hierarchical structure for pragmatic reasons. For more on the 'double alternative' model of alternative public spheres, see Schiller (2006).
3. Empirical research on conflicts *within* community stations, and how they are overcome (or not), can point to important strategies for developing better coalitional strategies *between* them too. Attempts at forging a coalitional strategy between grassroots community radio stations, and to regularly address these sorts of challenges, include the emergence of the Grassroots Radio Coalition in 1996 (Durlin and Melio 2003 [1996]). For a decade this network has sustained conversation *between* local community stations about how to implement *within* them the aspirations

contained in their missions. Thus, at least in the realm of community radio, efforts exist to transform a series of locally embedded specific counterpublics into a broader alternative public sphere. For more extended elaboration of this point, see Schiller (2006).

4. Here, I reference specifically a Burawoyian conception of counterhegemonic processes in civil society (2003). For a fuller treatment of this idea and its relationship to community media than is possible in these pages, please see Schiller (2006), esp. ch. 1.

# 11
## Representing the Public of the Cinema's Public Sphere

*Shawn Shimpach*

The emergence of Hollywood cinema is a significant moment in the history of modern media's role in the changing conditions of equal participation in rational discourse idealized by Jürgen Habermas from eighteenth-century bourgeois public life (Habermas 1989; 2006 (2001, 1989)). On the one hand, as Miriam Hansen notes, 'For Habermas, the industrial dissemination of cultural products is structurally incompatible with the possibility of public discourse' (Hansen 1991, 11). On the other hand, John Durham Peters reminds that 'Membership in a collective whose scale rules out face-to-face interaction or acquaintance, such as the nation, needs representation or some mediating fiction of the whole' in order 'to allow a common backdrop for participation' (Peters 1993, 565). The modern public sphere depends on representations of the public as a necessary precondition, but such representations seem inevitably inscribed in practices of private economic considerations. This situation not only complicates theories of communication and rational–critical debate premised upon face-to-face encounters, but it also complicates the process by which private individuals can participate in the public sphere.

Peters notes that for Habermas the public sphere is 'a site governed neither by the intimacy of the family, the authority of the state, nor the exchange of the market, but by the "public reason of private citizens"' (Peters 1993, 542). For the public reason of private citizens to prevail, however, these citizens must have a way to be both private and public simultaneously. Moreover, in large modern societies, this must occur in relation to the representation or mediating fiction of the public. Michael Warner describes the essence of this pre-condition for entry into the public sphere as an imagined relationship between private self and public-ness that takes the form of self-alienation (Warner 1992; 2002). As Warner explains the problem, 'No one really inhabits the general public. This is true not only because it is by definition general but also because everyone brings to such a category the particularities from which they have to abstract themselves' in order to fit the category and participate (Warner 1992, 396–7). A credible process needs to exist to allow for this abstraction, so that the common public can emerge from so many particularities. There needs to be a representation of the public to the public that allows individuals to imagine themselves in this abstracted, or self-alienated way. Otherwise the particularities can threaten to overtake the commonality and throw the very idea of the public into crisis.

The Hollywood cinema emerged during the Progressive Era, a moment of intense cultural and political pressure when the particularities of different people and populations threatened to overwhelm the basis for a collective, common public. Indeed Progressive reformers took the burgeoning nickelodeon phenomenon as an important indicator of the collapse of a recognizable common culture and, therefore, an important site of reform and intervention. Motion pictures were of particular interest for reformers because they offered a public gathering place – neither part of the state nor part of the family – *and* at the same time they provided mediated communication that could be widely distributed and easily comprehended. In exposing the need to police and reform this combination, Progressives utilized social scientific methodologies and exhaustively publicized their results. These efforts were instrumental in effecting the cinema's transformation, refining this new mode of address from that of short, suspect attractions for working-class and immigrant audiences into respectable, internally coherent narratives of socially acceptable appeal. Eventually, however, the very practices employed by Progressive reformers, the near ubiquity of statistics used to represent the motion picture audience as an object of reform, had the effect of routinizing the representation of a new form of public-ness and produced a viable mediating fiction of the public organized around and through this new mode of address. Through their attention to the rising phenomenon of the motion pictures and their statistical representations of its audience, Progressive reformers (abetted by the era's sympathetic journalists) helped define and clearly establish a new form of mediation between private individuals and public participation, bringing the mass public into awareness of itself and its distinctness.[1]

Making the decision to go to the movies in this context became about imagining oneself as a certain type of person, as one of a certain kind of many, mediating 'a self-relation different from that of personal life' (Warner 1992, 378), and therefore negotiating private experience with the public sphere. Moreover this act of becoming public was inscribed in the content and conditions of the filmgoing practice. Formulated as a viable new cultural category, the audience came to represent a means of imagining entry into a category of public existence. Detailing such a history demonstrates the complex processes at work behind the observation that 'Modern media are means for imagining community' (Peters 1993, 566). It does so by illustrating the way in which under certain historical conditions, powerful forms of representation can serve to construct and define a relationship between private and public through new modes of address.[2]

## The transformation of the cinema

Initially the cinematic mode of address favored what has been retrospectively theorized as an alternative public sphere – accessible to ethnicities, classes, and genders marginalized by the hegemonic structures of the bourgeois public sphere (Hansen 1991; Stokes and Maltby 2001). As Progressive reform efforts drew attention to the nickelodeon audience, however, the cinema began a process of transformation that had the effect of placing limits on the diversity of viewing experiences and social interactions available.

The alternative public sphere gave way to a hegemonic mode of address. Regimes of bourgeois taste, decorum, and behavior were introduced and regulated at the sites of exhibition, where requirements for air quality and fire safety met with new guidelines for seating and lighting often meant to regulate moral safety as much as physical safety (Pearson 1987; Uricchio and Pearson 1993). Textually the cinema was transformed from a 'cinema of attractions'[3] into a reliably narrative cinema, witnessing the 'formulation of the classical style' (Bordwell *et al*. 1985) and the 'origin of American narrative film' (Gunning 1994). The films of this period not only highlighted 'quality' topics (Uricchio and Pearson 1993), but they began emphasizing characters 'whose motivations are indicated within the film,' thus becoming more standardized in their intelligibility (predictably internally coherent) and more uniform in their address (less reliant on the context of reception) in ways understood to correct for nickelodeon viewing practices and to attract a more sophisticated (and thus 'better' class of) audience than had heretofore been observed and surveyed by Progressive reformers (Gunning 1998, 264).

Such transformations of both the content and the actual exhibition sites, where interaction with other spectators was correspondingly discouraged, had the effect of limiting, if not access, then expression of alternative forms of public sphere gathering (Hansen 1991). What had been an alternative public sphere of working class and immigrant practices of sociability became a bourgeois public space presuming practices identified by Progressives as attributes of a common culture and securing the hegemonic power of Hollywood's mode of address. However, the process that led to and allowed for these transformations did not simply render the audience into isolated individuals spellbound in the darkness. The broader context for these transformations reveals that they had a double effect. The cinema became industrially and culturally respectable and textually self-contained and consistent, but at the same time the audience became public.

These transformations were made possible – even necessary – because of proliferating representations of the motion picture audience as a statistically demonstrable problem in need of intervention and reform. It was Progressive reformers who publicized representations of the nickelodeon audience that influenced perceptions of the cinema and informed decisions leading to its transformation during these years. Moreover, Progressive methodologies continued to be deployed even after transformations were effected and the nickelodeon itself had disappeared. If the communal experience of nickelodeon attendance was reformed and transformed out of existence, motion picture attendance, despite some appearances to the contrary (i.e. the isolating effect of the darkened theatre and the socially policed practices of respectable spectatorship), nevertheless remained a public activity. During and after the transformations of the cinema, certain, prevalent representations of the audience continued to reinforce the idea of the *public* nature of the cinematic address.

## Progressive reform and the motion picture audience

This new, public form of address was of particular significance amidst an almost generalized collapse in confidence in a recognizable common culture in the United States. The first decades of the twentieth century in the United States were marked by what has been characterized as a 'demographic panic about the quantity and quality of the U.S. population' (Greene 1999, 39). Such a panic was occasioned by a number of coinciding developments: the closing of the frontier implying that America was now filling up;[4] a massive influx of immigration, challenging assimilationist assumptions about U.S. citizenship; and unprecedented internal migration, resulting from the radical economic shifts that characterized the rapid industrialization and urbanization of the Gilded Age. At virtually the same time, foundational myths of the promise of the frontier, ready and eager assimilation, and equality of economic opportunity were called into question, severely imperiling well-cherished understandings of the United States' national character. At such a moment, the ability of strangers to imagine commonality – a shared common public – was under great pressure.

Progressive reformers saw themselves as the modern, rational voice of reason positioned between extremes, fighting for a recognizable common culture. Demonstrating this approach, Progressives by 1916 could report that 'the last decade or so in this country may be characterized as years of social, industrial, and civic investigating, scrutinizing, researching, surveying, with a view to meeting the new human needs discovered – a process predicated on the desire for peaceful, but not necessarily slow social evolution, rather than wasteful, upturning revolution' (Harrison 1916, 27). The social and economic problems of the nineteenth century, leading to a crisis in the common culture, it was believed, could be solved by the measured and rational deployment of the modern technology and science that had also developed over the nineteenth century. Only through the transparent, unbiased, expert application of the sciences to human conditions could progress be made (Hofstadter 1955; Wiebe 1967; Link and McCormick 1983).

Therefore when Progressive reformers encountered the emerging cinema, it was not only what was on the screen that mattered to them, but also who was watching. Initial interest in the nickelodeon centered on the age, gender, and class make-up of its audiences, who gathered in unruly groups, within darkened storefronts rife with dangers and improprieties. Civic investigating produced statistical representations of this audience as a predictor of how they behaved and were influenced by the movies, inevitably signaling the need for intervention and reform. The techniques of statistically compiling an audience, however, began a process that allowed for the imagination of a common public among strangers.

Reformers at first drew on whatever sources they could find that might produce compelling facts. As early as 1907, in an issue of the social work journal *Charities and the Commons*, for example, 'the rapid increase of five cent theaters' was noted as a 'matter of common observation' (Kingsley 1907, 295). Nevertheless the article cited a number of sources in an effort to provide numeric evidence supporting this 'common observation.' These included an April, 1907 edition of *The Moving Picture World* ('our estimate is that the attendance at all of Chicago places combined averages 100,000 daily'), personal interviews with theater managers as to revenue, and an advertisement for Mills Amusement Company found on the back cover of *Ridgway's Weekly Magazine* (a part of which mentioned the monthly take from one location on State Street – $3,000) (Kingsley 1907, 295). The motion picture audience in this 1907 article was thus rendered in several numerical and statistical forms: averages per diem, income, and monthly revenue. At this point the nickelodeon phenomenon was barely two years old and just beginning to register in public discourse and consciousness.

Soon organized surveys were conducted in municipalities around the nation.[5] The results of these surveys, drawing on amateur understandings of social science techniques, were combined with anecdotal evidence and then, following the era's ethos of exposure, widely disseminated. By 1908, John Collier, for example, published the results of research conducted for the People's Institute of New York in several social work magazines (Collier 1908; Collier 1910), concluding that 'The nickelodeon is now the core of the cheap amusement problem. *Considered numerically it is four times more important than all the standard theaters of the city combined.* It entertains from three to four hundred thousand people daily, and between seventy-five and hundred thousand children' (Collier 1908, 74 emphasis added). This was such an important observation because it demonstrated that 'all the settlements and churches combined do not reach daily a tithe of the simple and impressionable folk that the nickelodeons reach and vitally impress every day' (Collier 1908, 75). Moreover, it considered and demonstrated this development numerically.

Such numbers were considered effective in establishing the necessity and urgency of taking the burgeoning motion picture phenomenon seriously. They operated as a type of 'factual propaganda' (Fisher 1974, 294), demonstrating how many and what types of people were attending motion pictures while implying through this very representation that the audience was subject to reform. This was consistent with the Progressive political theory of citizenry action that consisted primarily of 'publicity' of 'facts' that would inevitably imply 'problems' needing intervention.[6] As Shelby Harrison explained 'The successful working of this leaven of civic renewal depends upon the correcting power of facts, which must be gathered as carefully and faithfully as the truth-loving scientist in any field gathers them – plus such a telling of the facts as will make them common knowledge' (Harrison 1916, 27). Through their association with social science and their efficient summation of measurable facts, statistics lent credence to policy and interventionist proposals by offering scientific truth in a form readily digestible as common knowledge. Here was a representational form evidently devoid of sensationalism and unassailable in factuality yet when presented correctly quite powerful in ability to convey social attributes and generalize about populations. As a result, numbers were everywhere published in telling the facts of motion pictures and making social revelations into common knowledge.

By 1909 *Charities and the Commons* had changed its name to *The Survey*, suggesting the significance of number gathering as a condition of any kind of social engagement. That same year the magazine published a lengthy article about the increasing significance of motion pictures, rendering it in an impressive series of numerical revelations:

> Two-thirds of the entire theater-going public [are] entertained by this 'infant industry' with its $50,000,000 of invested capital and its 190 miles of film daily thrown upon the screen of 7,000 nickelodeons – this in round, bare figures is the extent of the new amusement that has sprung up within a decade and become popular only within four or five years (Palmer 1909, 356).

Such 'round, bare figures' defined the emerging film industry in terms of invested capital, quantity of film projected, and number of screens. Statistics were providing, in other words, a normative basis for public reason and Progressive action. This normative basis was also used when describing the motion picture audience:

> In New York city alone there are some 350 motion picture theaters with daily audiences of a quarter of a million or more and a Sunday attendance of half a million. Chicago entertains daily some 200,000 people in its 345 picture shows and Philadelphia's 158 nickelodeons claim audiences of 150,000 every day of the week (Palmer 1909, 356).

From this 1909 article, it is clear that the mere recitation of numbers was considered sufficient exposure to establish the 'extent of the new amusement.'

The statistics depicting the audience were published for a specific purpose: 'Its interest to social workers is apparent; for the great majority of moving picture audiences are made up of those who have little opportunity for other wholesome recreation' (Palmer 1909, 356–7). The implication is clear, the moving pictures require reform attention. At the same time, however, such reform efforts, at the very least, demonstrate, as Nikolas Rose writes, that 'the unruly population was rendered into a form in which it could be used in political arguments and administrative decisions' (Rose 1990, 6). This form of the audience signaled the emergence of an object – of discourse, of reform, of curiosity, but an object all the same. The barrage of statistics, presented in an objective, scientific forum and form, was already beginning to demonstrate that moviegoers at this early date constituted a public.

## Publicizing the audience

As exposure and publicity efforts expanded, statistical representations of the audience soon moved from social work periodicals to less specialized reform magazines and finally came to fill the pages of popular magazines with the widest distribution in the nation. A brief look through the archive of such publications provides evidence of the growing reach – to near ubiquity – of Progressive representations of the cinema-going public. It also demonstrates that the repetition of such numbers eventually produced a certain factual weariness wherein readers (and journalists alike) took the (numeric) fact of the audience as increasingly self-evident. This was a sure sign of the way such statistics, deployed to rouse middle class reform action in the name of a common culture, were producing an accepted, viable public category of the audience.

In its 1908 account of the 'Moving Picture Drama for the Multitude,' *The Independent* established the 'multitude' of its title in numerical terms: 'The moving picture drama furnishes great entertainment for the millions, literally reproducing comic, tragic, and great events to some sixteen million people a week at a nominal cost of a nickel or a dime'[7] (Walsh 1908, 306). The 'millions' and the more specific (if still imprecise) 'some sixteen million' were placed in the very first sentence to verify the claim made in his article's title that the audience for moving pictures did, indeed, constitute a 'multitude.' This authorized the writer, in the very next sentence, to assert without any further observation or study that 'the effect of this new form of pictorial drama on the public is without parallel in modern history' (Walsh 1908, 306). The moving pictures, it was demonstrated, were addressing a significant public.

Such a public was also increasingly national in scale:

> In the last two years 'nickelodeons' or moving picture theaters or exhibition halls have opened in nearly every city from the Klondike to Florida and [cities] from Maine to California supports [sic] from two or three to several hundred. . . . it is estimated that on an average two or three million people in this country attend the shows every day in the week (Walsh 1908, 306).

Such numbers were deployed not simply to bolster the argument, but to make it. Statistics, in no small part, constituted both the evidence and the argument that motion pictures were related to a new, national, and rapidly growing form of public gathering. Here was a dramatic opportunity for the public to begin to recognize itself in relation to this emerging media form.

The sheer proliferation of such straightforward statistics stood as evidence and argument in calls for the citizenry action upon motion pictures. Reformers saw initially a motion picture audience of children (or in other reports, women, workers, immigrants and all 'those who have little opportunity for other wholesome recreation') as an alarming feature needing reform in this statistically constructed category. The Protestant magazine *The Banner's* term for moving picture shows, 'Vaudettes,' did not catch on, but its representation of the problem audience was certainly familiar: 'New York City alone has at present about 350 Vaudettes, with daily attendance of over a quarter of a million persons on week days and twice that number on Sundays. It is estimated that within the United States over sixteen millions of people visit the Vaudettes every week' ((DeBeer 1909) reprinted in (Lindvall 2001, 25–29)). A 1911 edition of *The Outlook* claimed that 'the average daily attendance [at New York motion picture theatres] is between four million and five million, about twenty per cent being children' (1911).

At the same time, however, signs began to emerge that this category of the audience represented something in addition to factual propaganda for reform efforts. An August 1909 issue of *Current Literature: Religion and Ethics*, for example, began familiarly enough, using a 'conservative estimate' to place 'the number of people in New York City who daily visit the nickelodeon at 200,000.' This number was used to proclaim that regarding the 'nickel theater or "moving picture" show': 'Their enormous popularity is proof that they appeal to the foundation qualities of men.' Here such numbers not only constructed the audience as a (potential) problem, but in so doing, suggested a public sphere mediated by the cinematic practice. The magazine concluded its point by reminding readers that with the motion pictures, 'here is a tremendous factor in the imaginative life of the people, for good or for ill' ((Anonymous (*Patten 1909*) reprinted in (Lindvall 2001)).

Such numbers, therefore, need to be understood not merely as empirical data or even only as part of an argument for reform. These numbers not only produced the motion picture audience as a real problem, but more fundamentally, as real. Statistics found in accounts of the motion picture audience refined a portrayal of the public to itself. More so, they did it in a way that meant that at the movies, as Michael Warner puts it, 'we might recognize ourselves as addressees, but it is equally important that we remember that the speech was addressed to indefinite others, that in singling us out it does so not on the basis of our concrete identity but by virtue of our participation in the discourse alone and therefore in common with strangers' (Warner 2002, 77–8). Such self-alienation relies on representations of the public to itself.

The movies, statistics kept reminding, were made for a large, known public – the motion picture audience. By choosing to attend, one unavoidably chose to become a part of that public. In Warner's formulation, a public 'is a special kind of virtual social object, enabling a special mode of address' (Warner 2002, 55). As the motion picture audience was constructed with statistics, it became not only a concrete gathering of individuals, but 'a virtual social object' as well and the classical Hollywood cinema developed and was enabled as a special mode of address. As the cinema transformed, the emerging Hollywood style offered a mode of address both individual (internally coherent, psychologically motivated) and yet simultaneously generic and public (nationally distributed, publicly screened). To go to the movies and enter into this category of the motion picture audience, statistics everywhere reminded, was to imagine oneself as one part of a collective whole.

Indeed, at the very same time that motion pictures were developing internal coherence and other attributes of classical address, readers of general, mass-market magazines were learning to think of the motion picture audience as a virtual social object. For example, in 1910, *Harper's Weekly* claimed that five million attended one of 7,500 moving-picture houses each day (Inglis 1910). By 1912, *McClure's* insisted that 'not far from' 300,000 people attended the movies daily 'in New York City alone' (Musson and Grau 1912). From experts to reformers to all readers, an empirical, enumerated public object was being constructed, reproduced, and repeated.

Regardless, however, of the need for reform or the composition of the audience in a given article (even as these were the reasons for the articles being published), the cumulative effect was to establish the protocols for knowing (and potentially entering) this category. This was already beginning to be evident as early as 1910, just five years after the emergence of the nickelodeon phenomenon.[8] One study that year, focusing on school-aged children's motion picture attendance, was filled with the usual statistics:[9] 'Out of 350 pupils from ten to fourteen years of age all but thirty-four were habitués . . . of the moving-picture shows. One hundred and eighty-three went as often as once a week; one hundred and thirty went twice a week or oftener,' etc. (Jump 1911). At this early date, however, even the school children being studied were well aware of the standard questions (and, one might conjecture, the standard replies) when such studies were made. As the survey's author reported in *The Moving Picture World*, rather astonishingly:

> Having exhausted the list of inquiries which she had in mind, the principal asked, 'Do you think of any other question I ought to put to you?' And one young hopeful piped up, 'Wouldn't you like to know which theater we think is the healthiest, has best ventilation, etc.?' [sic] And when the teacher asked that question she got as frank an answer as she had received to her other queries. The lines of thought suggested by these statistics are many, but there is no time to follow them up now (Jump 1910).

And indeed little need either, if even the children who are the object of investigation could see where the study was leading. Going to the movies, already by this time, consisted of well-known protocols, conditions, behaviors, and potential dangers. It also apparently consisted of being frequently and predictably apprehended by social reformers. By 1910 the school children who regularly attended motion pictures knew what their attendance meant better than did their adult interrogators. In addition to exposing oneself to certain dangers (both physical and presumably textual as well), attendance meant exposing oneself to a certain publicness wherein the fact of one's attendance, its frequency, its timing, its location, its accompaniments and one's own age, gender, class, sometimes race, ethnicity, behaviors, criminality, etc. were legitimately open to scrutiny and publicity. One's particularities could be abstracted into statistical commonalities through motion picture attendance. Such a publicness was given form during these same years through the insistent publication and repetition of these statistics.

By 1915, as D. W. Griffith's *The Birth of a Nation* controversially established the cinema's artistic potential and solidified its transformations through an elaborate, sophisticated, and astonishly bald celebration of the Ku Klux Klan (it was promoted as the first film screened at the White House, signaling the cinema's arrival in the corridors of cultural respectability), a weariness with such factual propaganda could be detected. That same year an article in *The Atlantic Monthly* began with the by now clearly obligatory statistics: 'Various calculations have been made to determine the number of people who daily attend the movies in the United States, the figures ranging from an inside estimate of four million, to an outside figure of ten million. . . . Ten per cent of our population, then, are patrons of the motion pictures.' At this point, however, the author could not resist adding that 'these facts, I am aware, have been stated over and over, to the point of weariness, and various interpretations put upon them, or deductions drawn from them' (Eaton 1915, 48). Statistics were simply ubiquitous in describing the 'problem' of motion pictures, the audience. Indeed such statistics, 'to the point of weariness,' were evidently crucial to seeing the audience at all. Like the children surveyed in 1910, the reader and journalist here know the protocols for conceiving of audiences. Such factual weariness signals the viability of this cultural category – its self-evident nature – even as it articulates the public-ness of the audience.

*McClure's* had already understood this in 1914, when it made the loaded observation in its perhaps premature history of the cinema that 'What did most to improve the moving-picture show was the new underlying conception of its scope' (Musson and Grau 1912, 70). The facts and fact of the audience fundamentally changed the effective nature of the cinema, rendering it a specific yet public form of address. For readers now of nearly every form of periodical publication, statistics – to the point of weariness – meant not only the identification of a new social problem to address and reform, but also a recognition of the distinct reality of this new, public, cultural category called the motion picture audience.

## The public

Such articles established the motion picture audience as a distinct and pre-existing entity, out there to be known, measured, reformed and eventually entered into. Moreover, attending the movies came to mean submitting one's activities to such public scrutiny. As Richard Maxwell insists, this 'institutional identity, the media audience, forms by recombination of [discretely measured] component categories. A composite creature comes into being, with features that often mirror our own so well that our self-definition gets tied up with the way a media audience is said to behave' (Maxwell 2000). The public could recognize itself anew in relation to the emergence of this new, mass medium. Not only were motion pictures an increasingly respectable form of leisure, but they were also an entry into a category of public existence.

Progressive publicity made this into a compact, made it part of what it meant to *be* an audience. No matter how personal the experience of watching a movie, this publicity assured the movie's mode of address was understood to be public – the sheer numbers guaranteed that – and so becoming an audience involved the particular process of self-alienation that is a pre-condition for entering the public sphere. The complex mediation of public presence and mode of address (both gathering and watching) represented by motion pictures provided an early template for modern mass media in which 'we go "there" to see each other seeing each other' offering an early form of precondition in which the media 'sphere' offered a 'collective image of the collective' (Peters 1993, 566). This developed at an important moment of crisis in the history of both representation and the public sphere.

Habermas has been famously critical of social science approaches to measuring the public, effectively banishing from considerations of the public sphere statistics and such 'empirical social research' that 'returns with positivist pathos . . . in order to establish "public opinion" directly' (Habermas 1989, 239–40). The essence of the problem for him is that public opinion polling and statistics construct a public opinion from the aggregate measurement of many individuals. Indeed this is what was so compelling about statistics to Progressive Era reformers, the revelation of formerly invisible facts through the acquisition and statistical compilation of discretely measured data.[10] For Habermas, such a representation of the public fundamentally misunderstands the role of the public sphere. The public is not simply an empirically measurable amalgam of individuals (or individual opinions) but the result of individuals publicly interacting, debating, and arguing. Public opinion is not simply the majority of opinions held by individuals, but the emergent result of rational, critical debate between and among opinion holders (Habermas 1989, 236–50).

At the same time, his concern with the decline of critical, rational discourse amidst the rise of mere consumption seems directly applicable to the emergence of Hollywood cinema: 'When the laws of the market governing the sphere of commodity exchange and of social labor also pervaded the sphere reserved for private people as a public, rational–critical debate of public communication unraveled into acts of individuated reception, however uniform in mode' (Habermas 1989, 161). This chapter, however, has shown that individual reception was only *part* of the cinematic practice. Audience statistics *are* an aggregate of individual measurements, *but* their insistent reproduction as a representation of the motion picture audience meant that the viable (virtual) social object they constructed (the audience) was understood and could be experienced as a reflexive collectivity. For individual spectators, this construct of the audience was perhaps not necessary or really very important. For the public, however, the sense of the collective offered through this viable social object was a condition of existence.[11] No rational–critical debate can proceed without a public. The emergence of Hollywood cinema during the Progressive Era represents a moment when a mass media audience could recognize itself as a collectivity rather than an aggregate of individuals. While statistical representations of the motion picture audience may have very well, in and of themselves, signaled the rise of positivist pathos, through their insistent repetition to the point of factual weariness, they nevertheless offered the means for imagining a collective identity, organized around the cinematic mode of address.

## Notes

The author thanks Richard Butsch, Christopher Kamrath, Anna McCarthy, and John McMurria.

1. Warner makes a similar argument in connection with new media taking hold, demonstrating the way in which 'this statistical consciousness, combined with a vast network of non-state association and an equally vast body of print, brought a mass public into awareness of itself and its distinctness from the national state' during the 1840s as the Temperance Movement utilized the then emerging penny press newspapers in an early rehearsal of the much broader Progressive movement (Warner 2002, 269–71, quote on 271).
2. This is a rather different interpretation of Miriam Hansen's assertion that the cinema represents 'the emergence of qualitatively different types of publicity.' Hansen answers Habermas's concern about the commercial nature of media forms like the cinema by examining how 'the public dimension of the cinematic institution harbors a potentially autonomous dynamic,' which she suggests makes it more than 'a consumerist spectacle orchestrated from above' (Hansen 1991, 11). This chapter focuses on the complex processes and practices that render the public dimension of the cinema audience meaningful for the public sphere.
3. This phrase is usually attributed to Tom Gunning in collaboration with André Gaudreault (Gunning 1990).
4. Frederick Jackson Turner, for example, announced the literal closing of the American frontier in 1893 (Turner 1920) (see also Hodgson 1991, 4, 24).
5. For more on the Social Survey Movement in the United States, see: (Taylor 1919; Gordon 1973; Bulmer *et al.* 1991) For more on the relationship between social surveys and Progressive interest in motion pictures, see (Shimpach 2004).

6. For a brief introduction to the theory of citizenry action, the literature of exposure, and a sample article from this era, see (Gaonkar and Kamrath 1999).
7. *The Independent* was a Christian reform magazine. During the Progressive Era, even moral and religious concerns were embedded with notions of scientific authority, efficiency, and technology (Link and McCormick 1983, 22).
8. The emergence of the nickelodeon is typically traced to 1905 (Merritt 1976, 1985; Musser 1990).
9. The results of this survey were widely disseminated (Jump 1910; 1911).
10. The implication of knowable 'underlying causes' meant that statistics offered a theoretical and functional foundation for social reform (for background, see Hacking 1990).
11. This formulation is loosely derived from (Dayan 2005).

# 12
## The Psychedelic Public and Its Problems: Rock Music Festivals and Civil Society in the Sixties Counterculture

*Michael J. Kramer*

The camera zooms in on the stage at CNE Stadium. We are in Toronto first stop for the Festival Express, a multi-band rock concert touring across Canada by train in the summer of 1970. A bearded man in a leather jacket and tie-dyed shirt approaches the microphone. Below him, the crowd surges toward the entrances, pushed back by mounted police. Inspired by Woodstock and other large rock gatherings of the previous year, they demand free entry. But the bearded man has another idea.

'The thing we're trying to do is organize another sort of scene that we can have here,' says Jerry Garcia, lead guitarist and 'Captain Trips' in the quintessential psychedelic rock band, the Grateful Dead. 'And, we would like, if possible, to have about a half hour of just coolness, so that we can work something out that would be an alternative to all this hassling, and see if we can avoid getting people hurt.' You can almost feel the wind get knocked out of Garcia's gut as he says the word 'organize.' This consummate non-organizer, a musician whose formative concert experiences were the anarchic Acid Tests run by LSD-guru Ken Kesey and his Merry Pranksters, has fear and loathing in his eyes as he is forced to assert control over the crowd. Meanwhile, the audience will have none of it. Someone off camera shouts at Garcia: 'Let the people in, that's the only alternative!' (Smeaton, 2004).

Who were these 'people' that both Garcia and his heckler mentioned? For even the most anti-intellectual participants in the 1960s counterculture, and certainly for the more thoughtful among them, rock music raised vexing questions about who counted as 'the people.' Though rock was full of escapist pleasures, the music also sparked deep engagements with the dilemmas of mass-mediated public life. Not only at concerts and festivals, but also through recordings, radio, television, print publications, and countless informal conversations, rock made participants wonder: Who were 'the people' and what did they want? Were participants members of a subculture, of tribes, or of a new culture? Was rock merely part of a devious capitalist system that duped them by seeming like anticonsumerism in order to sell more product (Frank, 1997)?

Or, did rock herald a new, socialist electric commons? Rock music and its festivals became flash points in the counterculture's stormy relationship with
mass-mediation and mass consumerism.

'We demand that Transcontinental (Rip-off) Express to be free for everyone
and all tickets be refunded.' So read an 'Open Letter to a Closed Corporation,'
written by the leaders of the M4M movement to the Festival Express concert promoters. Formed at Toronto's experimental Rochdale College, M4M insisted that:

> there be free food, dope, and music for the people there, with no cops.
> Failing these totally reasonable and just demands, we demand that twenty
> per cent of the gate receipts be returned to the community in the following
> ways: money for already existing free food programs, day care centers . . . a
> collective bail fund . . . and equipment for the People's Party. (Dalton and
> Cott, 1970, 32)

For the leaders of the M4M movement, rock music brought issues of ownership to the fore. They believed that the music and its *accoutrements* should be
free, or a tithe should be levied on profits from the music for the 'community'
and the 'People's Party.' Behind their demands was the idea that rock belonged
as much to its audiences as it did to its makers and promoters.

For many participants in the counterculture, the free-festival precedent set
by Woodstock a year earlier pointed to similar conclusions. These enormous
gatherings seemed to create small cities with civic as well as commercial cultures. Festival populations could grow into the hundreds of thousands. People
got married, gave birth, and died. Festivals developed their own rules and codes
of neighborly connection and commitment. They also provided the setting for
dishonesty, cruelty, and violence. Rock festivals even increasingly demanded
the resources that any municipality would need: water, food, bathrooms, sewage
control, garbage collection, and extensive health care services. Because they
were so large, these gatherings transformed the economic transactions of
entertainment into something else: they created an associational life in which
participants explored the complexities of civil society (Frisch, 1996).

Moreover, because their images and sounds circulated through the mechanisms of mass culture as commercial products and reported news, rock music
festivals presented the possibility of a new civic culture to a far bigger audience.
As both direct and mediated experience, the festivals suggested that individuals
and groups might actively engage in the making of their social worlds rather
than be dominated by authoritative forces such as the state, with its police and
restrictive rules, or be alienated by the calculations of the market, with its
homogenous goods and services. Largely organized and populated by and for
the young, rock music festivals conveyed 'the energy of becoming free,' as Jerry
Garcia pointed out to a journalist, so they 'became free' (Lydon, 1970, 23).
They were proto-political spheres – emergent zones of civic interaction that
sprang from the marketplace, but took on a political air.

Not for everyone, though. The promoters of the Festival Express rejected the demands of the M4M movement and the idea that their concerts were more than just commercial entertainment. To promoter Ken Walker, 'M4M appealed to kids who figured they'd just wait around and get in for free. It's a bit like looters who see a store window busted and go in and take something themselves' (Dalton and Cott, 1970, 32). Although many of the musicians were sympathetic to the protesters, they also objected to the idea that they were expected to perform for free all the time.

Because of these contradictory perspectives on rock music concerts in the 1960s counterculture, the Festival Express tour provided a vivid example of the tensions between rock as a commodity and as the sound of a public coming into being. Writing in *Rolling Stone* magazine, journalists David Dalton and Jonathan Cott remembered that, 'It used to be that you could walk down streets at dusk and catch the entire new Beatles album drifting out, band overlapping and interconnecting. The music somehow realized and extended the senses...' (Dalton and Cott, 1970, 34). For Dalton and Cott, the music was mobile, and therefore egalitarian. In contrast, they noticed that the 'festival structure is finally pyramidical – groups playing in order of financial draw . . . stadium walls enclosing performers and audiences, blocking out the kids standing outside. It is this boundary implicit in the structure that undermines the boundlessness of the music.' The ease with which rock circulated to public spaces called for an open use of the music as a soundtrack to public life. However, the music's existence as a commercial form, and the resources and labor expended to create the music, demanded a closed format for rock.

Beyond economic considerations, there were also aesthetic issues. Speaking with a journalist a few months after Festival Express, Jerry Garcia raised questions about the politicization of music as art. He agreed that rock was a public phenomenon to be shared, but he was troubled by the 'pseudo-political reality' that the Grateful Dead 'find when we go out on tour.' When his band traveled to perform at festivals, 'because there are people there, radicals say it's a political festival now, not a music festival.' Garcia, however, objected to the narrowing of aesthetic and musical experiences to 'a political plane.' 'I don't want to take over anybody's mind,' he explained, 'but I don't want anybody else to take over anybody's mind.' To Garcia, rather than politicize music, there was 'something uniquely groovy about the musical experience; it is its own beginning and end. It threatens no one' (Lydon, 1970, 23). While certain members of the counterculture saw rock's mass gatherings as political, Garcia wanted to draw a line between aesthetics and politics. This is no surprise coming from a person whose livelihood depended on rock. But, Garcia recognized that the music did have effects on its audiences. While he rejected politics, Garcia hinted at the civic function rock might play in opening up a space where minds were engaged, but not 'taken over.'

Like Garcia, other participants in the counterculture heard something 'groovy' in rock's circulation not as political doctrine, but rather as expressive experience capable of sparking civic engagement. For many, rock provided a way for feelings of 'community' to circulate through the electronic technologies of postwar mass culture. The music's 'secret,' the journalist Michael Lydon wrote, 'was not the dancing, the lightshows, the posters, the long sets, or the complete lack of stage act, but the idea that all of them together were the creation and recreation of a community.' Rock made it seem as if you 'could be making your own music for your friends – folk music in a special sense.' However, the mediation of rock by mass culture also compromised rock's capacities for communal connection. As Lydon warned, rock beckoned with its promise of community precisely because it spoke to the larger allure of contemporary mass culture. 'Rock and roll, rather some other art, became the prime expression of that community' because the music symbolized the 'machine and all, the miracle beauty of American mass production, a mythic past, a global fantasy, an instantaneous communications network, and a maker of super-heroes' (Lydon, 1969, 18).

Yet, Lydon contended, since 'the machine, with all its flashy fraudulences, is not a foreign growth on rock, but its very essence,' rock was far more than just a folk music you could create among friends. Mass culture's 'flashy fraudulences' could not be ignored. 'There's no way to combine wanting that and wanting 'just folks' too,' Lydon decided (Lydon, 1969, 18). Rock music, Lydon argued, miraculously promised both 'community' and the technological power of mass culture. But, as he pointed out, deep tensions lurked in this tantalizing combination. It was difficult to synthesize folksy community with mass culture's 'flashy fraudulences' in order to create a robust, democratic public life.

Lydon was not the first to notice these contradictions between community and mass culture. In the United States, Walter Lippmann argued in the 1920s that only a 'phantom public' could exist in complex, modern societies (Lippmann, 1925). Responding to Lippmann, John Dewey maintained faith in the creation of an authentic public rooted in the idea of community but capable of responding to the demands of modernity. Dewey's exploration of this 'public and its problems' presaged issues that rock music raised in the 1960s. 'The Great Society created by steam and electricity may be a society, but it is no community,' Dewey wrote years before Lyndon Johnson's bold but ill-fated 'Great Society' programs of the mid-1960s (Dewey, 1927, 98). Identifying the very contradictions between face-to-face connection and mass culture that Michael Lydon later discovered in rock music, Dewey nonetheless believed that a 'Great Community' could come into being. He insisted that, 'The Great Community, in the sense of free and full intercommunication, is conceivable' (Dewey, 1927, 211). But, Dewey thought, 'the essential need . . . is the improvement of the methods and conditions of debate, discussion, and persuasion. That is *the* problem of the public' (Dewey, 1927, 208).

For Dewey, art became a crucial means in making 'the Great Community' a reality. Through its creation of shared symbols, Dewey argued, art as a mode of 'free social inquiry' could provide the means of harnessing the power of mass production and communication for democratic purposes. Individuals could then assemble into life-enriching communities both on the local level and in larger configurations of interlinked and overlapping associations, from the state to the marketplace. In Dewey's thinking:

> the highest and most difficult kind of inquiry and a subtle, delicate, vivid, and responsive art of communication must take possession of the physical machinery of transmission and circulation and breathe life into it. When the machine age has thus perfected its machinery it will be a means of life and not its despotic master. Democracy will come into its own, for democracy is a name for a life of free and enriching communion. . . . It will have its consummation when free social inquiry is indissolubly wedded to the art of full and moving communication. (Dewey, 1927, 184)

Dewey contended that aesthetics, in particular 'art as experience,' could transform the tyrannical forces of mass society into a more democratic public life (Dewey, 1934). Several decades later, and even more enmeshed in a complex, technological, consumer society, participants in the counterculture heard in rock music precisely the potential for this transformation. If Dewey wrote of *The Public and Its Problems* and advocated for *Art As Experience*, then rock music provided the soundtrack for the psychedelic public and its problems. Within the context of mass culture, the music seemed able to link private, intimate encounters to larger public, collective concerns. However, it did so problematically. Rock revealed the difficulties that a functioning civil society faced in the age of mass mediation and mass consumption. The music did not present a consistent ideology that carried listeners to common conclusions and values. Instead, it generated a fractured aesthetic and social space for debate and conflict. Rock was not a coherent subculture, but rather an amorphous public sphere.

This was not, however, Jürgen Habermas's (1962, 1964) idealized public sphere of the bourgeois Enlightenment. Nonetheless, in precisely the setting of mass culture that Habermas argued destroyed the public sphere, rock music, especially festivals, wound up fostering engagement with public life and its problems.[1] As Grateful Dead manager Rock Scully told journalists David Dalton and Jonathan Cott, 'The problems involved in Festivals have cost us a lot of thought.' To Scully, the hierarchical structure of these mass events was an 'unnatural form.' Instead, Scully imagined festivals could be 'spontaneous. It has to be announced as other than an all-star line up. All these kids will come together to celebrate a solstice, say, and it will become people's music' (Dalton and Cott, 1970, 34). Participating in debates about rock, Scully both identified problems with concert festivals, and sought to invent solutions. Joining the psychedelic public, he pursued ideas, perspectives, and actions that might transform rock into a 'people's music.'

Scully's comments suggested parallels with Habermas's original definition of the public sphere even though rock's version was new in crucial ways. 'A portion of the public sphere,' Habermas wrote in his famous 1964 encyclo-pedia article, 'comes into being in every conversation in which private indi-viduals assemble to form a public body.' Talking with Dalton and Cott, Scully helped create their 'portion of the public sphere.' Moreover, in Habermas's view, citizens in the public sphere 'behave neither like business or professional people transacting private affairs, nor like members of a constitu-tional order subject to the legal constraints of a state bureaucracy' (Habermas, 1964, 49). Scully seemed to do precisely this: he put aside his commercial position as manager of the Dead (and he certainly did not want to join a gov-ernmental bureaucracy of any kind) in order to consider the larger common good. Scully entered into deliberation about the psychedelic public and the problems it faced.

Nonetheless, especially when it came to matters of mass mediation and con-sumption, rock did not replicate Habermas's original conceptualization of the public sphere. Habermas claimed that with the expansion of mass culture, 'the public sphere. . .was replaced by the pseudo-public or sham-private world of culture consumption' (Habermas, 1962, 160). But, for Scully and other counter-cultural participants, even through rock was implicated in consumerism the music's festival concerts nonetheless provided moments for deliberation and action. Of course, rock's electronic roar often went along with selfishness, hedonism, and escapist debauchery, but the music also inspired debate and discussion. Even Habermas himself came to conclude that rock concerts could be included in the '*occasional* or arranged publics of particular presentations and events' (Habermas, 1996, 374). Rock attracted what a Chicago promoter of free concerts called, in a letter to *Rolling Stone*, a 'commitment to a viable, dialogue-producing activity' (Dunne, 1970, 3).

We see the 'dialogue-producing activity' occur in the film *Festival Express* when, partying on the train as it headed to the next concert site, a reporter with the Grateful Dead guitarist argued Bob Weir about whether the Festival Express concerts should be free. 'All these kids got uptight because the admis-sion was too high and they decided they were going to have a riot,' Weir responded to the reporter's questions about what he thought of the M4M movement protests during the Festival Express concerts. Weir gestures to his own head and long hair: 'They busted some cop's head and they busted it wide open. He's got a plate in his head now and he may still be in critical condition.' Turning the floor back to the reporter, Weir asks, 'Is that worth sixteen fucking dollars?'

'Okay, but how many kids got busted wide open too?' the reporter, a young woman in glasses, retorts. She and Weir confront each other directly, uncom-fortably, but also in a spirit of engagement rather than mutual dismissal. Along with the other musicians and reporters in the train car, they created a kind of mini-public sphere, one that we might imagine forming wherever rock's sounds circulated. Their conversation also brought to the surface a pressing issue: rock music as a commercial transaction also generated confrontations with state power. Rock became not only commercial, but also a generator of civil society, especially when political groups such as the M4M movement demanded that festivals should be free. Resonating between the market and the state, the music fostered contested spaces of associational life. Mounted police and concertgoers confronted one another in this space. So too, this zone of engagement continued when participants such as the reporter and the Dead gathered to debate what had happened.

'Is that worth sixteen dollars?' Weir asks again, 'Nearly killing some cop.' He pauses, thinking carefully about his terms. 'Nearly killing a person,' he corrects himself. In Weir's choice of words, the problem of who constituted 'the people' manifested itself. Was the cop a 'person' – a member of the community that rock created at festival gatherings – or was he simply an alien presence, a repressive agent of the state? Neither Weir nor any other participant would have spoken about the police such abstract terms, but their colloquial language addressed these crucial issues of inclusion and power. As the conversation continued, Jerry Garcia echoed Weir's thinking about 'the people' involved in rock festivals. 'Jerry Garcia objected to her using the word "pigs",' David Dalton and Jonathan Cott wrote. To Garcia, 'If you call people pigs, that's what they will become. We're not trying to alienate people, we're more interested in getting the whole thing together' (Dalton and Cott, 1970, 32). Bob Weir concurred, telling the reporter, 'And those cops out there, I talked to a lot of them. They were all boss, they were all good people.' For the two guitarists in the Grateful Dead, rock did not distinguish who was part of a concert's public and who was not, but rather opened up participation.

But just as rock music could enable debate, so too, its involvement with mass mediation could impede deliberation. In *Festival Express*, the presence of the camera interrupted the proceedings between the reporter, Weir, and Garcia. Musician Kenny Gradney, getting fed up with the reporter's questions, lifted up an issue of the Canadian underground newspaper *Youthbeat*, which was sympathetic to the festival protesters. 'I want to show the camera,' he declares. In front of the newspaper, which now takes up the entire frame, Gradney addressed the movie audience instead of the reporter. His contribution to the debate was to raise his middle finger to the newspaper itself. Bob Weir finally ends the conversation by saying in response to the reporter's complaints about ticket prices, 'If you want something for nothing, jerk off' (Dalton and Cott, 1970, 32). The spirit of debate and deliberation had broken down, in part because of the presence of the camera (Gitlin, 1980).

But the conversation was not quite over. As *Youthbeat* and Gradney's middle finger filled up the screen, Jerry Garcia quipped, 'Must we put up with yellow journalism?' The joke was rich with references, linking the controversy over free rock festivals to a deep history of pseudo-public spheres that passed off sensationalistic manipulations of public opinion for objective reporting. Bringing this awareness to the debate about rock music and public life, Garcia's comment suggested that ironic playfulness might serve as one mode of furthering public engagement despite the power of mass-mediated technologies to overtake debates and conversations. While Kenny Gradney's angry turn to the camera ended the conversation and dissolved the mini-public sphere on the train car, Garcia offered another strategy for continuing the energy of civic interaction. His joke signaled that a sensibility of critical awareness and public-spiritedness might persevere, perhaps even thrive, through irreverence and wry humor rather than direct confrontation. The conversation could continue in the channels of mass culture, but only in code, indirectly and ironically.[2]

So too, one should not forget that despite Weir and Garcia's criticisms of the reporter, the Grateful Dead did perform a free concert. The group organized a show in Toronto's Coronation Park not only to prevent violence and to head off confrontation between the protesters and police, but also because they were engaged in the dilemmas of the rock festival. Through performance as well as conversation, they participated in debates about how the counterculture might pose alternatives to the problems and flaws of mass society. As Garcia remarked, the Grateful Dead were 'not trying to alienate people,' but instead were 'interested in getting the whole thing together' (Lydon, 1970, 23). Through rock music, they attempted to contribute to a psychedelic public life that might satisfy the needs and overcome the alienations of mass culture. 'We're trying to organize a free stage, man,' Garcia explains from the CNE Stadium stage after his heckler quiets down. 'You don't have to go for it, you can believe it or not, but that's where it's at, right now' (Smeaton, 2004).

In *Festival Express*, we glimpse footage of this free concert. The late afternoon sun shines in peacefully upon the band members, who are perched atop two flatbed trucks with their equipment, much as they had been during the many free concerts they gave in their hometown of San Francisco during the mid-1960s. The band performs the song 'Friend of the Devil,' a folksy, Kerouacian tale about an individual seeking salvation in a lonely and difficult world. We see a small crowd gathered around the band. A young man with sideburns nods appreciatively, as if he might start to cry. A teenage girl stands up in a purple tie-dye shirt to dance, leaning and bobbing her head like a chicken. The faces of the audience are not absent-minded, but intently focused on the music and the secrets it might reveal.

As the title of the song, 'Friend of the Devil,' suggested, the music was filled with demons – it did not establish a paradise, but rather explored the difficulties of finding peace. The tune was haunted by past sins as it repeatedly rolled through its descending, major-key bass line. But, a spirit of collective aesthetic engagement emerged in the song as well, both in the harmony singing of the Dead and in the audience's responses to the performance. Occupying the public space of Coronation Park, between the setting sun and the reverberating amplifiers, the Dead and their listeners addressed issues of identity and survival, shared commitments and individual freedom, through 'Friend of the Devil' (Smeaton, 2004). They joined a process that Nicholas Bromell described when he wrote, 'Rock was fun, but it was also a vital and spontaneous public philosophizing, a medium through which important questions were raised and rehearsed, and sometimes focused, and sometimes (rarely) answered' (Bromell, 2000, 16).

Like 'Friend of the Devil,' other performances in the film *Festival Express* also sustained a 'medium' for grappling with the problems of public life. For example, in Winnipeg, the Buddy Guy Blues Band performed a song, 'Money (That's What I Want).' Written by Berry Gordy, Jr., owner of Motown, and covered most famously by the Beatles, *'Money'* resonated with the struggle over free admission at the Festival Express concerts. Guy further explored tensions between the interests of performers and audiences when the guitarist suddenly descended to the stadium field, followed by yards of uncoiling electrical cord. Soloing angrily, his guitar signal overdriven and distorted, Guy walked the line between the power of the stage and full communion with his listeners. He was tethered to the electric speakers, yet he sought to move among the people. In this performance, through aesthetic expression, Guy played the blues of the counterculture's public life, where participants were both empowered and trapped by mass culture's technologies.

Raw and powerful as those technologies were, rock music festivals also seemed capable of surprising subtleties. The music became something like the art as experience that John Dewey imagined: the 'subtle, delicate, vivid, and responsive art of communication' that might 'take possession of the physical machinery of transmission and circulation and breathe life into it.' Concerts did not offer solutions, but rather made public ongoing dilemmas and problems. Questions of race, for example, manifested themselves in Buddy Guy's presence and in the prominence of African-American-based musical forms. Guy's performance of 'Money,' just to take one example, presented a blues-based song written by Motown's African-American owner. But, Berry Gordy Jr had himself been eager to cross over to white audiences. Then the song was covered by the Beatles, white musicians from Britain. Now, at Festival Express, 'Money' was appropriated again by an African-American musician, this time a Chicago bluesman performing before a largely white Canadian audience. Similarly, questions of women's places in the counterculture moved from the private sphere into public life through Janis Joplin's performances. Guy, Joplin, and others did not solve the problems of the psychedelic public. Rather, they offered forms of artistic expression through which participants could explore the difficulties of attaining equality and freedom in the modern world. What rock music in *Festival Express* offered was not the utopian realization of an ideal civil society or a perfect public sphere, but the chance to address postwar American mass culture's deep imperfections – and also, the opportunity to investigate its dramatic possibilities for community.

As Nicholas Bromell pointed out, rock rarely provided answers, but it did attract utopian hopes. Rock's modifications of the public sphere drew theorists such as Marshall McLuhan to the music. Based at the University of Toronto, where he had helped organize the very same experimental Rochdale College at which the M4M movement took shape, McLuhan placed a full-page photo-graph of Andy Warhol's Exploding Plastic Inevitable multimedia show in his 1967 book, *The Medium Is the Massage*. McLuhan chose a photograph of the Velvet Underground in performance. With disorienting film montages behind them, the photograph hinted at the ways in which the band, and Warhol's multimedia show in general, explored the extremes of electronic bombardment of the senses.

Because the Exploding Plastic Inevitable and the Velvet Underground focused so intently on electronic stimulation, McLuhan thought that their music addressed the multiplicity of meanings, feelings, and sensations that listeners experienced in the mass-mediated world. 'Bang!,' McLuhan wrote on the page following the Exploding Plastic Inevitable photograph, 'The ear favors no particular 'point of view.' We are *enveloped* by sound. It forms a seamless web around us. . . . the ear world is a world of simultaneous relationships' (McLuhan, 1967, 110). For McLuhan, rock music as electrified sound offered a new kind of 'ear world,' one in which 'simultaneous relationships' replaced hier-archical social structures. And with the technologies of mass communication, public life took on new configurations. As early as 1964, the same year that Habermas published his famous encyclopedia entry about the public sphere, McLuhan argued that popular music was especially important in creating new environments of public interaction. 'When the LP and Hi-Fi and stereo arrived, a depth approach to musical experience also came in.' This is because, according to McLuhan, music allowed entrance into a world of experiential engagement. 'Anything that is approached in depth acquires as much interest as the greatest matters,' he wrote. 'Because "depth" means "in interrelationship," not in isola-tion' (McLuhan, 1964, 282). McLuhan believed that precisely the same modes of mass-cultural experience and interaction that Habermas thought corrupted the public sphere brought about a new kind of public, which he famously called the 'global village' (McLuhan, 1968). Like Dewey before him, McLuhan thought that mass media, properly harnessed, could foster rather than destroy the community necessary for a flourishing democratic public life.[3]

In both McLuhan's utopian vision and Habermas's sharp critique, however, mass culture created a crisis of representation. How would art symbolize experience in this new world of what McLuhan called 'interrelationship'? And how would aesthetic forms such as popular music relate to questions of politi-cal representation, when, to quote Habermas, 'public discussion deals with . . . the activity of the state' (Habermas, 1964, 49)? Rock music did not answer these questions, but it made them apparent, allowing participants in the counterculture to address, measure, contest, and negotiate the problems of representation at a crucial historical juncture, when the modern gave way to the postmodern (DeKoven, 2004; Whelan 1988–89; Gloag, 2001). The use of mul-tiple screen shots in films such as *Festival Express*, which purposefully imitated the *Woodstock* documentary film, suggested the difficulties of representing the psychedelic public. One frame simply could not capture all that went on at a rock festival. The overlapping experiences of participants demanded more than one vantage point. Only then did the dizzying, kaleidoscopic quality of the psychedelic public begin to emerge. A mass-cultural form of art capable of circulating widely, rock music did not create one, unified public sphere. Rather, in a world increasingly fragmented by mass mediation and mass consumerism, rock provided multiple entrances into communal connection and shared inquiry.[4]

Though never assembling one 'Great Community,' rock generated what John Dewey imagined as 'full and free intercommunication' about common interests and problems. Not only at the festivals, but also in their wake, public engagement continued. For instance, in J. R. Young's *Rolling Stone* review of the phonograph album culled from Woodstock, a boy named Bill borrowed from Abbie Hoffman's book title to declare, 'I *live* in Woodstock Nation . . . I mean how many were actually there . . . We'll never know. But it doesn't make any difference. The Woodstock actuality has become a media trip' (Young, 1970, 38; Hoffman, 1969). To this countercultural participant, Marshall McLuhan was right: not just attendance at the concert itself, but also its mass-mediated forms offered a chance to become one of 'the people' in the psychedelic public.

Later in Young's review, a friend who actually attended the festival critiqued Bill's obsessive consumption of the Woodstock album and film. Suddenly the review itself became a public sphere – a debate among multiple participants. 'He'd been sold a bill of goods,' the friend insisted, 'a product that had little to do with anything but money.' Carrying on the conversation, a girl in Young's review responded to this attack on Bill, saying to the Woodstock attendee, 'But you *were* there. You are Woodstock nation, and if it comes down to this, then that's sad. That's why there will never really be a Woodstock Nation. You won't let anybody live on the land' (Young, 1970, 39). In these exchanges, Young demonstrated how the issues generated *at* rock music festivals could travel *through* mass culture to reach and include additional participants. The 'land' of Woodstock Nation was not only at the actual site of the festival, but also in its mass-mediated representation. As Habermas himself wrote in 1964, 'In a large public body this kind of communication requires specific means for transmitting information and influencing those who receive it. Today newspapers and magazines, radio and television are the media of the public sphere' (Habermas, 1964, 49).

As if to emphasize even more that debate could occur in this larger realm of mass-mediation, *Rolling Stone* ran another analysis of the very same *Woodstock* album alongside Young's review (Ward, 1970, 38). In this additional essay, the critic Ed Ward not only explored issues of mass mediation, but also of mass consumption. Ward claimed that the Woodstock album, and the festival from which the album came, epitomized the tensions facing countercultural participants in the psychedelic public – tensions between rock as a mode of civic culture and as a form of mass entertainment. To Ward, the *Woodstock* album made apparent the problem of sustaining authentic community within the channels of mass culture. Referring to the December 1969 Altamont Speedway concert, where the Hells Angels were hired as security but wound up killing an audience member (Maysles 1970), Ward wrote of the troubling questions raised by the *Woodstock* album:

> This is what I like to call the Metaphor of Altamont. Are all those bodies in line there really the kids who'll be bringing us a new day, with a brand new lifestyle, or are they just empty receptacles lined up waiting to be filled with entertainment . . . like empty Coke bottles on line at the bottling plant?

For Ward, rock festivals sharpened the key dilemma of the psychedelic public: could rock music inspire an inclusive, interactive public life, or would it deteriorate into passive spectatorship and horrifying violence? Was rock the harbinger of a 'new day' or did it merely fill up listeners as if they were 'empty Coke bottles' waiting to be smashed?

Rock raised this crucial problem for Ward and others not only because it was a form of mass culture, but also because it was sound. As John Dewey had argued decades earlier than even Marshall McLuhan, 'the connections of the ear with vital and out-going thought and emotion are immensely closer and more varied than those of the eye. Vision is a spectator; hearing is a participator' (Dewey, 1927, 218–19). Though it could still render audiences either passive or violent, rock music also enabled 'connections of the ear' at festivals. Moreover, precisely because it was a technological product of Dewey's 'Great Society,' rock also resonated more broadly in mass culture. The responses that the music generated, both at festivals and in their mass-mediated reverberations, represented efforts to enact Dewey's 'Great Community.'

The attempts to create a 'Great Community' within dense networks of mass-communication and consumption fostered a new sort of public sphere; however, rock's complicity in mass culture also compromised rock. As pop music scholars have noted, the music could not offer or enact a structural critique of capitalism (Frith, 1981; Lipsitz 1994; Grossberg 1997). Instead, rock only enabled considerations and contestations of the psychedelic public. To borrow Raymond Williams's famous formulation, the music did not shift *structures of feeling* in postwar mass culture, but it did allow participants to engage in what might be called *seizures of feeling* (Williams, 1978). As immaterial goods such as sound became increasingly commodified, feelings themselves became products. By focusing so intently on the feelings of rock as artistic experience, members of the psychedelic public in a sense seized the means of production: they plugged into and temporarily played the electronic frequencies of mass culture. They did so only in fleeting moments of seizure. Nonetheless, many developed a consciousness of their predicament through aesthetic experiences of rock.

Because rock music both seized and was seized by the larger forces of mediation and consumption, it became a lightning rod that both harnessed and grounded the stormy energies of the counterculture. The music became a flash point, especially at the festivals of the late 1960s and early 1970s, for the challenges of achieving community in mass culture. In particular, rock attracted experimentations with modes of associational interaction that might make mass culture more just, democratic, and libratory for 'the people.' The music rang with a willingness to entertain civic experiments. But, the central problem of the counterculture's psychedelic public – what Dewey called the challenge of 'freeing and perfecting the processes of inquiry and of dissemination of their conclusions' – remained long after rock's last acid flash and electrifying thunderbolt of feedback had faded (Dewey, 1927, 208).

## Notes

1. This argument draws upon Kluge and Negt (1972), Calhoun (1992), Robbins (1993), and Warner (2002).
2. On irony and citizenship, see Rorty (1985) and (1989).
3. For an interpretation of McLuhan as antidemocratic antimodernist, see Brick (1998).
4. On representations of the public sphere, see Latour (2005).

# 13
## Popular Culture and the Public Sphere: Currents of Feeling and Social Control in Talk Shows and Reality TV

*Peter Lunt and Mervi Pantti*

The growing role of mediation in the creativity, richness, diversity and sheer ubiquity of popular culture challenge Habermas' (1989) idea that radical democracy can be grounded in the differentiation between everyday life and the institutional spheres of politics and commerce. In a recent account of the contemporary relevance of the public sphere concept, McKee (2005) sets about reconstructing an account of the public sphere that reflects the multiple connections between social institutions, everyday life and popular culture. Writing against the grain of the many dissenting voices concerned at the increasing mediatization of everyday life and an increasingly populist agenda in public life, McKee develops the idea that the public sphere can be adapted to fit a contemporary mediated plurality of modes of engagement, if not emancipation.

This chapter explores the links between the changing landscape of mediated sociality and the public sphere in relation to two case studies: sensationalist talk shows and reality TV shows. The focus will be on the way that these genres engage participants and their audiences through emotions. We explore two key problematizations of the role of popular culture in the public sphere: firstly, the irrelevance and incongruity between emotional expression and political engagement, and, secondly, the idea that the emotions are the site for new forms of social control, and therefore undermining the potential for popular culture to act as a vehicle for the formation of a public.

The relationship between the public and the media industry is certainly complex. From the point of view of Habermas' analysis the critical point is that popular culture both reflects everyday life with all its pleasures and limitations and constitutes the public primarily as a consuming audience (Livingstone, 2005). These two dimensions of mediation prompt Habermas to disallow the production, content and reception of media a role in legitimate public engagement in the political process. In reaction to the way that Habermas lays out his view, much has been made of his elitist bias. However, on a theoretical level at least, Habermas is not straightforwardly elitist in relation to popular culture. For Habermas everyday life is to be celebrated and protected, and to achieve this it must be differentiated from power and from the processes of the economy.

Habermas was making these arguments against the background of postwar political consensus and the welfare state and their immanent crisis in the 1960s. He seeks to protect everyday life from the encroachment of the market and the state (in combination as part of the welfare contract) and the transformation of publics into consumers and audiences. This raises the question of what purchase these critiques have in an era where welfare policy is being radically restructured, where media systems are globalized and where everyday life has grown in importance, richness and diversity, in contrast to the pessimistic view of the conforming masses of the post-war period.

Another important dimension here is experience. Habermas aligns experience with the social logics of the lifeworld and therefore excludes it from the public sphere. In contrast, Negt and Kluge (1993) suggest an alternative view of the proletarian public sphere in which identity is not understood in terms of rules and roles paralleling the social system with the consequent need to develop a component of the social system (the public sphere) that affords a specific kind of role identity (disinterested discussant in the public sphere). Instead, they argue that the expression of identities and the interstices and creative possibilities of the intersection between culture, commerce and politics opens up possibilities for public engagement. In response to these various themes McKee (2005) suggests that there has been a transformation in the concept of the public sphere away from the metaphor of a context or receptacle for legitimate political engagement or deliberation. Instead, any form of public engagement, even popular culture, is included in the public sphere.

Emotions are at the center of both the distinctions that Habermas draws between the lifeworld, the system world and the public sphere and also those drawn by his critics. Habermas' account of the need for a public sphere partly reflects the dangers that he sees in the expressive order of everyday life where commitments potentially 'distort' communication. Equally, the cold rationality of the instrumental reason of the system world threatens commitment and value. In his attempt to create the conditions for rational critical discussion, Habermas works up the logic of exclusion and containment. Behind Habermas' thinking is a traditional distinction between reason and emotion, which has been challenged in recent studies on emotions in social and political sciences (e.g. Williams, 2001; Marcus, 2002).

Yet any attempt to include commitment and emotional expression in public life has to deal with the inherent problems of the potential for emotions to drive out other forms of rationality and of the problem that emotions are a key site of contemporary social ordering. We will explore these two problems for an emotionally inclusive public sphere, which includes popular culture. The analysis of the *Jerry Springer Show* argues against the idea that popular culture is outside of processes of deliberation and reflection because of the emotional dimension of the programs. The analysis of reality TV shows then confronts the question as to whether the confessional elements of reality TV are an example of the colonization of the lifeworld. In contrast some analysts see that there is a need to engage the emotions of citizens (not just consumers) and that this requires a return to questions of commitment and values.

Another important theme that complicates the relationship between popular culture and the mediated public sphere is the recent work on counter publics. Fenton and Downey (in prep) give the example of DIY political culture, where local groups agree to take action over an issue that affects their everyday lives. They do this partly because they think that the normal processes of representation and advocacy in the public sphere will not address their concerns. Such actions involve commitment and there is an affective dimension to this action, even if it is often a temporary elision based on a specific interest. Habermas would want to distance the public sphere proper from such acts and only give them a legitimate role in times of crisis. Here we are up against Habermas' interpretation of the political ramifications of life political movements, which he sees as a bursting into the public sphere of highly emotional expressions of grievance and concern. For Habermas such acts are not able to play a direct role in deliberation.

At the center of concerns about the contemporary cultural sphere and its role in public life, therefore, are concerns about the meaning of emotional expression: either as a pollutant of the possibility of reasonable argument and detached deliberation in the public sphere or as the locus of new forms of social control that produce docile bodies. Popular culture engages these issues, which is partly why Habermas will not give it a role in political communication. The question we confront here is whether Habermas' theoretical containment of emotional expression in popular culture is justified? The next section of the paper explores the theoretical questions in public sphere theory of the relation between popular culture and the public sphere in particular focusing on the issues surrounding the spectacular and emotional aspects of talk shows and the importance of the confessional to reality TV.

## The sensationalist talk show

The account of the talk show as public sphere in the academic literature has changed as the shows themselves have shifted from early examples that focused on the public discussion of personal and social issues (e.g. *Donahue*) through therapeutic versions (e.g. *Oprah!*) and more recent sensationalist programs exploring personal conflict and revelation of personal secrets (e.g. *The Jerry Springer Show*) (see Livingstone and Lunt, 1994; Shattuc, 1997; Gamson, 1998; Dovey, 2000; Tolson, 2001; Illouz, 2003). Although most of these commentators go beyond the repudiation of talk shows as trash TV, relevance of talk shows to the public sphere debate has been questioned.

Initially the link between the talk show genre and the public sphere came from the idea that the genre offers unprecedented access to the public to appear on television. However, the control of content and access, the role of the hosts in structuring dialogue and the characteristics of argumentation (talk shows seemed have more in common with a personal quarrel than a rational critical discussion) raise doubts about the relevance of the public sphere concept to the analysis of this genre. These doubts were only increased by the recognition that talk shows often followed populist agendas, were primarily structured around sensationalism and entertainment and emphasized the expression of personal interests.

These points suggest a gap between the reality of interactions on talk shows and the ideal of a relatively neutral space where consensus can develop out of rational critical discussion. It is tempting to conclude that talk shows have nothing to do with serious questions of public engagement and that they illustrate the importance of distinguishing between ideas and representations that merely circulate in public rather than those which potentially constitute a public sphere.

Two different notions of the public sphere are in play here: one being a general term for what is available in the public realm and one that focuses on the question of the role that media play in the political process (McKee, 2005). Despite the above misgivings, talk shows are still seen to contribute to public engagement and expression although they might not be related to the public sphere as a technical construct in social and political theory and in practice they might not have much influence in the political sphere. Whilst talk shows cannot easily be defended as occasioning autonomous rational critical discussion leading to consensus, they do express something important and characteristic about public opinion and involvement in contemporary civic culture.

Shattuc (1997) and Gamson (1998) argue that talk shows do play a role in public life by providing an opportunity for otherwise marginalized voices and expressions to be seen and heard. Livingstone and Lunt (1994) suggest that talk shows are a candidate for an oppositional public sphere, emphasizes the expression of interested points of view and aiming at compromise rather than consensus. So, talk shows have a potentially democratizing aspect, not by virtue of offering opportunities for discussion, but through juxtaposition: creating novel combinations of people who normally live separate lives and giving them the opportunity to express their opinions about an issue of topical concern and relevance to them (Lunt and Stenner, 2005). Such opportunities can be seen as part of the democratization of culture and of the role of cultural forms in the broader public sphere (Gamson, 1999).

## Emotions, expression and the public sphere

*The Jerry Springer Show* creates entertainment from the emotions that emerge during the real-time presentation of personal conflict and scandalous revelations and accusations: 'It seems to revel in the excitable, and is always on the edge of taste and public decency. Participants curse and swear, and physically and verbally threaten one another. Fights break out, in-house bouncers are called in, and the studio audience go wild. [–] *The Jerry Springer Show* is flagrantly and self-consciously trash television, refusing to take itself seriously, constantly challenging the censors' (Lunt and Stenner, 2005: 63).

Lunt and Stenner (2005) invite us to consider *The Jerry Springer Show* as an emotional public sphere that parallels the bourgeois public sphere in the way that it encourages, manages and reflects upon emotional conflict in a public context. Arguing against the settlement based on the separation between the public sphere and popular culture, they write that ideas from Habermas' discussion of deliberation and radical democracy have considerable purchase for a cultural analysis of the show, which on the surface seems to be the antithesis of rational critical discussion.

Committed personal expression is often at the center of the analysis of talk shows where it is either valorized or seen as the means by which participants are enrolled in normative conceptions of the subject. Both the Habermasian inheritance in public sphere theory and the analysis of the talk show as a cultural forum for the expression of marginal voices buy into similar assumptions concerning the opposition of rational critical discussion and emotional expression. This is complemented by the analysis that authenticity and expression in talk shows is key to questions of identity and is contrasted with rational and critical discussion.

Another similarity is Habermas' concern with the pollution of the potential of the public sphere. Habermas shares with cultural analysis the valorization of the lifeworld as a source of innovation and as a means of the expression of concerns and interests. In both cases there is a tendency to regard the emotions as a potential danger to public engagement. This distrust of the emotions parallels Habermas' concerns that the expression of interest can disrupt the potential for deliberation. A similar ambivalence towards emotional expression is also discernable: emotions are central to the committed expression of personal beliefs but this very fact challenges the potential for the production of a reasoned public.

Livingstone and Lunt (1994) examine the importance of emotional expression in authenticating personal accounts on talk shows. However, they also demonstrate that those in the subject position of ordinary people in discussion-based talk shows are made into the object of discussion and debate among experts and commentators. Emotional expression both authenticates and limits the role of the participants in the ensuing debate. Shattuc (1997) makes similar points about the essential role of the public expression of feeling in therapeutic talk shows, which both affords people the opportunity to express their feelings and concerns but also positions them as objects of analytic review. In her analysis of *Oprah*, Illouz (2003) argues for a basic ambivalence in the cultural analysis of the talk show and demonstrates the difficulties of both an optimistic account of talk shows as public sphere and a pessimistic view of talk shows as simply reflecting a cultural obsession with the psychological.

What emerges is a complex view of talk shows as combining information and entertainment in novel ways. Livingstone and Lunt (1994) argue that a variety of devices are used to distance emotional expression from commentary through the sequencing of contributions of lay participants and expert commentators. In contrast to the discussion-based and therapeutic talk shows, *The Jerry Springer Show* reverses the ordering and implicit hierarchy of emotion and critical discussion. The shift in the talk show genre can be understood as a reversal of the attempt in earlier versions to contain emotional expression to allow for a reasonable level of discussion. *The Jerry Springer Show* is organized so as to encourage emotional expression and to guard against the potentially disruptive influence of rational critical discussion!

Attention to the production of the show allows us to elaborate this interpretation. Although emotional expressions, usually of interpersonal conflict and the revelation of secrets, are highly salient, the program is the product of a variety of other production features. Among these features is the way that the sequences of contributions to the program are organized along the lines of a debate (Lunt and Stenner, 2005). The protagonists are usually presented in the following order: an aggrieved party, or someone who wants to reveal a secret or tell someone like it is, is introduced first, encouraged through neutral questioning by the host to state their concern to say what warrants them feeling the way they do and what action they would like to take against the person they are complaining against. In the meantime the person who is the subject of the complaint is shown in a small window on the screen usually shaking their head in disagreement. This second person is then introduced and invited to contest the claim made against them or hear the complaint or secret that concerns them. A guest who supports the original complainant and, in turn, a fourth party who supports the person complained against are then introduced to tell their stories and make their accusations. This ordering of contributions reflects a traditional debate format. Much of the language may be vernacular and much of the expression might be emotional, but these are structured as claims, warrants, evidence, counterclaims and rebuttals that give the whole a forensic quality.

The program host does not just direct this sequence but also uses a variety of techniques to interrogate the stories, arguments and claims made by the participants. The interrogation takes a particular rhetorical form reflecting a public inquiry with Springer as the chair and the participants giving the evidence. Their evidence is a combination of their experiences and their accounts. Springer probes the evidence, sometimes questioning their sincerity, sometimes their right to say the things that they do on the show. But significantly, the host rarely challenges the truthfulness of the claims and counter claims made.

The sequences of expression, argument and interrogation have other features. Time is compressed as each participant is afforded less and less time, building the antipathy between the guests to a point of tension which often breaks out into cursing or physical confrontation. The guests are seated in a line facing out to the audience who play the role of a Greek chorus by reacting volubly and emotionally to the nuances of the claims and counter claims. If physical confrontation occurs then an important component of the props for the show spring into action; minders leap forward to restrain the participants, gently pulling them apart and returning them to their seats to continue the clash of difference.

Lunt and Stenner (2005) interpret these elements as constituting a machine for the production and interrogation of emotions. What is more, they also argue that the program is a hybrid of spectacle and rationalization (or reflection). Despite the focus on entertainment and the confliction elements, there are a surprising variety of parallels between the programs and Habermas' conception of the bourgeois public sphere. The shows are excessive to be sure but those excesses reflect social problems in the contemporary life. These problems arise from distorted communication in everyday life because the politics of identity are incompatible with the demands of social relationships. The extreme formulations of personal problems on Springer articulate, maybe in a distilled form, problems of communication, and the solution, whilst not a public conversation, is nevertheless a public airing. The idea is that the problems of human relationships can be helped by the oxygen of publicity in a controlled space where people can express their deepest conflicts, fears and secrets in a way that has become difficult in everyday life.

The participants on *The Jerry Springer Show* also represent some of those ordinarily excluded from the mass media on the grounds of social position, looks and cultural capital; a democratization of popular culture. The tension between personal and institutional interests, which is handled by exclusion in Habermas, are embraced and combined in *The Jerry Springer Show* where equality of rights of expression are combined with commentary and public reaction. In his interrogation of the guests, Springer deploys both moral questioning of participants and ethical rules of thumb as part of his summing up at the end of the show. The background assumption about the prevailing nature of interpersonal relationships is that individuals are mislead by the intrusion of identity politics of everyday life, leading to insuperable problems of distorted communication which people lack the resources to deal with. In this context, a public, ritualized occasion is needed to introduce direct, unmediated emotional engagement.

Habermas has often been criticized for ignoring the issues of social inclusion (e.g. Fraser, 1992). *The Jerry Springer Show* confronts the contemporary problems of emotional expression and identity: this is one of the places where identity and life politics has ended up whereas it was doomed to exclusion and containment in Habermas' proposals. It is not just that individuals would be left without a voice under proposals for a rational critical public sphere. There are also a range of social problems related to identity politics that could not be discussed because they are not tractable in the language of rational critical discussion and do not lend themselves to resolution in the formation of consensus. Under this view many of the problems of contemporary life need the development of a public expressive order.

## Confessional culture: reality TV and emotions

In our second case study we encounter another critical problem for the idea of a role for popular culture in public life. Is personal, emotionally laden expression in public a site of social control rather than an opportunity for civic engagement?

Furedi (2004) charts the rise of psychological terms in the British newspapers since the mid-1990s. There is a remarkable similarity in the rapid rise in the numbers of mentions of a cluster of psychological terms such as 'self-esteem', 'trauma', 'stress', 'syndrome', and 'counseling'. Before the mid 1990s these terms were rarely used; 'self-esteem', for example, had zero mentions from 1980 to 1986. It slowly rose to around 500 mentions a year by 1995, but then rapidly escalated to over 3000 mentions by 1999. According to Furedi the imperative to emotional confession in what he terms 'therapy culture' leads to individuals focusing on their own vulnerability and orienting to social networks and institutions through a culture of litigation and complaint, leading to the de-politicization of public life. Furedi's analysis is a version of the Foucaultian analysis of discursive control, exemplified by the dispersal of the confessional from the church to the field of medicine and psychology and now popular culture. The idea is that this form of social control works through individuals internalizing a self-reflexive psychological discourse, leading to inner directed conforming and passive subjects.

This view has considerable resonance, especially with those features of the mediation of public life that seem to undermine the potential for a civil society. McKee (2005) sums up the challenges to serious engagement in public life through popular culture as follows: Fragmentation of social groups because of the way that popular culture addresses individuals; trivialization as diversion from critical social, political and economic issues; spectacle which focuses on performing the self rather than engagement in public debate or deliberation; commercialization through which audiences are positioned as consumers of culture and political communication rather than as participants; apathy resulting from obsession with internal life as a basis for action rather than participation in civil society.

Emotional expression seems implicated in all of these aspects of contemporary cultural life. The expansion of genre such as reality TV seems to support these arguments for the diverting nature of popular culture because of its focus on the emotions associated with internal reflection and public confession. Whilst writers such as Furedi (2004) take the development of representations of the internal life as an evident cause for concern, others (e.g. McKee, 2005; Lunt and Stenner, 2005) have argued that a closer interpretation of these emergent genre do raise the possibility of a more positive relationship between popular culture and the public sphere. In addition, the analysis of mediation as an enrolment of the subject indicate that the interpretation of popular culture as exclusively a site of social control might be supplemented by more positive accounts of the transformation of life-political movements and a broader cultural basis to participation in the public sphere.

There have been a number of commentaries on the confessional quality of new genre in popular TV (e.g. Grindstaff, 1997; Dovey, 2000; White, 2002; Illouz, 2003). Here we explore the place of confessional expression in reality TV and reflect on the issue of the confessional as a site of social control. The following analysis arises from an examination of a number of reality TV formats (Aslama and Pantti, 2006). In total, thirty-nine episodes of reality programs were analyzed from the following shows: *The Bachelor* (USA), *The Bachelorette* (USA), *Expedition Robinson* (Sweden), *Extreme Escapades* (Finland), *Faking It* (UK), *Fat Club* (UK), *Idols* (Finland), *Popstars* (Finland), *Shipmates* (USA), and *Temptation Island* (USA). All of the programs examined belong to the 'third phase' of reality programming, mixing the earlier 'action/incident' programs (e.g. *999*) and 'docusoap' formats (e.g. *Hotel* and *Airport*) with game-show interest in tests and challenges and incorporating elements of the talent contest (Corner, 2004: 291–2).

Most of these examples of reality TV involve groups of people interacting over a period of time in a specific setting. However, most of the interactions that are screened take the form of dialogues or small groups. Situations involving interaction amongst the larger group of participants are mostly confined to the formal and ritual moments of reality TV: in the run up to a gaming moment in a show when participants gather together, when the judgment to evict is about to be made, or at mealtimes. These set piece occasions do involve some emotional expression but mainly in the form of expression of empathy or surprise, for example, in game show reality formats following the announcement of the person who is to be evicted. The predominant forms of social interaction, however, are the more intimate moments of interaction. The interplay of emotions between dyads and small groups in the broader setting of a community of characters is the primary form that the unstructured interactions take in reality TV. The interaction between pairs of characters often takes the form of the speech act of declaration (of love, friendship, honesty). One party is typically the silent recipient of these declarations, which take the form of a personal narrative (often of self-revelation). Another common form of interaction is the confrontation often focused around provoking a reaction that might 'reveal' aspects of the protagonist to the other participants and the home audience and linked to the competition of identities, which is at the core of much reality TV.

Complementing the group interactions and the various smaller scale interpersonal interactions are more formal interviews conducted by a host or monologues in which participants speak direct to the camera. In reality TV these interviews and monologues are moments of emotional revelation oriented towards either expression of backstage issues, or the tensions surrounding emotional control in performance (e.g. *Popstars*). These interviews contrast to the melodrama of interaction in dating shows and game-show reality TV. A special case of the emotionally oriented factual interview in the context of reality TV is the therapeutic interview, reflecting the role of hosts such as Oprah in therapeutic talk shows (Illouz, 2003; Lunt and Stenner, 2005) and more generally the deployment of therapeutic techniques in the supportive role of the host in enabling and structuring the contributions of lay participants in talk shows (Livingstone and Lunt, 2004). In the talk show these techniques, derived from clinical interviewing and therapeutic practice, are mainly deployed to generate the conditions under which individuals can tell their own stories. They protect the space for a monologue in which the individual can express their feelings on the topic at hand or reveal their emotional secret. In the talk show genre these personal stories both authenticate the accounts given of the topic of the show as reflecting people's experience and concerns and opens those accounts up as data which experts are asked to account for (Livingstone and Lunt, 1994).

In shows such as *Big Brother* these reflections on the relationships developing between participants take the form of a moment detached from the interaction space of the reality TV program in an anteroom or pod. An interviewer is sometimes linked through an audio feed and sometimes participants speak direct to camera in a monologue. The aim of the interview is to provide moments of reflection on the interaction in the house rather than the expression of evidence about the person's life outside the show, as is the case in talk shows. Another moment at which an interview is presented in reality TV shows is when a guest has been voted off or eliminated from the program. An interview format is then used to provide the last reflections of the individual on their experiences of being on the show, their views about the remaining participants and as a bridge to their potential celebrity in the world outside the program.

The programs are structured around these moments of personal revelation in interactions, interviews or monologues direct to camera much the same way that talk shows are structured around the 'money-shot' of emotional expression or conflict (Grindstaff, 1997; Lunt and Stenner, 2005). These are the 'moments of truth' where the 'true feelings' of participants in reality TV shows leak out and which the audience have been speculating about and waiting for (Hill, 2005). These apparently spontaneous expressions of true feelings about the situation unfolding in reality TV take a variety of forms, which reflect the diversity of genre legacies of reality TV. For example, use of the interview room in programs such as *Big Brother* and *The Real World* deploy the technique that was developed in the use of video diaries in documentary. A monologue is delivered direct to camera reflecting on conditions of life (in this case life on the reality TV show). These situations take on the appearance of melodramatic confession: asides which comment on the unfolding interaction in the programs and placing the audience in the ironic position, as they become party to the secret feelings of an individual towards the other participants.

The link between confessional and therapeutic discourse presents a theoretical link to contemporary theories of social control. It is suggested that the growing salience of therapeutic discourse is a contemporary form of the confessional in which individuals construct themselves, through reflection on their motives, relationships and actions, as a psychological subject open to scrutiny of a higher authority (Furedi, 2004). However, the analysis of different forms of confession in reality TV suggest that the confessional has a variety of functions: in small group interaction confession functions to provoke a fellow participant or to reveal, through their reactions something about the others as much as about the self. Similarly, interviews and direct to camera monologues have a variety of functions in relation to the dynamics of the relationships within the show and between the participants and the audience rather than simply serving to express the psychological state of the confessor. There are, for example, subtle issues of address in the distinction between different examples of confessional discourses oriented directly to the audience at home which position the audience as overhearers of what the person would like to say to another participant of the show. Alternatively, in confessional monologues and interviews, participants present an appeal aimed at persuading the home audience not to vote them off the program or more indirectly to persuade the public and the media industry that they are worthy of a shot at celebrity.

Evidently emotional expression in the form of confession takes a variety of forms in the context of reality TV (Aslama and Pantti, 2006). In many programs all of these variants are in play supporting the idea that these are hybrid genre, which give participants a context to play out a variety of performances of the self. We suggest that the confessional voice in monologue in reality TV combines the promise of authenticity to the viewer and the opportunity to have (briefly) the power to create television to the participant. It thus combines the interests of the participants and viewers in a distilled moment of the private appearing in the public. Confessional monologues are organized around the idea of expression and reflection and present a variety of points of view. The participant reflects on and examines their inner life and the interaction order of the TV program. The production of reality TV makes claims to reality, and the audience is given the role of interpreting and judging the underlying motives and character of the participants (Hill, 2005).

These are the reasons why emotional confession in a monologue or interview is a core part of the production and reception of reality TV. Furthermore, these themes are central to the production of the reality TV genre itself where questions of simulation and reality, of authenticity and performance, the expression of inner feelings and the management of identity are all highlighted as the central production theme, the main issue of participation for those on the programs and the challenge posed for the audience (Aslama and Pantti, 2006).

## Reflections and conclusions

We have seen that emotions, as a central feature of both sensational talk shows and reality TV, present dilemmas for the relationship between popular culture and the public sphere. In the talk show case the issue focused on the distinction between the needs for rational critical dialogue and the formation of consensus in the public sphere and the needs of emotional engagement and expression in the lifeworld. In the case of reality TV the tension is between understanding emotionally laden confessional monologues as moments of opportunity for individuals in the public sphere and as reflecting discursive social control.

The expression of emotion is important to public engagement but does this inevitably mean that there is a gap between popular culture and the public sphere? And what implications does this have for the limits of the public sphere to represent public taste and opinion? We suggest that these cases illustrate the challenge that these two genre of popular television raise for debates in public sphere theory over popular culture and the public sphere and in interpreting the implications of the spread of reflexive discourse of the self in the contemporary cultural scene. Do these media constructions of public reflection mirror the increasing centrality of the reflexive project of the self (Giddens, 2001) or is this the working through of a regime of social control that operates through the internalization of norms of self-restraint backed by the dispersal of psychological categories that enroll the individual to the social?

On the issue of whether the mediation of the confessional, as exemplified by monologues or interviews focused on the revelation of internal feelings, is an example of the dispersal of social control through confessing subjects, Shattuc (1997) and White (1992) argue that there are important differences between mediated self-expression and the confessional of the church and the psychotherapeutic context. An important dimension of this is the public nature of mediated performances of confession. Similarly, Lunt and Stenner (2005) argued that *The Jerry Springer Show* exteriorizes through public display what otherwise would be a private engagement in the church confessional and in psychotherapy.

These arguments are supported by the idea that the mediation of emotional conflict (in talk shows) and expressive confession (in reality TV) are not best seen as attempts to replicate or represent everyday social interactions. They are 'strange situations', specific to the media context rather than attempts to represent something that 'happens' either in the inner world of the participants or their private lives. All of which challenges the notion that representing the public is best achieved through the construction of consensus in public opinion. In contrast, popular culture emphasizes difference and conflicting representations and it is the playing through of these differences and conflicts that constitutes the challenge to the contemporary public sphere. This is precisely the opposite of the idea of leaving personal identity behind and engaging in a public dialogue aimed at mutual self-understanding and formation of consensus. Talk shows and reality TV offer a view of the public sphere as a mediated public space that operates to display differences and conflict and in which the lessons to be learned are to do with the way that identity combines personal and social commitments and has to be performed in socially structured contexts rather than understood as the expression of an inner, psychological state.

The mediation of the public sphere, we suggest, should not lead us to want to draw a strong line between the public sphere and popular culture. Popular culture can all too readily be seen as fragmented, trivial, a managed show of publicity and implicated in producing passive and docile rather than engaged and active publics. This is the tendency in Habermas' work but also in many of his critics who argue for a limited role for popular culture in the expression of currents of feeling in the lifeworld, which is differentiated from the 'real' sphere of political influence. In contrast, we have suggested that the examples of sensational talk shows and reality TV demonstrate the importance of popular culture in reflecting critical dimensions of the contemporary public sphere. These include the pragmatic coming together of 'teams' of people in a given social situation; the focus on diversity and the expressive voice in public affairs; the relative decline of the authority claims of television and the consequent implications for what constitutes the public service in television; and the insertion of previously excluded voices into the public sphere as a transformation of life politics.

# 14
# The Revolution Will Be Televised: Free Speech TV, Democratic Communication and the Public Sphere

*Todd Fraley*

Democracy, understood as an ongoing process striving to find and protect the common good, demands equal and unrestricted participation among active, engaged, and informed citizens. An egalitarian public sphere is central to this process, as it represents a space where citizens are afforded the opportunity to deliberate and have an impact on the essence of democracy – decision making. Continuously contested, critiqued, praised, questioned, and even reworked, Jurgen Habermas' ideal strived to create 'a network for communicating information and points of view . . . filtered and synthesized in such a way that they coalesce into . . . public opinions' (Habermas, 2002, p. 359). Many scholars question the possibilities of fashioning such a space, but this ideal retains support with those who believe the public sphere is 'indispensable as a model of what a good society should achieve.' (Schudson, 1992, p. 160).

One key addition to the work of Habermas is the idea that democracy requires one overarching, common, or official public sphere consisting of multiple, competing and alternative publics in which participants negotiate differences about policy that concern them all. Members of these counterpublics 'invent and circulate counterdiscourses to formulate oppositional interpretations of their identities, interests and needs . . . [while] reducing the extent of . . . disadvantage in official public spheres' (Fraser, 1992, p. 123). As Nicholas Garnham (1992) suggests counterpublics alone are not sufficient, 'there must be a single public sphere, even if we might want to conceive of this single public sphere as made up of a series of subsidiary public spheres, each organized around its own political structure, media system, and sent of norms and interests (p. 371). Alternative, oppositional, and/or independent spheres may not compare in size to the mainstream public sphere, but they may nevertheless be effective, as these competing spheres overlap and create the potential for social change. For example, the feminist movement of the 1970s disseminated a marginalized perspective of domestic violence through 'sustained discursive contestation' and moved the issue from a private interest to a common concern (Fraser, 1992, p. 129).

Today, Habermas' 'network for communicating information and points of view' is to a large degree supplied by media. Peter Dahlgren (1995) suggests that television in particular has become, 'for better or worse, the major institution of the public sphere in modern society' (p. x). Historically, mediated forms of communication have restricted access to mediated public spheres, and substituted vigorous participation with managed discussion. Highlighting serious consequences of this influence, Robert McChesney (2004) outlines how corporate domination 'causes serious problems for a functioning democracy and healthy culture' (p. 7). The potential exists to utilize communication technologies in ways that allow for and encourage full participation among diverse citizens, yet most people become 'unofficial communicators' effectively removed from the debate (Drew, 1995). Today that issue remains fundamental to any discussion of the role of media in generating and sustaining an official public sphere built upon alternative public spheres. But creating democratic communication systems are problems of implementation and access, not technological deficiencies. Circumventing these shortcomings in attempts to serve the public interest, progressive organizations and individuals have established alternative media outlets to expand the public sphere. The goal is not to silence the perspective privileged by corporate media, but instead to provide media access for other viewpoints and ensure an informed public.

Following these ideas, this chapter examines the continued development of alternative mediated public spheres created by existing counterpublics that integrate competing and conflicting perspectives into an overarching public sphere as a counter to the current flow of information emanating from mainstream media. The next few pages offer a brief overview of alternative media and alternative publics and their attempts to construct an egalitarian public sphere. Following that discussion, I shift my focus to the efforts of Free Speech TV, a component of an expanding network of alternative and independent media essential to the success of counterpublics to shape common concerns among citizens. Free Speech TV is one of many examples of the ongoing process of creating media spaces for alternative public spheres of all stripes that is essential to sustaining an overarching public sphere. A weekly newspaper, a website, or a 24-hour satellite channel are merely components of the public sphere, but they are important parts to the process of involving a broad spectrum of citizens in public dialog.

## Media, democracy and the public sphere

James Curran (1991) suggests a goal to 'recreate the media as a public sphere in a form that is relatively autonomous from both government and the market' (p. 52). 'He argues that an adequate media system should enable the full range of political and economic interests to be represented in the public domain . . .' (Curran, 1991, p. 47). A mediated public sphere should, therefore, represent all significant interests in society, facilitate participation in the public domain, enable contributions to public debate and input in the framing of public policy (Curran, 1991, p. 30). Ultimately, media should 'assist the realization of common objectives of society through agreement or compromise between conflicting interests . . . by facilitating democratic procedures for resolving conflict and defining collectively agreed aims' (Curran as cited in Thornton, 2002, p. 10).

The public sphere requires exchanges of viewpoints and interaction among citizens and counterpublics and media fosters this process as audience members become citizens (Dahlgren, 1995). Counterpublics have attempted to use communication technologies to create and develop alternative mediated public spheres but they continue to face problems of implementation and access. As 'ordinary people' gain knowledge and take initiative, these restrictions can be surmounted. Profit-driven corporate media privilege one-way communication, stifling participation among citizens in a mediated public sphere (Kellner, n.d., p. 9), but if TV is the most influential communication device, alternative TV has the potential to create spaces of resistance (Anderson & Goldson, 1993, p. 57).

The US tradition of alternative television uses public access TV[1] and satellite technology to circulate views of counterpublics often marginalized by mainstream media. Dee Dee Halleck (1984; 2002) argues that satellite technology is a powerful organizing tool and central to the creation of an alternative public sphere. Two organizations using this technology successfully are Deep Dish TV and Paper Tiger TV (Halleck, 2002; Kellner, 1992). Twenty-five years after its creation, Paper Tiger continues to appear on public access cable channels across the country and remains an organization of local media volunteers creating programs that analyze and critique mainstream media, culture and politics. Deep Dish TV, a network of community access channels sharing programming via satellite technology, was founded in 1986. Its existence helps grassroots media projects searching for an outlet and proves that satellite distribution is a powerful political tool that encourages 'active engagement with television: for people to become part of a community of interest that engages with issues of interest and reacts to events' (Halleck, 167, p. 2002).

Both organizations assist media volunteers and activists by providing critical space for media productions and offering workshops as a way to help others learn how to use and create media. By distributing media productions from all over the world, Deep Dish and Paper Tiger allow individuals to communicate beyond the local as their programs circulate nationally, thanks to satellite and video technology. Halleck (2002) explains that, while traditionally 'alternative views have remained localized,' the infrastructure of alternative networks allows for rapid and widespread dissemination that enables and encourages organization and strategizing (p. 106). A collaboration between Deep Dish and Paper Tiger, the Gulf Crisis TV Project helped groups opposed to the first war in Iraq find and share their voices by linking local video-producers, peace activists, and a national public access outlet (Halleck, 2002). Such efforts serve as effective models for utilizing the participatory aspects of public access TV, encouraging individuals and groups to create their own media and value their own perspective (Anderson & Goldson, 1993). The potential of these resources to 'provide for widespread dissemination of . . . issue oriented media is an emancipatory moment yet to be realized' (Halleck, 1984, p. 317). Similarly, Douglas Kellner (1992) outlines the possibilities of a 'public interest satellite channel . . . [offering] real debate over issues of public concern' achieved by 'expand[ing] the current spectrum of ideas and information' (p. 109).

## FSTV and the public sphere

Responding both to democracy's need for news and to the limitations of news from mainstream corporate media, Free Speech TV, a national satellite television channel, expands on previous attempts and assists current efforts to create an alternative, mediated public sphere by incorporating the ideas, concerns, and organizational strategies of its predecessors utilizing public access television and satellite technology. Launched in 1995, FSTV began as a public access channel airing documentaries and striving for diversity in content. A publicly supported, independent non-profit TV channel airing on Dish Satellite Network and on 156 community access cable stations in 33 states, FSTV works with independent media producers to create programming focused on providing important context to social and political issues in a manner that educates and urges action (Fruchter, 2002). Communication technology serves as a tool to achieve its mission of 'working with activists and artists . . . to cultivate an informed and active citizenry in order to advance social change' (www.freespeech.org). Central to this process is the creation of a mediated public sphere for progressives and traditionally marginalized voices to expand their efforts, broaden their communicative networks, and ultimately forge alliances with other individuals and groups. In this manner, FSTV is similar to alternative newspapers in the mid-1960s, that Bodroghkozy explains served as information, communication, and community-building forums (2001, p. 11).

FSTV is part of a growing alternative media system that creates what Downing (2003) refers to as a 'counter-public sphere [that operates] . . . in close relationship to political and social movements' (Downing, 2003, p. 253). Over the course of a day, viewers watch programming dedicated to 'promoting participatory democracy, grassroots organizing, and cross-community dialogue,' as well as providing a 'platform for voices and points of view traditionally excluded from television . . . at home and abroad' (www.freespeech.org). The efforts of Free Speech TV during the 1999 WTO protests in Seattle demonstrate how counterpublics utilize communication technology to create an alternative public sphere that documents their efforts and reveals their reality. These protests documented the utility of mediated forms of communication in fostering the creation of new alliances among disjointed and disparate groups working towards a similar goal (Kellner, n.d.).

During the 1999 Seattle WTO protests, media activists bypassed corporate media and informed the public about complex reasons behind the protests, and documented police actions against demonstrators (Downing, 2003, p. 242). Also during this time, 'video-documentaries were . . . edited together from footage shot by many different videographers' (Kidd, 2003, p. 243), and resulted in *Showdown in Seattle: Five Days that Shook the WTO*, a program that circulated via the web and FSTV.

Planning the media strategy for Seattle began six months prior to the protest, with a goal of creating a media center that produced 'a daily newspaper, thirty minutes of satellite TV every day, radio, miscellaneous other coverage, and the website' through collaborations with media activists from Paper Tiger, Deep Dish, and Free Speech TV (Morris, 2004, p. 329). By establishing daily web updates and creating documentaries like *This is What Democracy Looks Like* and *Showdown in Seattle*, activists challenged episodic mainstream media frames by providing thematic coverage with relevant context, and independent media worked to 'widen outreach and participation of activists from various movements' (Morris, 2004, p. 330). These efforts continued during the World Bank/IMF protests in Washington DC and Cancun, as well as in Quebec City to protest the FTAA (Kellner, n.d.).

Based on the response to this programming, FSTV created the *Mobile-Eyes* series that incorporates investigative reporting on critical issues and 'partners with social justice organizations' (Mamoun, n.d., p. 2). Referred to as 'national teach-ins', *Mobile-Eyes* has investigated the US military, media ownership, US Foreign Policy, the peace movement, and the World Social Forum, along with other topics often underreported in mainstream media. It often includes live broadcasts from demonstrations and interviews with movement leaders (Mamoun, p. 2). It is supported by a web presence complete with action alerts, contact information, and online forums that enable collaboration among counterpublics that were not possible a few years ago (Mamoun, n.d.).

*Mobile Eyes* offers an example of how FSTV helps establish an alternative public sphere and independent media network that serves as a global social justice movement press (Morris, 2004). FSTV introduces information unavailable within mainstream media outlets, and creates access to media outlets through collaborations with, reliance on, and support for independent producers and progressive media operations like Big Noise Tactical Media, Guerilla News Network, and Undercurrents. As Schiller explains in Chapter 10 on low power FM radio, counterpublics are creating 'opportunities . . . for "ordinary people" to exercise their communicative agency as producers of media' (p. 00), except in this case they are speaking to a nationwide audience rather than a local community.

By using FSTV as an outlet for disseminating information, media activists and citizens share perspectives and allow spaces for voices historically 'shut out of the established media or . . . effectively absent' (Downing, 1984, p. 35). As Kellner (1992) explains, these open-access communication systems allow individuals and groups to circulate important points of view while presenting opportunities for relationship building and political organizing.

To establish Eley's 'structured setting . . . where negotiation . . . takes place' (1992, p. 306) FSTV's must reach beyond activists to other concerned citizens. Lacking the benefit of *TV Guide* printing Deep Dish TV's lineup to publicize and attract broader audiences, Halleck (1984) argues for a strategy of consistent scheduling. Similarly, FSTV offers regularly scheduled daily, weekly, and monthly programming (Fruchter, 2002). Throughout the course of the day, viewers can watch Democracy Now! (DN) an hour-long news program at 8am, 12pm, 7pm or 12am. The remainder of the day FSTV airs programs such as *GAY USA*, a weekly news program devoted to gay, lesbian, bisexual, and transgender issues; *Fallujah*, a program documenting the American destruction of Fallujah; *Blacked Out Media*, an alternative news media and experimental showcase for creative works; or *Globalization at Gunpoint*, part of an ongoing series investigating US military involvement in Iraq and its impact on Iraq's culture and economy. Viewers are also exposed to critical perspectives regarding local, state, and national issues through independently produced news programs such as *Liberty News, Dyke TV, Chicago Independent Television* and *I.N.N World Report*.

FSTV programming includes films such as *This is What Democracy Looks Like* or *Kilometer 0*, two documentaries created by media activists to offer detailed accounts of the efforts and positions of those protesting the policies of the WTO and IMF in Seattle and Cancun. *Guerilla Video Primer* is an educational program teaching individuals step by step how to make media, document events, and communicate effectively in a media culture that continues to neglect and silence critical voices. Programming discussions may include Arundhati Roy offering an informed and passionate critique of US foreign policy to a capacity filled auditorium or scholars, activists, and professionals contemplating the war on terror in a Guerilla News Network production titled *Aftermath: Unanswered Questions from 9/11*. These efforts are important as they help counterpublics disseminate information, create discursive contestation, and establish what Fraser (1992) called *common* concern within the official/overarching public sphere.

The programming of FSTV exhibits the possibilities of creating an important alternative mediated public sphere that helps incorporate dissent and conflict into the 'official public sphere' in an attempt to arrive at the common good. The reality is that individual citizens participate in numerous publics and create overlap among the many alternative public spheres and ultimately develop a larger public sphere where participants accept, expect, and negotiate differences (Fraser, 1992, p. 127).

## Democracy Now!: informing the public

Mainstream news reporting typically presents a fragmented picture that often lacks serious analysis or critical thought and is ultimately of little use to citizens (Bennett, 2001, p. 5). In response, Paper Tiger TV and Deep Dish collaborated on covering one major news event, creating the Gulf Crisis TV Project to document resistance and opposition to the first Gulf War (Halleck, 2002). In the wake of 9-11, FSTV provided context for the attacks that was missing from mainstream media and offered global voices of dissent an opportunity to critique the US response (Fruchter, 2002). This coverage led to FSTV introducing the daily news program, *Democracy Now* (*DN*) hosted by journalist Amy Goodman. Launched in 1996 as part of Pacifica Radio, *DN* describes itself as a national, listener-sponsored public radio and TV show, pioneering the largest community radio collaboration in the country and committed to bringing the voices of marginalized to the airwaves. Billed as 'Resistance radio: The exception to the rulers,' *DN* claims to bring life to the ideas and voices that share a 'commitment to truth, democracy, justice, diversity, equality, and peace' (www.democracynow.org).

Pacifica Radio founder Lewis Hill believed that 'radio and the press should not be run by entrepreneurs motivated by profits but by journalists and artists whose motive would be the most objective and enlightening programming possible' (as cited in Downing, 1984, p. 75). He envisioned a form of media providing access to sources of news not commonly brought together in the same medium while promoting full distribution of public information (www.pacificaradio.org). As a televised broadcast of a radio show, *DN* host Amy Goodman barely acknowledges the presence of the camera. Shedding the familiarity of a professionally clad anchor greeting an audience from behind a wrap-around desk located in a technologically advanced studio, Goodman, donning a headset, t-shirt, and leather vest, takes her place in the center of a cramped room decorated with wall-to-wall newspaper clippings and a table covered with notepads and the day's papers. As the program begins and Goodman prepares to discuss the day's top stories, she motions to her producer to bring the music down. Seeming less a figure of power and importance, Goodman instead reminds one of a friend waiting to talk about the rising death toll for American troops in Iraq, NSA spying, or US foreign policy. Beyond these differences in appearance, *DN* offer viewers a critical approach and a non-traditional lens that shapes understanding by discussing perspectives that are competing with the official public sphere but nonetheless are circulating throughout the public consciousness.

Prior to the 2003 US invasion of Iraq, ABC, NBC, and CBS sidestepped the discussion surrounding the mystery of Hussein's weapons of mass destruction and questions concerning the justifications for war, and focused on the acceptance of a UN resolution against Iraq as well as the Iraqi Parliament's unanimous rejection of said resolution. Mainstream media coverage contained commentary from State Department or White House correspondents quoting senior government officials. As talk of the passing of the UN resolution and Iraq's response to the resolution earned center stage, mainstream media reminded audiences of the unanimous support the resolution received and the US-established timeline for Hussein's response.

By contrast, *DN* furnished different context, incorporated different sources, and offered analysis that included discussions of Saudi Arabia's decision to prohibit the US from using their facilities in the event of war, Turkey's questions concerning the UN resolution, and anti-war protests across the nation and around the world. *DN* also used the UN resolution to interview Denis Halliday, former UN Assistant Secretary-General and UN Humanitarian Coordinator in Iraq, who called the resolution a 'charade' and 'dangerously ambiguous.' Concerning Iraq's weapons capabilities, Halliday explained that Iraq has no capacity to deliver chemical agents and cited a Pentagon memo stating Iraq poses 'no serious threat.' After an extensive breakdown of the resolution's text and the changes requested by Russia and France, Halliday reiterated the US role in supplying arms to Iraq, placed the current conflict into historical context, and incorporated perspectives that revealed the complexities of US foreign policy. FSTV's inclusion of diverse and marginalized voices in the daily lineup built upon 'The War and Peace Report' a daily newscast created by Deep Dish, FSTV, and New York City's Downtown Community Television Center that served as a 'forum for grief, anger, and informed discussion' (Halleck, 2002, p. 108). More importantly, it established a diverse, informative, and controversial discussion within a sustained alternative public sphere.

Collaborating with Big Noise Tactical Media, self-described as 'a not-for-profit, all volunteer collective of media makers around the world,' *DN* developed a segment called *Iraq Journal* that contained discussions with individuals invisible within US nightly news. Iraqi families, artists, and community leaders, demonstrated the impact of war on the citizens. Iraq emerges as people and a culture, as it becomes more than just a location on a map with which the US has had a long and tumultuous relationship. These conversations continue online at FSTV's website and on community boards created by FSTV to allow individuals to share their voices and establish relationships.

By working with volunteers, artists, and other progressive media outlets understanding the power and mobility of modern media technology, *DN* and FSTV establish an alternative public sphere for important but often silenced counterpublics and surmount barriers limiting the discourse of the public sphere.

## Conclusion

For three days in November 2003, roughly1600 media activists and independent media producers descended upon Madison, Wisconsin for the first National Conference on Media Reform. Discussions centered on the critical components of democratic media and a better understanding of an independent global press. The weekend included workshops and panels designed specifically for those looking to learn about the global independent media network and offered a glimpse of the support network created by media activists.

Furthermore, this event highlighted numerous organizations fighting for media and social reform by linking media and democracy. Mainstream media outlets were noticeably absent, but tape recorders and cameras were rolling, and in instances where technology allowed, events were streamed live on the web. Whether Senator Russ Feingold or FCC Commissioner Jonathan Adelstein was giving a speech or John Doe was talking about low power radio, their comments were documented and disseminated. Keynote speeches by Jesse Jackson, Bill Moyers, Naomi Klein, Studs Terkel, and many others were filmed, taped, and prepared for broadcast by individuals representing different Indymedia affiliates.[2] During the closing session, a meeting was announced to allow citizens involved with recording the event to collaborate on a National Conference on Media Reform documentary. Sessions and speeches were aired on Free Speech TV and made available on their website. Participating in the public sphere became less of a theoretical question and more of a reality as citizens voiced their concerns and shared their perspectives.

The public sphere demands open discussion and the possibilities of answering back as each individual contributes their voice to the great chorus (Mills, 2000, p. 299). Seemingly impossible and certainly frustrating, the public sphere must allow for each and every willing voice to be heard, understood, and integrated into the larger discussion. Journalist William Greider explains that, 'It's not [that] every citizen expects to speak personally in the governing dialogue, but every citizen is entitled to feel authentically represented' (1992, p. 14). Hence, Thomas Jefferson believed, 'where the press is free, and every man able to read, all is safe.' To agree with this contention is to understand the significance of free media to that public domain where individuals interact and openly discuss important issues of the day in an attempt to articulate public opinion and locate the common good. While mediated communication has evolved beyond the printed word, the centrality of Jefferson's notion still rings true. Citing French sociologist Gabriel Tarde, Michael Schudson (1997) asserts, the importance is 'not that everyone need read the newspaper [because]. . . . One pen suffices to set off a million tongues' (p. 305). That is the value of a media system that includes FSTV and embraces the spirit of a public sphere.

The belief and willingness to participate in the conversation of democracy, coupled with an understanding of and access to communication technology is essential to a public sphere that Peter Dahlgren (1995) argues demands new forms and strategies. FSTV exposes the possibilities, potential, and frustrations inherent in communication technologies to create alternative public spheres that provide the foundation for an overarching and egalitarian public sphere. While TV is 'not a substitute for political organization and struggle, [it is] a vehicle for participants . . . to provide information about their activities and to involve people in their efforts' (Kellner, 1992, p. 107). This is key to a truly democratic society, is vital to realizing Habermas' ideal, and demonstrates the value of a network like FSTV.

A public sphere committed to the common good cannot flourish under corporate and state controlled media, but is only established, sustained and protected by an ongoing process of creating democratic media. But finding ways in which modern media structures can be transformed to give a voice to the voiceless and ensure participation remains a key concern. FSTV has not perfected this form of communication, but it is continuing the tradition of counterpublics employing mediated forms of communication to create a comfortable space – or as Habermas wrote, 'a network for communicating information and points of view' – to engage in deliberation and influence the state without fear of retribution. In the end, mediated communication among multiple, alternative, and/or counterpublic spheres accessible to all citizens and guaranteeing the circulation of equal, independent, and critical voices makes it easier to support Fraser's contention that there is 'no reason in principle to rule out such a society in which social equality and cultural diversity exist with participatory democracy' (1992, p. 126–7).

## Notes

1. Communities negotiate with local cable television franchises to support public, educational, and governmental (PEG) TV, better known as Public Access. Cable operators are required to negotiate for a *franchise* in the cities they serve. Making equipment and air time available to ordinary citizens for non-commercial uses on a first come, first serve basis can be part of this negotiation. For more info on governmental regulations pertaining to cable franchises see www.fcc.gov, http://www.democraticmedia.org/ddc/CCCIntro.php, and, http://www.freepress.net/defendlocalaccess/=benefits.
2. Visit http://www.freepress.net/conference/recordings.php to view and listen to the conference.

# 15
# Lost in Space: Television's Missing Publics

*Virginia Nightingale*

Television today is a multi-headed hydra, a medium with multiple lives and diverse modes of connection with its viewers – it is a medium in perpetual transition. As broadcast TV it offers news, entertainment and advertising in a magazine format. As Cable TV it offers thematic or genre-based product flows. As Internet TV it offers pay per view and program downloads, chat and other interactive options. As mobile tv it offers program alerts, mobisodes, TV program highlight downloads and special offers from program sponsors. While the digital platforms have been slow to develop original content modes, those now being developed are shaped by a convergence process that is changing fundamentally the nature of the tacit 'contract' between audiences and entertainment. This change, the change from free-to-air services to pay-services that involve multiple contractual arrangements between clients and providers, means that television's capacity to communicate the public sphere to the masses can no longer be taken for granted.

Since its introduction across the developed world in the nineteen fifties, broadcast television has played a vital role in the mass communication of the public sphere. Political parties and politicians have used broadcast television to publicize their activities, to persuade the electorate to their points of view, to bolster their credibility, and as the primary instrument of explanation and persuasion in relation to programs of economics, health, education and social security. Advertisers have used broadcast TV to promote products and services. Emergency services have used broadcast television to deliver warnings and guidance to the public on how to handle dangerous situations. Broadcast television has become perhaps the only environment (outside of the polling booth) where most people experience a sense of connection to the public sphere. Television and radio contributed to the endurance and stability of political process from the mid to the late twentieth century. This was achieved through the mass media's stage-management of the public sphere, and by its capacity to efficiently deliver mass audiences for public information. This stage-management concentrated immense power and wealth in the hands of entrepreneurial media owners by gifting to them the power inherent in editorializing the public sphere.

185

Many of the mass communication functions broadcast TV performed are proving to be redundant in the context of the internet and as the secondary impacts of media convergence become obvious. As a result, the nature of the restructuring of television seriously compromises its capacity to continue to host the public sphere in the ways it has until now, and potentially this has profound implications for the reshaping of public life. Even if we consider television's constructed public sphere to have been fraudulent – a counterfeit public sphere – we cannot avoid addressing the problem of how to imagine the real public sphere without access to the masses through broadcast television. Yet this scenario is already upon us and demonstrated by the persistent shrinkage of free-to-air television audiences.

Fortunati (2005) has suggested that one way of describing the impact of convergence today is to recognize that traditional media are transforming themselves to fit the new communications environment produced by convergence, while at the same time the internet is equipping itself with media like capacities. In other words, the internet is trying to become more like television to attract larger audiences [it is 'mediatizing'], and television is trying to become more like the internet [it is 'internetizing']. This chapter tracks the way this process is playing out in the context of multiplatform television. It explores three convergence-related changes that possess the potential to dramatically alter the nature of the mediated public sphere: the changed competition context of the television industry; the substitution of free-to-air broadcasting services with pay-per-view commodities; and the reshaping of the media text as 'content' commodity rather than primarily as an agent of discourse.

Optimistic visions of this convergence as a technological sublime (Lévy, 1997) were easier to accept as an ideal before September 11 and its aftermath, before the persecution of the young by major media companies for file sharing began, before the internet demonstrated its efficiency as a tool for the black economy as much as for the common wealth and health, before the significance of the 'culture wars' predicted by Castells (1998) began to demonstrate their destructive potential. Castells (2001) has long recognised the potential of the network society to assist the expansion of the black economy and to compromise elected governments. Responses to the emerging cyberculture are demonstrating conclusively that large, self-organizing communities are prepared to act against the interests of others to achieve their sectional interests, and that the basis for taking such action increasingly occurs with no reference whatsoever to humanity in general, let alone a public sphere. In other words, the system seems to lack an overarching sense of public interest, which suggests it will prove problematic as a replacement for even a dysfunctional public sphere in the production of 'the social bond'.

## Competition and the television industry

Historically the introduction of broadcast TV was considered a public good, so the industry infrastructure, established to protect fledgling television industries, was underwritten by national governments, by limiting competition within the television industry and/or by establishing television broadcasting as a public service. Whether publicly or commercially funded, the number of television stations operating in any one market was limited by both decree and economics. But in a commercial TV environment, the competition between television stations was contained by limiting the number of stations serving a particular market to the amount of advertising revenue that market could generate. Since advertising revenue is limited, it was clearly in the interests of the channels to ensure that competition was also limited. The competitive relationship between channels led them to minimize programming differences in order to attract as large a share as possible of the available mass audience. Neuman (1991, p. 145ff) has explained that this occurs as a result of 'the economic pressures towards homogenization' which ensure that the more similar the products offered by competitors, the more evenly the available consumer base will be divided between them.

Limited competition in turn led to television industry practices that clearly could not be justified on the basis of audience preferences – like scheduling based on the 'least objectionable program' (Webster *et al.*, 2000: 164). Such practices ensured that most people were exposed to very similar programs and information. The public knowledge generated by shared exposure creates an imagined public sphere that is all the more convincing to its audiences because the media also represents the public to itself. This in turn exacerbates a mass media phenomenon Niklas Luhmann described as, 'the reproduction of *non-transparency of effects* through *transparency of knowledge*' (Luhmann, 2000, 1996, p. 103, italics in original). Luhmann argued that the public believes that it has access to all the relevant information because cross-checking available sources reveals consistency among them. But this consistency is itself a product of limited competition or, in Neuman's terminology, the 'economic pressures towards homogenization' rather than the analysis of diverse sources, so cross-checking simply reinforces the seamless operation of the communication system. In addition, the media routinely represent the public to itself in the form of opinion polls and surveys, and therefore are often the only source of information the public has about itself beyond the local parameters of work and home life. So lack of diversity of sources and complete dependence on the media for a sense beyond the local of what others might think about social and political issues, allowed audiences to assume that the public sphere hosted by the mass media is an accurate representation of what they needed to know to participate as citizens in the democratic process.

The strategies broadcast TV developed to maintain mass audiences are proving inadequate to the changed conditions of a digital media environment. It's standard content forms are not sufficiently multi-purpose to transfer easily to digital platforms; scarce youth audiences now drive production that is increasingly poorly attuned to mainstream interests; file sharing undermines the strategies that previously controlled syndication and staged release across international territories; and its scheduling practices heighten broadcast TV's vulnerability to technologies that allow viewers to avoid advertising. The mass audience is fragmenting as a result of competition from digital media – cable and satellite television services, the internet, online gaming; mobile media, DVDs (www.journalism.org, 2006). The mainstream audience is no longer bound by the constraints of 'lowest common denominator' viewing (Neuman, 1991) or by scheduling designed to present not the best but the 'least objectionable program' (Webster *et al.*). Predictably, audiences are choosing entertainment options with more personalized appeal from a broader range of options, and advertisers are following their targeted audiences to these new destinations.

A compromised capacity to deliver the mainstream (in terms of ratings) means not only that broadcast TV is compromised in its capacity to deliver mass audiences, but also that advertisers will increasingly buy advertising space from other, more easily customizable media [thus diminishing the funds available for new television program development]. Governments will become increasingly reluctant to fund or subsidise public broadcasting services that address the interests of shrinking components of the general public. The declining attractiveness of existing TV genres for key audience demographics causes existing audiences to be revalued by both advertisers and the television industry. Napoli (2003, Ch 4) has discussed the process of audience valuation in the USA and demonstrated why the key demographics for commercial TV broadcasting are by definition audiences who rarely watch – the youth audience and young male viewers in particular. Broadcast TV actively rewards customer disloyalty because advertisers are willing to pay more for access to the scarce youth audience. As television content is increasingly tailored to their interests, other segments of the mainstream opt out of services that are not sensitive to their interests. Decline thus becomes a self-fulfilling prophecy for the broadcast TV industry, and its role as host or intermediary in the public sphere becomes less and less relevant (Nightingale, 2004a).

## Substituting 'free-to-air' with 'user-pays'

In the shift to its new digital platforms, free-to-air broadcasting is being replaced by television commodities and services which invariably involve user-pays or pay-per-view choices. Convergence is hastening the 'disintermediation' of broadcast TV because, as the mass audience fragments, so does the advertiser funding on which the industry relies (Nightingale, 2004). Advertisers are now able to avoid the 'waste coverage' inherent in broadcast TV advertising and to focus specifically on existing customers and prospects who share similar media profiles and can therefore be expected to be more receptive to the advertising message. In a recent comment to the *Wall Street Journal Online* (May 23, 2005), Adam Klein of the EMI Group is reported as describing mobile phones as 'a very attractive environment' for content delivery because, 'Whereas people are used to getting content free online, they are accustomed to seeing items tacked onto their phone bill.' While mobile TV is in its infancy, it has already gained considerable publicity for its capacity to raise revenue from downloads of program highlights for shows like *Big Brother* and *Idol*.

From a television industry perspective, enhanced formats like *Big Brother* and *Idol* offer some hope that free-to-air TV might retain its primary position in the television hierarchy in spite of convergence. Enhanced programs offer the prospect of bringing fragmenting audiences back under industry control. This view is evident in the publicity for the *Enhanced TV Show and Mobile TV Forum* industry conference (London, September 2005). The conference was promoted as 'delivering the future of broadcasting' by demonstrating the power of both enhanced TV and mobile tv to build program loyalty, increase telephone revenues, and to deliver a new channel (mobile tv) to the television market (www.enhanced-television.com). In this context, the third screen (mobile tv) is presented as a vehicle for the delivery of broadcast program spin-offs, and indeed there is evidence that in 2005 the third screen delivered substantial revenue linked to downloadable highlights. During the 2005 UK series of *Big Brother* for example, the mobile phone operator 3 offered both highlight downloads and live streaming of the program for cell phone screens. Writing for *The Times* newspaper in Britain, Sabbagh (2005) disclosed that 'Highlights of the reality show were downloaded 360,000 times at 50p a time. A 75p-a-minute live television stream was also watched on 90,000 occasions, according to information released to *The Times*.'

The 'enhancement' project replaces dwindling advertiser funding with viewer/user funding. In this scenario, broadcast TV companies continue to control production of television programs and series, but programs are chosen for their capacity to generate revenue directly from the viewer[1] by including interactive enhancements as part of the initial product design. In this capacity *Big Brother* continues to be a winning format. In its 2006 Australian series, audiences were encouraged not only to vote contestants off the program, but also to vote for whom they thought should stay. Instead of just one phone call viewers now make at least two phone calls – thus doubling the potential income generated by the voting enhancement. This voting strategy also provides extremely useful feedback to the production team on what makes contestants popular with the audience, thus creating a feedback loop that ensures the program is progressively tailored to the interests of its high profit customers. So, when Rob O'Neill reported in 2004 that Jane Roscoe's research had demonstrated a core fan audience for Australian *Big Brother* of approximately 35,000 fans, the finding was quickly translated into an industry revenue strategy where the profitable loyal fan base is offered even more opportunities to pay to participate. This is a text book example of what advertisers refer to as 'profitability targeting' (Duncan, 2005, pp. 232–4). In this case, the costs of digital enhancement have been passed on to the consumer-audience, so that enhancements are also spin-offs that deliver independent and increasingly substantial revenue streams for broadcasters, production companies and the telcos. The digital enhancement of its programs therefore has offered broadcast

TV a reprieve from the inexorable decline in overall audience size by providing the means to raise additional revenue directly from its loyal audiences, who also double as its primary online customer base.

The technical arrangements for digital enhancement are complex and involve audiences in multiple contractual financial agreements. Nightingale and Dwyer (2006) have shown that viewers have three options to access interactive enhancements (e.g. voting, auction sites, chat lines, sponsor links, etc.) for enhanced programs like *Big Brother*: the telephone landline, their Internet connection or their cell phone. Each of these choices involves the audience consumer in a (series of) financial transaction(s) with their cell phone service provider, their telephone (landline) service provider, or their internet service provider. The various service providers reimburse the vote processing company a set percentage of the resulting revenue for the business generated, and the vote processing company in turn reimburses predetermined percentages of the telephone transactions back to the TV production company and the television channel. The complexity of the processes and agreements by which revenue is both raised and redistributed makes it extremely difficult to for the public to protest about these arrangements, or to argue for better or cheaper services since they are by definition commodities and therefore can no longer be considered as communication rights.

Even though it is routinely represented to the audience as an opportunity to participate in a democratic process, votes become commodities in this context. In a wonderful sleight-of-hand, program presenters borrow the language and style of the hustings to rally viewers to pay to participate (Nightingale and Dwyer, 2006). While the emphasis on 'participation' may suggest that TV voting actually grooms the audience for public sphere activity,

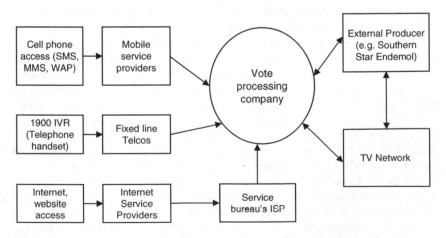

*Figure 15.1*

the lack of transparency in the voting process and its commercial cl
must also be taken into account, since the similarities to the democratic principle of one person one vote is strongly challenged by this position. Admittedly,
Coleman (2003) has suggested that since democracy is a work-in-progress
(each democratic nation adapting the practice of democracy to its own special
conditions), the way it is practiced should be expected to change, especially
if the percentage of the population voting in elections continues to decline.
The problem with the television voting comparison is that it requires a redefinition of democratic process. This would be a democracy based on purchasing
power justified presumably on the basis that in such a system everyone has the
option not of voting but of purchasing one or many votes. The problem of the
shift from participation as citizen's right, to participation on the basis of one's
capacity to purchase votes is central to my concern about the lack of transparency indicated by the rhetoric on television voting.

## The commercialized text: the case of branded entertainment

Use the branded entertainment team that puts who, what & where before
content development; the team who's creative development starts with
understanding the business, the audience, their world and where they
consume their entertainment. The team that creates games, film and
TV that is motivationally relevant to it's audience (Advertisement for
www.cocojambo.com).

The communication challenge posed for broadcast television by the ramifications of convergence is echoed in its impact on the advertising industry
because both industries collaborated in providing services to the publics, markets and communities of broadcasting's mass audience (Nightingale, 2004b).
The advertising industry response has been quite different from that of
broadcast television. Since advertising always served two masters – its clients
and the media industries – it has taken the opportunity offered by the convergence challenge to lessen its dependence on traditional media and television in particular. Instead of advertising products, the advertising industry
now tells brand stories. Lury (2004) and Ardvisson (2006) have both recently
provided excellent accounts of the consolidation of brands as 'communication media' (Lury, 2004, ch. 1) and as 'information capital' (Ardvisson, 2006,
ch. 6). Their work demonstrates that not only is the brand a medium of communication but it can also be argued to be the model for understanding the
website as an internet genre.

Brand communication is a much more diverse activity than product promotion and over the last five years or so it has shifted the industry's orientation
away from advertising [as opposed to publicity, direct mail, etc.] and away
from television as its preferred medium and focused instead on a practice
commonly referred to as 'media neutral' planning. The central idea in media

neutral planning is that the communicative purpose of the advertising campaign, who it aims to persuade to what course of action, should drive the selection of media channels. Assumptions that television is necessarily the first choice for advertising have been reconsidered, and media planning is increasingly designed around segmentation based on profitability. This has made targeting a more highly developed 'art' since demographic, geographic and psychographic segmentation now play secondary roles to customer segmentation, where the most profitable customers and those who share similar media profiles to them, becomes the key to defining target audiences (Duncan, 2004, ch. 7). In the late 1990s, Turow had expressed concern that the segmentation practices of the advertising industry had had a negative impact on the public sphere because, 'Marketers' concerns with diversity act to push groups away from one another rather than to encourage them to learn about the strengths of coming together to share experiences and discuss issues from different viewpoints' (Turow, 1997, pp. 199–200). His concern echoed and amplified Meehan's earlier complaint that the television industry primarily serves the 'consumerist class' rather than the general public (Meehan, 2003). The advertising industry's narrow focus on existing and more profitable customers shows that these trends continue to influence the reshaping of audience formations and their links to the public sphere.

By fragmenting the general public on the basis of personal consumption patterns, the 'hypersegmentation' to which Turow referred exerts an even more divisive impact on the public sphere today, but for a rather different reason than he suggested. Confronted by the challenge of convergence and television's shrinking audiences, the advertising industry has invented new ways to enact advertising in an online environment. The transfer of brand representation from the mass media to the internet has facilitated a complete reorganization of way brands manage their interactions with customers. So in addition to audience fragmentation, the mass communication system as a whole appears set to face a reduction in advertiser interest in television and mass marketing, and its replacement by promotion and personalized approaches to the stimulation of consumption. The internet allows advertisers to cultivate virtual communities among brand customers and contacts and to both personalize and customize their communication with them. However, online communications tend not to have the same emotional impact as television, and so the advertising industry has been searching for ways of producing richer content for online distribution of brand communications. One such adventure has been the investment in branded entertainment.

One of the earliest iterations of branded entertainment, involving a return to sponsorship and product placement, was McDonalds sponsorship of the internet game, *The Sims* (Walsh, 2002). This sponsorship allowed game participants to both frequent the McDonalds outlets in *The Sims* and to open their own McDonalds' franchise within the game environment – i.e. to engage with the brand both as consumer and as franchisee. More recently however this type of branded entertainment has been applied to product placement within entertainment products designed for distribution by both the internet and other more traditional distribution means. So for example, the advertising company, *Hypnotic*, defines branded entertainment as, 'the combination of traditional marketing, entertainment content and branding tactics' (www.hypnotic.com) and licenses the use of brand names and brand messages in short films or by music artists. The products developed are primarily (though not solely) promoted and marketed through the internet. Just as enhanced TV has been used to internetize broadcast TV, branded entertainment is an advertising industry attempt to mediatize the internet, and to bridge the gap between entertainment and advertising. The reason why sponsorship and product placement have regained popularity, especially in the online environment, is that it has proved effective in taking advertising to the internet sites where target audiences (young males in particular) are active. Rather than using banner ads, pop ups or click through, branded entertainment embeds the advertising in the entertainment product in ways that inseparably meld the brand with the product/content (e.g. Rodgers, 2004).

More innovative approaches to online advertising have taken advantage of the ubiquity of the brand website, where custom-designed weblogs offer the site user additional benefits like access to expert advice sponsored by the company, or access to the knowledge work of other site users. Genealogy sites like Ancestry.com are good examples. They have established themselves as brands that offer access to a wide range of family history research data sources, alongside chat, bulletin boards and managed email. They actively advertise products and services relevant to the interests of their subscribers. Customers are able to make contact with people researching names linked to their own genealogies or to any names at all. Such web-based services have created thriving family research businesses with active and often diverse global consumer audiences. It is hardly surprising then that in December 2005 the British Media company, ITV, paid the sum of £120 m for the website Friends Reunited, the parent company of another genealogy site – Genes Reunited. The press release states that, 'The acquisition is part of a strategy to build content based businesses which create and monetize direct consumer revenue for ITV' (www.itvplc.com/itv/news/releases/pr2005/2005-12-06). The decision also seems likely to have been motivated by the popularity of a family history series, *Who Do You Think You Are?*, produced by the BBC in collaboration with *Ancestry* in 2005 and 2006 (http://www.scotroots.com/who-do-you-think-you-are.htm). These industry activities are important because they demonstrate how interchangeable advertising and content development have become in the world of converged media since in this case the broadcast TV content effectively now works as advertising for the brand/websites by motivating new customers to sign up and by reminding lapsed customers to update their knowledge about the site and what it offers. It also demonstrates how central the content work of audience members is to the ongoing work of the brand/site.

In 2001 and 2002, the car manufacturer BMW experimented with a new approach to online advertising by using a series of short films to revitalize the brand and promote the release of its latest model car. It produced a series of eight award winning internet short films made by renowned film directors featuring its new car. The internet (rather than broadcast TV) was used as the primary medium for the advertising campaign. The campaign used viral techniques, encouraging people who viewed the films to send them on to friends and acquaintances, thus using online networking to do the work of distribution. Accounts of the series found in advertising texts (Duncan, 2004, pp. 386–8) and on the web (www.bmwusa.com/bmwexperience/filmspr.htm) indicate that the initiative was successful as internet advertising [BMW claims the films were viewed over 100 million times, and Duncan that more than 20 million viewers accessed the streaming video website]. The films were also used as a promotional give-away (in DVD form), to launch BMW's own cable channel, and to promote the brand as 'innovative', 'first of its kind' and the sort of company you can rely on. In addition, the films linked viewers to live promotions that exploited the capacity of the internet to generate 'smart mob' activism (Rheingold, 2002). Though the 'activism' reported by Duncan constituted little more than an act of brand loyalty and curiosity (Duncan, 2004, p. 387) it provides evidence that the films and other promotional activities pursued by BMW resulted in strong commitment to the brand among the films' viewers. For reasons that have not been disclosed, the films were removed from the internet on 21 October 2005. Yet this example has now become part of advertising lore – a demonstration of the capacity of internet networking to deliver mass audiences.

The differences between these two examples are interesting. The success of the family history initiatives is a product of the size of the online subscription base for the Internet businesses and the mass appeal of the broadcast programs. While the collaboration between content creators and the internet businesses pushes new subscribers to the online services and some viewers to the broadcast programs, it also delivers a personalized take on national and local history and its impact on ordinary individuals. The television programs contribute 'content' to the ongoing work of both the site and its subscribers, and justify the development and maintenance of both local and national resources (public records, historical buildings and artifacts, etc.). The sites assist the establishment of offline local history groups who educate others in the skills of family history research and in some cases encourage an interest in the study of the impact of history and politics on the everyday lives of ordinary people. While not overtly politicizing site members or broadcast TV viewers, the convergence of broadcast TV and internet sites in this case works to enrich both the online and offline worlds. The BMW example is, on the surface, quite different. While it proved highly effective in distributing a brand message to millions of internet users, its purpose was primarily oriented to consumption and brand promotion. It refers its audiences recursively back to the brand, and actively distracts attention away from the social, environmental, economic and political issues that surround the motorcar. The BMW films have encouraged advertiser confidence in the usefulness of branded entertainment that doubles as Arts sponsorship primarily because the BMW short films are taken to have proved that the emotion that television provides can be delivered online. Both examples illustrate aspects of the ways the internet operates, 'as an economic space in its own right, an arena for both the production and the consumption of branded content' (Ardvisson, 2006, p. 104).

Ardvisson (2006) has also argued that the internet 'shows a close technological fit with capital's strategic response to mass intellectuality: branding' (ibid., p. 96). In his view, companies like BMW are currently participating in a phenomenon he calls the 'mediatization of consumption' whereby the brand expands beyond its traditional narrow product range (automobiles in this case) into a product array it does not necessarily produce but that bears its name (lifestyle goods like designer kitchen equipment or fashion accessories). Porsche AG is another example. It is a majority shareholder in the Porsche Design Group, a company that includes Porsche Design Studio, Porsche Design and Porsche Design Drivers' Selection (http://www.answers.com/topic/porsche-design-group, accessed 7 June 2006). The products developed by Porsche Design include luggage and leather, accessories, timepieces, home products and eyewear, while the Porsche Design Studio projects create the designs for these products alongside transportation, architecture and interior design and design process projects (http://www.porsche-design.com/live/PORSCHE_DESIGN_en.PorscheDesign, accessed 7 June 2006). The Eddie Bauer department store's design for the Ford SUV achieves a similar purpose. A profile of a profitable client group (Eddie Bauer customers) is identified as a good match with the profile of Ford's SUV owners. By targeting the two customer groups both brands stand to benefit. Ardvisson suggests that brands are mediatising consumption through such arrangements. The brand becomes less dependent on conventional advertising because it is strongly associated with the consumption environments referenced by each brand. In this sense the brand presents itself through 'environment' rather than through 'representation'. He argues that in this context,

> The internet has the capacity to create all-encompassing environments centered around a particular brand; environments where all actions, where activity in general, is always already anticipated by the program of the brand' (Ardvisson, 2006, p. 96).

What seems to be happening here is that 'mass intellectuality' is groomed to serve the brand which nourishes an apolitical micro 'public' sphere devoted to itself and its users. The problem is that this productivity is not holistic and the brand therefore embodies a contradiction inherent in informational capitalism, as Ardvisson concedes (p. 137). The brand is increasingly dependent on the social production (participation) of its client base in its world view, but it is reduced in its capacity to control that participation.

Media convergence both produces and exacerbates the crisis in informational capitalism. Converged media require different sorts of content – content that is valued for the contribution it makes to the vitality of an arena of consumption linked to one or many brands. Ebay, Google, Yahoo! and other search sites are valued for their capacity to locate specific information and sites, and to facilitate the trade in branded commodities. Online 'content' is increasingly designed around a cycle of inter-linked media forms – for example: product/program releases, website, fan club, fanzine, instant messaging service (IMS), mobile phone alerts, etc. – each designed to maximize the capacity of the content idea to generate revenue and to stimulate the micro publics of brand culture. It is developed as a set of merchandisable propositions to serve the brand's environment of consumption. The diversity of online content requires texts to be multi-purpose, content-delivery hubs – places that offer differential access to components of a core text (or brand) in accordance with consumer interests and willingness to pay. The hub text provides access to the different types of text-related data collected at the site. As a result, the discursive significance of text is diminished as is its potential to contribute to public sphere discourse beyond the apolitical micro spheres of everyday consumption. This makes it impossible for the internet to replace broadcast TV as a host to the public sphere.

## Concluding remarks

As Castells (2001, p. 129) has suggested, digital media have amplifed and deepened the pre-existing socio-cultural shift from place-based affiliation to 'networked individualism'. Networked individualism is affiliative, ephemeral and task-based (Castells, 2001, p. 125) – a 'social pattern' (p. 131) rather than a 'community' [as it is so often described]. This particular shift is linked to processes that can be dated to the beginning of the Industrial Revolution and its inherent internationalizating tendencies (Mattelart, 2000). On re-reading early audience researchers like Merton (Merton, 1979, 1949) and Lazarsfeld (Katz and Lazarsfeld, 1955), it is obvious that in the 1940s and 1950s the mass media both facilitated and accelerated a shift to voluntary affiliation as the organizational template for social life by creating new forms of social capital linked to media use. Now in the early twenty-first century the mass media are being displaced as the primary bearers of commercial messages and, as a result, the place-based voluntary affiliation of the mid-twentieth century is also being replaced by an internet mediated communications system organized through brand-based affiliations.

In this context, the nature of 'voluntary' affiliation is becoming increasingly commercial in nature and the space where affiliation is enacted is global and virtual rather than local and place-based. Effectively convergence has assisted a process whereby affiliation has been mediatized [i.e. it is expressed and enacted online] and where identity and agency are determined prescribed by where we buy and from whom it originates. Brands and branding therefore play a coordinating role in the continuing separation of place from space and in the disassociation of the citizen from the consumer. In spite of its occasional hosting of interest specific net activism (Rheingold, 2002) the brand-based model of communication increasingly dominating the internet seems likely to prove an uncomfortable environment for the type of bipartisan debate that has traditionally characterized understandings of the nature of a public sphere.

## Note

1. It is important at this juncture to question the ethics of the shift of the funding for free-to-air TV from advertisers to the audiences for peripheral services like downloads, alerts and other interactive novelties, at the very least because of the debt burden it is creating for the young. Premium services are usually specifically directed at the young who form a strong component of the so-called 'early adopter' market. In Australia, mobile phone debt sits alongside debt for other life-essentials like education and motor vehicles. The concern in Australia is that the new debt burdens carried by the young leave them unable to secure the more substantial loans required for housing and employment infrastructure.

# 16
## From Public Sphere to Civic Culture: Young Citizens' Internet Use

*Peter Dahlgren and Tobias Olsson*

During the last decade or so, basically ever since access to the internet reached a high proportion of people all over the western world, its ability to revitalize the public sphere has been discussed. Within the discussion, utopian as well as less hopeful future visions have been heard. On the one hand, authors have aired and identified new hope for the public sphere on the internet (cf. Malina, 1999; Slater, 2003); on the other hand, sceptical analyses have concluded that the internet is just another extension of corporate powers (McChesney, 1999), or a device selling back to people the ability to interact, an opportunity that one-way media such as radio and television have stolen from them (Holmes, 1997).

These ideas – whether critical or not – on the internet's ability to contribute to a more vibrant public sphere have mostly been developed from theoretical reflections. Quite often it has been a case of 'reading off the effects' of the internet by analysing aspects of its form. It has, for example, been asserted that the net's interactivity, co-presence of vertical and horizontal communication, disintermediation, speed and its absence of boundaries (Bentivegna, 2002) would foreground a new, different public sphere. Just a couple of examples from the by now quite encompassing literature on the subject (cf. Hague & Loader, 1999; Axford & Huggins, 2001; Jenkins & Thorburn, 2003) can underscore this point.

We can for instance note Mark Poster's (Poster, 1997) ideas about the internet (together with other digital media) taking us to a 'second media age' in which we can expect the development of a new kind of public sphere, 'postmodern' in character and hardly recognizable by 'modern' standards. Here we can also mention James Slevin's (Slevin, 2000) analysis of the internet as recreating the dialogic character of the public sphere, a character that has been marginalized by one-way media such as newspapers, TV and radio. Another, less hopeful analysis of the net drawing conclusions about consequences based on its form has been presented by Oscar Gandy in his reflection on what he calls 'the real digital divide': the divide between citizens and consumers that threatens to undermine all hopes about a more vibrant public sphere (Gandy, 2002).

When it comes to empirical studies on the internet as an institution of the public sphere, studies focusing on what is happening on-line have been numerous. We can for instance note the collection by Tsagarousianou *et al.* (1998), which presents and analyses different efforts in digitalizing municipal communication in various cities. Another frequent type of study is analyses of on-line forums. In a considerable way, they have looked into the dynamics of on-line discussions and to what extent the internet develops (or not) into a Habermasian inclusive, rational and deliberating public sphere (Hill & Hughes, 1998; Hale *et al.*, 1999; Wilhelm, 1999; Dahlberg, 2001a; 2001b; Holt, 2004). Also, a couple of studies have looked into political activism on the internet, how big as well as small political actors make use of the internet in pursuing their own goals (McCaughey & Ayers, 2003; van de Donk *et al.*, 2004; de Jong & Stammers, 2005).

Overall, there are numerous studies conducted on the users of internet, not least focusing on everyday practices and perception of among various groups (cf. Bakardijeva & Smith, 2001; Olsson, forthcoming. See also the volume edited by Wellman and Haythorthwaite, 2002; Warschauer, 2003, nicely synthesizes what we know so far about the users). However, such studies are rarely framed by theories of the public sphere. Much of the research to date has largely been statistical studies. One example is Anthony Wilhelm's book *Digital Democracy* (2000) in which he, among other things, discusses the emerging information underclass that seems to be 'immune to progress' and thus is at risk of never becoming part of the new internet-public sphere.

To our knowledge, then, there is a lack of qualitative studies paying attention to use and perception of the internet, analysing it from the point of view of theories of the public sphere. This chapter aims at presenting precisely such an analysis. It brings data from a Swedish study of use and perception of the media in general and the internet in particular among young, active citizens.

The research project on which this chapter is based focuses a specific set of internet users: young (16–19 years old), active citizens. The empirical material of the chapter draws upon two different studies within the project, one study of twenty young, active citizens affiliated with the political parties' youth organizations, and one study of some thirty young, active citizens affiliated with various alternative, extra-parliamentarian political movements, such as the alter-globalisation movement and the Animal Rights movement. Both studies rely on data from in-depth interviews with the respondents, mainly on their use and perception of media in general and the internet in particular (Olsson, 2004; 2005).

Among the respondents there is a general middle class bias and except for three or four exceptions they are all pursuing theoretical high school programs preparing them for future university studies. It is also worth mentioning that they have been recruited to the study from two different areas in Sweden. Half of the interviewees live in a Swedish big city area and half of them live in a smaller city in a rural area. Both of the areas are located in southern Sweden, which is the by far most populated parts of the country.

In the next section we develop a specific approach to the ideas on the public sphere by introducing the concept *civic culture*. Thereafter, in the empirical sections, we will illustrate and discuss in what ways the internet can be a resource to the development of civic culture.

## Civic cultures: resources for the public sphere

For all its compelling qualities, the perspective of the public sphere still leaves unclear a number of important issues. A key conceptual issue is that, while it asserts that people should, from a normative perspective, participate in the public sphere, this theoretic horizon does not have much to say about *why* or *how* people actually participate in the public sphere, and ignores a number of obvious reasons such as why they may choose not to participate. Yet it is precisely this theme of participation that has moved to the center of discussions in Western democracies. As the tensions and dilemmas of democracy have become all the more debated in the past decade, among the key questions being asked is why is political participation on the decline, at least within the contexts of formalised politics? And, in a related manner, how are we to understand the rise of newer forms of engagement? More generally, we could pose the question as follows: what factors contribute to people *acting* as citizens, i.e., engaging themselves in the public sphere and political life (however we may care to define the parameters of the political)? We offer here a short overview of what we call the civic culture perspective (Dahlgren, 2000; 2003) as a way to conceptualise the factors that can promote or impede participation in the public sphere. We use the plural form 'civic cultures' to underscore that there are many ways of enacting citizenship in late modern society.

Citizenship as a concept traditionally builds upon a set of rights and obligations, historically evolved in society, and underscores universalism and equality. In the modern world it has usually been linked to the nation-state. More recently, citizenship has become an object of contemporary social theory (cf. Isin and Turner, 2002). For our purposes, a major strand of such studies highlights the subjective side of citizenship, as a dimension of our plural, composite identities (cf. Mouffe, 1993; 1999; Clarke, 1996; Preston, 1997; Isin and Wood, 1999). This perspective argues that civic agency requires that one can see oneself as a citizen, that this social category be a part of one's sense of self – even if the actual word 'citizen' may not be a part of the vocabulary. This identity has to do with a sense of belonging to – and perceived possibilities for participating in – societal development.

Yet such identities cannot be fostered in a vacuum; they need to be culturally embedded in the minds sets, practical activities, and symbolic milieu of everyday life. Thus, we use the concept of civic cultures to refer to these resources upon which citizens – individually and collectively – draw to facilitate their participation. In a sense, civic cultures can be seen as prerequisites for engagement in the public sphere: without access to some viable version of civic cultures, people will not be participating. Via their participation in the public sphere, citizens in turn strengthen civic cultures. Yet, while civic cultures are empowering, they are also vulnerable: like all domains of culture, they can easily be affected by political and economic power. For our concerns, it is the media's relevance for civic cultures that is central.

Conceptually, civic cultures can be modelled as an integrated circuit with five parameters of mutual reciprocity. While identity can be seen as the key element, it must be understood as embedded in this circuit, interplaying with the other parameters. The five elements, discussed briefly below, are: values, affinity and trust, knowledge and competencies, practices, and identities. In deploying them, we underscore a constructionist stance and highlight that the meaning that characterise civic cultures at any given point in time are both dynamic and socially contingent. While conceptually offering an understanding of the preconditions for participation in the public sphere, the civic cultures notion, via these parameters, also provides a tool for the analysis of empirical data. Each parameter serves as a starting point for inquiry: of media output, as well as – such as in our case here – of respondents' discussions about their political participation and media use.

*Values* must have their anchoring in everyday life; a political system will never achieve a democratic character if the world of the everyday reflects anti-democratic normative dispositions. In short, democracy requires civic cultures that underscore commitment to the rules of the game.

For *affinity and trust*, we have in mind here something less ambitious than 'community' – rather, a minimal sense of commonality among citizens in heterogeneous late modern societies, a sense that they belong to the same social and political entities, despite all other differences and conflicts. Civic affinity blurs into civic trust. Here too we aim for a modest level. Certainly a degree of trust in government and other major institutions is important, but in the civic context we must also add trust between citizens. They have to deal with each other to cooperate, to make things work.

*Knowledge*, in the form of reliable, referential cognisance of the social world is indispensable for the vitality of democracy, even if the forms of knowledge – and its access, acquisition, and even modalities – may be evolving via new media cultures. A subset of knowledge is competence, and in particular, the skills to deal communicatively in the socio-political world are pivotal.

Democracy must be embodied in concrete, recurring *practices* – individual, group, and collective – relevant for diverse situations. Elections can be seen as a routine form of practice in this regard, but civic cultures requires many other practices, for example, organising campaigns, holding meetings and mobilising actions. One of the key practices of civic cultures is discussion, which of course is a cornerstone of the public sphere. In time, practices become traditions, and experience becomes collective memory. Today's democracy needs to be able to refer to a past, without being locked in it. New practices and traditions can and must evolve to ensure that democracy does not stagnate.

This brings us back to *identities*. It should be clear by now that this sense of self is predicated on the interplay with the other parameters of civic cultures. Thus, values may reinforce affinity and trust, which in turn can encourage certain practices, and these practices may have positive impact on knowledge, and so forth. We can envision both positive and negative spirals in this regard.

## The internet and civic culture: empirical illustrations

### Knowledge

The internet certainly appears to be an important resource when it comes to gaining *knowledge* in a couple of different but interrelated ways. To start with, the respondents spend a lot of time keeping up to date on the news through the internet (Olsson, 2004), which might not be too surprising, since a lot of other studies already have showed that this is a widespread practice among Swedish internet users (Bergström, 2005). Instead, two other practices related to the young, active citizens' habit of collecting relevant information appear more interesting. Firstly, their use of the internet to seek information from various *primary sources* and, secondly, their seeking what we might call *alternative information* through the internet.

When it comes to seeking information from primary sources, the empirical material provides several examples. One of them is from the interview with Marcus, who is 18 years old and holds an important position within a youth organization affiliated with one of the Swedish political parties. Marcus lives in the study's big city area and is very interested in a future as a politician:

> Interviewer: Could you mention some of the web pages that you regularly follow on the internet?
> Marcus: Yes, well . . . I of course follow the other youth organizations' web pages, but then I also check up on . . . extremists on the political left as well as the political right. Especially the left wing extremists are growing fast and I try to understand why they do that. What kind of rhetoric are they using? What are they actually saying? And when it comes to the right wing extremists I just check up on them and try to debate with them. But as soon as something happens [involving] these organizations, I usually go to their web pages to see what it's all about rather than trusting second hand information [the media], which usually isn't right.

Marcus starts by telling that he 'of course' follows the other youth organizations through the internet, checking up on their campaigns and new arguments. But besides that, he also stays up to date on the left and right wing extremists' whereabouts, not least when they are involved in the news. Then he goes to their web pages to get their perspective on the issue rather than solely relying on the media's representation of the event. In this way, Marcus tries as hard as possible to get hold of first hand political information.

To seek out political first hand information on the internet is very much a standard practice among the politically active respondents, among the young people affiliated with the political parties' youth organizations as well as the respondents within the alterative political organizations. But the active citizens within the latter group also engage in another practice that certainly tells to what great extent the internet has been shaped into a resource to their political activity – they use the internet to seek out and collect *alternative* (or non-mainstream) information.

Rita is 17 years old and she is an activist within the alter-globalisation movement. She lives in a big city area and she is in her second year in high school. To her – as to all other 'alternative' activists in the study – the internet is an important resource when it comes to seek out information connected to her political interests:

> Interviewer: Mmmm. . . . But I thought. . . . When it comes to your ideas on important political issues. . . . The media [traditional media, such as TV, radio and newspapers] covers that. Aren't you interested in that?
> Rita: Yes, well of course. . . . That's what I read in the papers and what I watch when I watch TV, of course. But . . . anyhow. . . . There're a lot of internet sights where there're a lot of people who are interested in [for instance] environmental issues and. . . . You know, you talk to people and get to know about forthcoming events. There you can read and also check up on things. . . . That's an important way of reaching out and I guess that's [the kind of information] I try to seek out on the internet.

Rita carefully makes the point that she is not too impressed by the traditional news media's way of presenting news about her areas of political interest (newspapers, TV-news etc.). The themes that are of special interest to her – environmental issues and global equality – are hardly covered by traditional media, and when they are covered, they are not appropriately dealt with, in her view; they just tend to reproduce the mainstream interpretation of the issues. Instead, for her, the internet makes up a much better source of information when it comes to – for instance – issues of alter-globalisation.

It is thus obvious that these young, active citizens have shaped the internet into an important tool for seeking out and collect information valuable to them in their role as active citizens. That the use of the net is an all-important communicative competence – decisive for their participation – is readily apparent.

## Values

Another parameter of civic culture is *loyalty to democratic values and procedures.* Also in this respect the young, active citizens have shaped the new information and communication technology into a civic resource. The internet's contribution to the shaping of loyalty to values and procedures is not a sur-face phenomenon, it happens on the 'inside' rather than the outside, in an implicit manner. As such it is rather difficult to bring up empirical examples to illustrate this point. However, it is possible to at least 'sense' their exis-tence out of the concrete practices that the respondents present. Thus, it can be argued that as the young, active citizens use the internet, they inevitably become involved in discussions and debates; even if this takes place largely on sites where they encounter like-minded participants, this tends to culti-vate a loyalty towards democratic values and procedures. In terms of demo-cratic values, we can distinguish between substantive ones such as equality, liberty, justice, solidarity, and procedural ones, like openness, reciprocity, responsibility, accountability, and tolerance. Both types seem to be implic-itly supported, the procedural ones via practical adherence and the substan-tive ones through being applied to specific issues. The participation in these debates, in which several of the respondents are active, could very well help foster such loyalty, at least to the extent that they resemble the communicative ethos of a democratic discussion.

### Affinity and trust

Similarly, the *trust* parameter within the notion of civic cultures is not directly revealed through interview data. On the other hand we have good reasons to claim that at least trust towards other citizens evolves out of the affinity man-ifested by the internet practices of the young, active citizens. Citizens have to deal with each other to make their common endeavors work, whether at the level of neighbourhood, nation-state or the global arena. If there exists a nom-inal degree of affinity, for example, conflicts can then become enacted between 'adversaries' rather than 'enemies', as Mouffe (1999) puts it, since an awareness of a shared civic commonality is operative.

In dealing with people of similar political persuasion, a degree of trust is likely to emerge. To what extent it carries over to people with differing views would need to be explored further. Also, trust in democratic institutions would seemingly rise with the practices of participation. Putnam (2000:136) distin-guishes between 'thick' trust based on established personal relationships, and 'thin trust', the generalised honesty and expectations of reciprocity that we accord people we don't know personally but whom we feel we can have satisfactory exchange with. We would hypothesize that trust is thicker among those working within the youth groups of the political parties; they are more tightly knit organizationally, and seemingly socialized along simi-lar lines. The extra-parliamentarian activists are more heterogenous, although within any one group there is probably thicker trust. Without such affinity and trust, there can be no civic networking, for example.

Another obvious example is the respondents' extensive use of the internet as a resource for co-ordinating their political activities. For instance, Asta, who is only 16 years old but already holds an important local level position within her political organization, describes in more detail in which way the internet is a resource for co-ordination:

> Interviewer: [B]ut you also said Green Globalisation . . .
> Asta: E-mail lists. . . . We've got one for [the local group]. You subscribe to that list and then you can hand out . . . if you want to send something to all members in this [local area]. . . . I use that quite a lot to hand out schedules and calls for meeting . . .
> Interviewer: That's locally, but do you have one for the regional level?
> Asta: Yes, one for the region as well as one for the whole nation. We also have a newspaper . . . for all members. Then we also have. . . . There are networks too, like "the network for the forests" and they also have e-mail lists. We also have a list for the people in the board, there we mostly . . . well . . . send protocols and discuss places to meet and when we've to set up the next meeting.

In the extract Asta, who comes from the big city area in southern Sweden, quite carefully describes how she and her alter-globalisation movement make use of the internet. To start with they use e-mail lists on the local level. Through them, she receives and delivers information on new meetings and schedules, for instance. But she also mentions the regional lists from which she continuously gets information. Her organization – Green Globalisation – also makes use of e-mail lists on a national level, including all Swedish activists. Then the movement also have additional lists partially outside the movements 'formal' organization, such as specific networks connecting activists within the movement who have similar special interests.

Asta's story is by no means unique to the young, active citizens. Pretty much all respondents tell similar stories about how their various organizations make use of the internet as a tool for organizing their activities. Through this co-ordination, Asta as well as the other active citizens learn about how political organizations work and how to co-ordinate political activities. It is not a too long shot to imagine that these practices also create trust to political action itself, even though it takes some analytical creativity.

Of course, we should also add here, the internet is not the only component. It is just one resource out of many making the young, active citizens learning about political organizing and action and thus creating trust. Nevertheless, the interviews make it quite obvious that the internet has been shaped into an important tool in this respect, a fact that should not be overlooked in our efforts to understand the internet's contribution to civic culture. We of course must not lose sight of the fact that loyalty to democratic values, trust, and affinity for other citizens are no doubt easier to achieve in a communicative environment where ideological homogeneity prevails. The real test of course is what happens in more heterogeneous public sphere contexts, but this lies outside our immediate research horizons.

## Practices

The next parameter in civic culture, *practices*, alludes to less abstract aspects, for instance political conversations, which is of course central. On this point it is certainly easy to bring empirical illustrations of the young, active citizens' shaping of the internet into a tool for civic action. We have already seen how the internet has been turned into a resource, putting the respondents in touch with internal debates within their organizations, especially among the active citizens affiliated with the political parties' youth organizations. The participation in these debates can of course also be interpreted as an important aspect of the useful experiences (practices – that become in a sense routines, and across time become established as traditions) that strengthen civic culture.

Stefan is 18 years old and a member of one of the political parties' youth organization. Stefan is in his second year in high school but he has already started to plan for a future as a journalist. Among the young interviewees he is one of the most ambitious when it comes to collecting experiences from participation in various debates:

> Interviewer: The last time you participated in a debate [on the internet], what was it about?
> Stefan: Yes, well . . . it was the European monetary union. I discussed it with people on the [oppositional party] web site.
> Interviewer: What do you think of that? When I visited your meeting . . . your idea of this campaign . . . it aims at reaching a lot of people, but the debates on the internet – on the other side – hardly include any people?
> Stefan: No, it is mostly for myself, to test arguments and to see what kind of response I get. To try to ask a good question and see how they react to it.
> Interviewer: How do they react then?
> Stefan: It can be anything from not bothering to answer to a long answer stating how terribly wrong I am [laughter].

Stefan's use of the internet is extensive. He uses it a lot in school and he is also a member of several internet communities. Besides that, he uses the internet as a tool for his political engagement and in this extract he presents how he uses the internet in order to get better at debating – he uses antagonistic political parties' web based public spheres. It is quite interesting to note how Stefan deliberately looks for opposition in these discussions. He is not hoping to make his reader change their points of view. Instead, he is looking for counter arguments, because they can help him to enhance his arguments and develop rhetorical skills.

We should also keep in mind that, as with all talk, civic discussion is embedded in sets of tacit rules, and shaped by mechanisms of social etiquette about talk that can either promote or hinder the practices of public discussion (Eliasoph, 1998). Such attributes would of course require more detailed analysis.

But the young, active citizens also make use of the internet in other ways when it comes to concrete civic practices. An interesting example can be found in the interview with Sara (she is 16 years old and lives just outside the study's big city area), who is involved in the alter-globalisation movement, but who also calls herself an antifascist and a feminist. In the interview she explains how she lately has started to make use of the internet as a resource in her everyday activism:

> Sara: [We're into] ad-busting, that's something new, where we. . . . You know . . . unethical commercials. . . . We collect information about the company in question in order to make sure that we're right to criticise them. Then we've – if it is perhaps sexist commercials – balloons that say: 'You can't buy me', that we put on the ads. Or: 'The ad has been taken away due to its unethical message'. . . .
> Interviewer: What's the name of the web site?
> Sara: [Addestruction.org (in Swedish: reklamsabotage.org)]. . . . But you have to be careful, you need to check on your facts before you move on to action. If you get it wrong it'll be destructive for the whole organization.
> Interviewer: How does it work?
> Sara: They've got. . . . They've for instance. . . . You can order and then print these balloons and they also have instructions about how you can go about. But we're careful not to destroy anything. We're only trying to make people open their eyes.

The latest addition to Sara's repertoire of everyday activism is the destruction of ads. Basically, what she and her activist friends are up to is the destruction of unethical, commercial messages, mainly changing their content by adding messages to them. In this practice of so-called 'culture-jamming', the internet is an indispensable resource. On websites such as reklamsabotage.org – which is a kind of Swedish equivalence to the internationally famous adbusters.org – she and her friends find the necessary material to this destruction: stickers with pre-printed alternative messages, models for posters and also a gallery to inspire the creation of alternative messages.

Stefan's participation in political debates on the internet and Sara's use of the internet as a resource for modest – and peaceful – everyday actions are but two out of many examples of how the young, active citizens have shaped the internet into a resource for various political activities, or rather – in this theoretical context – practices. These practices at least give some indications of how the internet can contribute to cultivating practices, routines, and traditions valuable to civic culture. Such practices help generate personal and social meaning to the ideals of democracy. They must have some element of the routine, of the taken for granted about them, if they are to be a part of a civic culture, yet the potential for spontaneous interventions, one-off, novel forms of practice, needs to be kept viable.

## Identity

Also when it comes to the *identity* aspect of civic culture, there are a lot of interesting issues to consider. In a way, we have already seen a great deal of the internet's contribution to the young, active citizens' identities as active citizens. Internet practices such as organizational co-ordination, participation in internal and external debates also have a qualitative, subjective side to them. As such they are also interesting as practices that encourage and cultivate the young, active citizens' view of themselves as citizens. All of these practices develops the respondents' connection to their organizations and/or movements and thus verify their views of themselves as active citizens.

But there are also more obvious examples of how the internet contributes to the cultivation of civic identity among the young, active citizens. Especially among the respondents within alternative movements the internet appears to be of crucial value to the cultivation of their activist identity. To them, the internet is, arguably, the most important resource to their continuous cultivation of the identity as active citizens, not least since they consider themselves to be marginalized by traditional news media – which hardly cover their issues and then tend to 'get it wrong'.

The interviews with the activists within the animal rights movement provide illustrative examples of their downgrading of traditional media and upgrading of the internet. For instance, Gina – who is 16 years old and still on her final year in elementary school – has elaborated ideas about what is the problem with traditional news media:

Interviewer: [Newspaper, what do you think of them?]
Gina: For reading about culture, they're good, but you can't really . . .
Interviewer: What's bad?
Gina: Perhaps that they get things wrong all the time, like in the case with the furrier's shop. It was this autumn, I think, and it got its thirtieth attack, I think, and the newspaper went: "Militant vegetarians have destroyed the shop." Then they just mention in passing that the attack in fact was conducted by a very specific organisation that's dealing with illegal actions. Thus, we [Rita's organization] end up [being blamed for things that we've not been involved in]. Cause we're legal! So I guess . . . how they put things. . . . They could be more accurate.

It is rather obvious that Gina is not too impressed by how the newspapers present her animal rights movement. Firstly, they are hardly represented in traditional news media and, secondly, her organization is misrepresented when they occasionally appear in the media – they are negatively angled and they quite often mistake her organization for a militant organization, while Gina insists that they are only into legal action.

On the other hand, through the internet, Gina can collect news and information valuable to her identity as an animal rights activist, she says, dor instance, through such everyday information as recipes. But she can also participate in various debates on relevant issues. Taken together, the internet community offers several opportunities to cultivate her alternative, activist identity. In sharp contrast to her view of traditional news media, she perceives the internet to be an important, not to say necessary resource to her identity as an active citizen.

## Conclusion

Here, using the concept of civic cultures, we have been able to give concrete examples of how, specifically, the internet has been shaped into a resource for young, politically active peoples' concrete everyday practices of pursuing their political interests. We have also been able to identify the significance of a number of everyday practices and other empirical parameters that we hardly would have been able to illuminate by the concept of the public sphere itself, with its weaker empirical referents to peoples' everyday lives.

A separate but interrelated contribution of the concept, civic cultures is that it encourages a slightly different empirical take on questions of the internet's contribution to the public sphere. In this respect, the notion 'culture' is especially important. It suggests that we pay close attention to peoples' everyday lives and the meanings that people attach to their own practices. As such, it also brings methodological recommendations arguing for qualitative approaches such as in-depth interviews, observations and perhaps the use of media diaries in our efforts in understanding the internet's significance for the public sphere. And, as we pointed out at the beginning of the article, these contributions have not been too numerous within research on the public sphere.

Finally, we would like to encourage others to take on such approaches to the study of the internet's contribution to the public sphere. Here we have been dealing with a very specific set of internet users, young and in various ways already politically active people. But we suggest that our perspective would be useful for studying just about any set of users in order to grasp the internet's significance for the public sphere. It would certainly help bring more nuances to our views of the internet as part of the public sphere than merely speculating about it by reading it off the internet's technological form.

# 17
## Blurring Boundaries in a 'Cyber-Greater China': Are Internet Bulletin Boards Constructing the Public Sphere in China?

*Yan Wu*

Traditional 'unifying media' deliver an authoritative discourse and thus 'assemble and sustain nations with real-time theatre' according to Nguyen and Alexander (1996: 108). On the other hand, the 'conversation model' and autonomy associated with computer-mediated communication (CMC) provides an alternative 'persuasive discourse' which challenges the authoritative discourse and 'provides the subject with a language for dialogue' (van Dijk, 2000; Mitra, 2001:32). Thus the decentralized nature of internet media may thaw the hegemonic control over public dialogue by dominant media and empower citizens. Internet bulletin boards and other interactive online communities may create a new sphere for public meeting and discussions, a potential for reunifying people and renewing revitalizing 'citizen-based democracy' (Rheingold, 1993).

In the Peoples Republic of China, online communities based on internet bulletin boards are changing the traditional political communities of official meetings, neighbourhood or organisation study groups, and private elite-dominated salons, and opening political discussion to ordinary Chinese. A survey conducted by the Chinese Academy of Social Sciences in 2001 on the impact of the internet on Chinese politics shows that 60.8 per cent of respondents believe that the internet gives them more opportunity to express their political opinions; 51 per cent think it gives them more opportunities to criticize government policies; 55.9 per cent think they have a better knowledge of politics, and 43.8 per cent think it will allow top officials to listen to public opinion from the common people (Guo, 2001). Online political discussion also goes beyond the geopolitical boundaries, to construct a virtual public sphere hardly anticipated before.

In this study of the *Qiangguo Luntan* Community (Strengthening-the-country Forum, hereafter, QGLT) (http://bbs.people.com.cn/bbs/start),[1] I focus on the role of bulletin boards in constructing political debate among Chinese, and on its democratizing potential in constructing a virtual public sphere in the cyberspace beyond the national boundary.

## QCLT: The Communist Party's Special zone for free speech

Mass media in China are still mainly state-owned and bear the responsibility of shaping public opinion in contemporary China. The Communist Party's control over media has constructed, to borrow Jakulbowicz's (1991) words, an 'official public sphere' dominating political discourse. Until recently, alternative and oppositional public spheres only existed marginally and more or less underground. Nevertheless, the emergence of a middle class and other changes in social strata following the economic reforms since the late 1970s have stimulated growth of a public power in China (Meng, 2000). Alternative and oppositional public spheres are expanding as a response to the public call for political participation, and have started to attenuate the effect of rigid political control.

Launched on 1 January 1997, *www.people.com.cn* was first created as 'the online news publishing platform'[2] of *People's Daily*, the Communist Party's 'mouthpiece' ever since its birth in 1948. This on-line party organ has been enjoying a prosperous development ever since. Its flagship QGLT has become 'the most popular Chinese-language bulletin boards'.[3]

QGLT was first used as a replacement for real life peaceful demonstration, which is extremely scarce in China, supporting claims that online communities cannot be disconnected from offline communities and should be examined in terms of offline political–economic contexts (Hauben and Hauben 1997; Jones, 1998; Baym, 2000). Set up on 9 May 1999, the second day after NATO's bombing of the Chinese embassy in Belgrade during the Kosovo Conflict, QGLT was first named as *Kangyi Luntan* (Protest Forum). More than 90,000 messages of civil protest had been posted since till the forum changed its name to QGLT on 19 June. *QGLT Current Affairs*, *QGLT In–Depth*, *China Forum* (in English) and 32 other forums on topics such as China–Japan relationship, local development, and so on were gradually set up within the community.

Any internet user can view QGLT sites, but only registered users can post. By May 2004, there have been nearly 450,000 registered users in QGLT community with an average daily increase of 200 new user names. The average number of daily visitors is 'near 1 million'. Broadband, with connection speed of 200 MBps, provides comparatively fast and steady input and output of data including audio-visual service.

Among scholars who have done research on the political application of bulletin boards in China, some celebrate electronic democracy, while others loathe internet use as new apparatuses for cultivating nationalism.

The digital utopian believers argue that bulletin boards entitle users to express themselves on current issues and break down the 'uniformity in public opinion' presented by the official media in China. Bulletin boards and other interactive internet facilities change the relationship between official media agenda-setting and public opinion forming (Min, 2001; Li and Qin, 2001; Tang and Shi, 2001; Chen and Deng, 2002). Meanwhile, other scholars argue that CMC is being used to cultivate nationalism and serve the communist party's administration (He, 2000; Huang and Lee, 2003). QGLT, according to Hughes, 'is a hotbed of nationalist fervour' and the Communist Party has been using internet for 'mobilize nationalism to legitimate its own claim to power' (2002: 218).

Alongside these visions of cybertopia and cyberghetto is another influence, online civic participation in Greater China.[4] Tay (1998) first used the term 'global Chinese community' to describe the communal formation through the online gathering of dispersed Chinese worldwide during the Indonesia Riots of May 1998.[5] Yang (2002, 2003) argues that online civic participation among Chinese worldwide has had visible influences on transnational politics and civil society through 'problem articulation, civic association and the mobilisation of activism' (2002). Chinese language distribution over a large geographic region worldwide facilitates the forming of a virtual public sphere, which might be viewed as a new approach to democratic progress and human rights problems in the Mainland. This chapter aims to examine the role of internet bulletin boards in a global context and answer the following questions: How do bulletin boards foster rational critical political discourse among Chinese individuals? Can isolated politically voices from individual gain understanding from online and form common actions? What is the limitation of the virtual public sphere in Greater China?

## Internet bulletin boards as Greater China's public sphere

The grassroots nature of internet bulletin boards connects ordinary individuals to each other in a totally new context, and allows them to form dialogue, discussion, and even debate over the commonly shared concerns. To better understand their interlocutors, participants of the online debate 'reflexively modify their pre-discursive positions in response to better arguments' (Dahlberg, 2001: 167). Hierarchy in social status in the real world no longer counts in the virtual debate as anonymity forms a 'new matrix of social relations' (Jones, 1998). Meanwhile, since online communities based on bulletin boards are no longer bound by geopolitical boundaries (Downing *et al.* 2001; 202; Castells, 2000), the political discussion online has the intrinsic capability of being global. Thus, a bulletin board, argues Rheingold, 'turns an ordinary person anywhere in the world into a publisher, an eyewitness reporter, an advocate, an organizer, a student or teacher, and potential participant in a worldwide citizen-to-citizen conversation' (Rheingold, 1993).

### Informing

One fatal weakness of modern journalism is that it provides little space for citizens who have no authority, celebrity or expertise to give their political opinions. Lewis *et al.* argue that 'the traditional top-down structure of political reporting' (2004: 163) excludes active citizen access to the media. Contrary to the traditional media, the internet provides a platform for those who want to speak out through posting on bulletin boards, news groups or web forums. Many QGLT postings contain news which otherwise would not be carried by the traditional media in China, which proves what Castells concludes that 'CMC could offer a chance to reverse traditional power games in the communication process' (2000: 391).

Circumventing the stringent censorship in official media, overseas news can always find a place on bulletin boards. This includes cross-posting of news from overseas Chinese media, users' translation of news in foreign languages, and original eyewitness 'reports' from overseas users. Overseas information has been playing an important role for breaking news events like the 9/11 Attack. 17 minutes after the first airliner crashed into the World Trade Centre, when the official media were still silent, a message about it from Hong Kong, coded in traditional Chinese (Big5), was posted on QGLT (Guo 2003). Similar examples could be found in postings from Taiwan regarding the earthquake in 2001 and the general elections. Heavy posters could also be found in the USA, Germany, Australia, Singapore, and other countries. When virtual proximity in the cyberspace creates a sense of locality, overseas Chinese users become information sources from their host countries to their home country.

Meanwhile, the informing role of bulletin boards can also be illustrated in domestic users' posting of their personal account of social changes and problems in the developing China. This individualized perspective of social news would be regarded as too 'insignificant' or too 'negative' to appear on the traditional media. Thanks to the anonymity of the Internet, stories and photos of the miserable livelihood of peasants, migrant workers, beggars, prostitute, the homeless, and the unemployed get 'published' on bulletin boards, which forms a contrast to the gilded image of economic prosperity presented in traditional media. Within QGLT, *Jieyu*, who comes from a village herself, constantly contributes articles on the equal rights of peasant migrant workers in the city (15/05/2002) and legal protection for their civil rights (16/05/2002). William[6] has been writing about the lack of social welfare and pension system for migrant workers since 2003. His articles were later adopted by *Southern Weekend* and several other media in China before it appeared on the website of an overseas labour rights organization based in the USA.

The survey conducted by the China Internet Network Information Centre reveals that among the total number of 94 million internet users in Mainland China (up to January 2005), 39.1 per cent identify their primary goal for getting online is 'to get information'. Among all the online sources obtained and browsed, overseas Chinese sites count for 7.0 per cent and overseas English sites 5.6 per cent. The informing role of internet reflects a growing public awareness of press freedom in China. The 'loss of right to speak', as a QGLT user wrote in his signature files: 'will eventually endanger the right to live'.

## Interpreting

The power relationship between information sending and receiving has been reversed on internet bulletin boards. Even within the officially administrated QGLT, comments on and analysis of current social political events provide a different perspective from the editorial pages of traditional media. In an attempt to write out their 'opinion pages', QGLT users usually rely on multi-textual information, personal experience and source before approaching news stories from a critical perspective. By doing so, the traditional 'passive audience' regain their right of constructing their own news narratives.

Tianjiali, a retired employee from a state-owned enterprise, frequently posts his 'news analyses' on QGLT. From my in-depth interview with him, I found that his media consumption includes television (watching headline news and investigative stories from China Central Television), newspapers (reading both local and national broadsheet papers), and internet. This intertextuality in media consumption helps to cultivate critical thinking in writing his news comments. One example is his analysis about a 'touching' story appeared on *Chongqing Evening* in July 2004. The local news reported a 6-year-old girl selling newspapers on the street and earning money for her father's medical operation. The local press focused on the little girl's filial duty to her parent and people's kindness in donating money, but Tianjiali raised his questioning about the social welfare system:

> I'm happy for the little girl for her receiving the attention of the media as well as the help from the society. However, who can support the other victims suffering from similar accidents? . . . Prestigious writer Liang Xiaosheng says, if we want to judge the rationality of a social system, we should look at how the poorest live their lives rather than how the richest spend their money. . . . We saw these people in need failing to get social support in time, so we know there must be something wrong with contemporary social mechanism. (31/07/2004 author's translation)

QGLT users' autonomy in interpreting 'detailed problems in China's development' is best exemplified by the *Special Discussion Channel on Strategic Development* (2001–02). Obtaining permission from the *people.com.cn* administration, 12 users volunteered to select topics, organize and moderate online discussions on development problems facing China. This was a response to users' enthusiasm for debating China's future and searching for solutions to problems. The discussion site continued for over a year until April 2002, during which 69 users actively participated; 134 articles of users' own observation of development problems were posted; 25 topical discussions were put on the agenda, ranging from domestic issues like 'Education and Social Welfare', 'Reform on Governmental Administrative System', 'Anti-corruption and Balance of Power', 'Reform of State-owned Enterprises', to the Taiwan issue and international relations.

Some academic works were abstracted, edited, or integrated into postings before they appeared on bulletin boards. The following piece appearing on QGLT is taken from a Sociologist Zhong Dajun's book on national treatment after China's joining WTO. National treatment, as a WTO principle, implies that both foreigners and locals should be treated without any discrimination within WTO member countries.[7] Zhong uses the concept of national treatment to argue that though China became a WTO country, discrimination against the rural population such as the deprivation of free migration could be found within its own territory. This unequal treatment among its own citizens results in widening gap between the city and countryside, and the rich and the poor. It is hard to imagine that such severe criticism on the official census registry system could be found on any other media than internet bulletin boards:

> This is a forced deprivation of the citizen rights of free migration and free choice of profession. This census registry system with Chinese character is more brutal than the racial segregation in the South African. . . . It can be compared only to the Nazi's concentration camp in some sense. (Shengdong Youqu 06/05/2003 author's translation)

## E-protesting

Internet bulletin boards in China are frequently used for fighting against social injustice, inequality, discrimination, or censorship. The idea behind online protesting is the separation between *civil society* and *the state* came from the eighteenth-century Enlightenment when the state came to be viewed as the antithesis of 'free association' or of a 'community of interests' (Hassan 2004: 101). Confrontations between civil society and the state could be found in the online protesting and demonstrations both at domestic and international levels.

The first large-scaled online protesting within a global Chinese community started in May 1998 when the anti-Chinese riot arose in Indonesia, and before the formation of QGLT. The World Huaren Federation (http://www.huaren.org) based in the USA launched its 'Yellow Ribbon' campaign and fervently condemned the violence targeting the Chinese community in Indonesia, especially the raping and killing of Chinese women. The 'Yellow Ribbon' campaign urged users around the world spread the news through emails and other forms of online communication, and call attention to the international public opinion to press the Indonesian government into taking action.[8] A protest thus spread like wild fire across the cyberspace and later triggered offline actions. Demonstrations were held in the USA, Canada, the UK, Peru, Hong Kong, the Philippines, Malaysia, Thailand, Singapore, mainland China, and Taiwan.[9] Under the pressure of international public opinion, an independent committee had been set up by the Indonesian government to investigate the riot against Chinese, especially the gang-raping and killing of Chinese women.

During the May riot, Zaobao Luntan (ZBLT) from Singapore, as a web forum affiliated to the *United Morning Post* in its early stage, played a significant role in welding together a Chinese community worldwide. Most Chinese users turned to ZBLT to seek information and voice their condemnation (Lin and Zhao, 2003).

In the following year, QGLT emerged in Beijing in the similar political context and has been a virtual venue for peaceful demonstration even since. The online protest against the Indonesia government or USA government was not a threat to and even supported by the Chinese Communist Party. But the online protest in Sun Zhigang's case in 2003 was directed at the Chinese government itself, pressing the government into abolishing the notorious *Regulations of Custody and Repatriation of Wanderers and Beggars in Cities.*[10] This online action proved bulletin boards' importance as venues for nation-wide civil rights movement.

Sun, a 27-year-old migrant employee in Guangdong province was detained on his way to an internet café on 17 March 2003 by the local police. Because he failed to produce an ID card and a Temporary Resident Permit, and he 'answered back', he was sent to the local custody and repatriation centre for migrant labours and was beaten to death!

Local China press *Southern Metropolis Daily* first reported Sun's case on 25 April both in its print media and its online service. Within hours, this news had been spread online all across the country. 'Tears shed and protest rose all over the Internet during one night' (Lin and Zhao 2003). Thousands of internet users had forwarded the article by email and posted it to bulletin boards. Hundreds of thousands of protest messages appeared on popular sites such as sina.com and sohu.com, decrying Sun's death and sharing their own experiences of being abused by police.[11] A memorial page to Sun, www.cn.netor.com was also set up and received hundreds of thousands of messages of outrage at the social injustice.

Similar tragedies like Sun's death had been covered by media before. However, it is the Internet connected people together and triggered a worldwide virtual protest among Chinese against the notorious deportation of migrant labours practice. Chinese internet bulletin boards worldwide, including famous current affair forums like QGLT and ZBLT, and oppositional voices like Humanity and Human Rights, played active roles in the following trial concerning Sun's case. QGLT users went beyond the sentiment and raised questions challenging the system: How can the public supervise the police if the police failed to perform their duties legally? The temporary Residents Registry System is based on discrimination and shows no respect to humanity. But why is it still in existence?

On 20 May 2003, a special channel 'the death of Sun Zhigang – public opinion – legal problems concerning the custody practice' was set up in QGLT.

Later it changed its name to 'The death of Sun Zhigang questioning the Custody and Repatriation system', which indicates that online public opinion shifted its focus from the media event to the relevant legal system. On 6 June, Professor He Weifang, a senior legal scholar requesting a revision of the custody and repatriation regulations from the government[12] hosted an online panel meeting with QGLT users. During the two-hour online interaction, 35 questions were raised. Comments on the custody's system, media's responsibilities, and the legal procedures for revising the administrative regulations against the Constitution were fervently discussed among users:

> The aim of legislation is to limit the power of the state, because the power of the state has its intrinsic nature of being invasive. If we failed in limiting the state power, the civil rights will be at danger. Sun's Case is a new proof (*Laoxin* author's translation)

> In China's Constitution, there are articles protecting citizen's lives, properties and freedom. . . . But various administrative regulations deprive our civil rights entitled by the Constitution. Meanwhile, the administration of justice in China is not independent, which leads to incidents of civil rights invasion in the real life. This is particularly obvious in [administrations'] invasion of public rights. . . (*He Weifang* author's translation)

On 9 June, it was announced that 18 police officers involved in Sun's death received sentence. In September 2003, the migrant detention centres in China were changed into voluntary service centres, and 'a revised administrative regulation allows any homeless person the right to refuse help from the government'.[13]

During the online protest in the Sun case, a strong sense of public awareness of civil rights could be detected from postings. Associated with this is a strong sense of social obligation found in QGLT users who believe they 'must' represent for people in lower social stratum. Thus, internet bulletin boards and web forums, as 'empowering' and 'emancipatory' technologies, nurture a sense of political equality among Chinese users, which is central to the deliberative ideal.

## E-organising

China has seen a continuous growth of online communities based on internet bulletin boards. Lawyers, journalists, environmentalists, nationalists, homosexuals, and even people who drive the same model of car started to find their peers in the cyberspace and the common interest usually take the communities from online to offline. At the same time, the potential to mobilize public opinion makes bulletin boards a new battlefield for political organising.

QGLT user Gordon is an internet café owner. Since the Communist Party's control over free flow of online information usually starts by closing down internet cafés, private owners running the business encounter great difficulties and risks. From March 2004, Gordon started posting articles questioning the *Administrative Regulations Over the Internet Access Service Business* (the *Regulations*) which is notorious for blocking public access to information and triggering corruptions. During the first 6 months of writing, Gordon had been contacted by internet café owners from all parts of China. A loose organisation National Internet Café Owners League was later set up in the summer. Keeping contact with each other in the cyberspace, this League launched it first nationwide nonviolent action in July 2004. They sent a petition letter with collective signature to the National People's Congress asking for reviewing the *Regulations* and protecting their Constitutional rights of running legal business.

Internet bulletin boards also have been actively used by NGOs and grassroots interest groups in mainland China. The number of NGOs in China reached 283,000 up to April 2005.[14] Internet has been actively used by environmental NGOs such as the Friends of Nature (www.fon.org.cn/) and the Green Earth Volunteers (www.chinagev.org) for networking members and promoting ecology protection ideas. Members from these environmental NGOs learn from the bulletin boards about coming events such as tree planting, better environmental schemes debating, or even participating in the governmental audition on controversial civil engineering projects.

One recent example of Chinese NGOs' civil participation was their efforts in stopping Yunnan provincial government from building 13 hydro-electricity dams on Nujiang River. Nujiang (Upper Salween) River, running through the Three Parallel Rivers Basin world heritage area in Southwest China, is 'one of last free-flowing international rivers in Asia'.[15] The proposed dam project will cause irreversible damage to the endangered flora and fauna in the area, and relocate at least 50,000 people. Chinese environmentalists have been networking each other and exploring media, including the internet, to campaign against Nujiang project since August 2003. They recruited international support from more than 60 countries in November 2003 when the Second International Meeting of Dam-Affected People and Their Allies held in Thailand. In a collective movement, a petition letter was sent to the UNESCO requesting its intervention into the issue. In the following February Chinese government announced that the hydropower project on Nujiang River had been postponed. This has been acclaimed by the national news agency Xinhua as 'the first time that NGOs in China changed plans made by a local government'.[16] Hassen (2004: 135) argues that 'the forms of struggle will have to change' in the digital age when the relationship among citizens, space and technology changes. Wang, the founder of the Green Earth Volunteers and a leading figure in this campaign, pointed out the importance of internet-based communication in Nujiang Action:

> We become more aware of the important networking role of media, especially, the internet in coordinating our action. A Chinese–English website

*Our Attachment to Nujiang River* (www.nujiang-river.ngo.cn) was set up in March 2004 to arouse public awareness of ecology protection with an online forum devoted to discussion about river reservation and ecology protection. (Interview with Wang 9 April 2005)

Media's principal role in shaping the public sphere will be fulfilled when 'they facilitate the formation of public opinion by providing an independent forum of debate; and they enable the people to shape the conduct of government by articulating their views' (Curran, 1991: 29). Thus, bulletin boards in China do have the potential for constructing the virtual public sphere online and contributing to the democratic progress.

## Limitations of the virtual public sphere in Greater China

Though bulletin boards are becoming instruments of self-organizing public debate at both local and transnational levels, its empowering capacity has inborn limitations. The virtual public sphere is vulnerable to government's intervention; political extremist voices spread online can undermine the deliberative democracy in embryo; the economic reform in China also brought about the 'digital divide' and the potential danger of the public sphere refeudalisation.

QGLT is still subject to stringent administrative regulations from the government and censorship within its newsroom. *The Regulations on Interactive Computer-Mediated Communication* which was passed by the Ministry of Information Industry on 8 October, 2000 stated that internet bulletin boards and other interactive online services must be put under tight control of government security institutions. Users must not post information that might reveal the nation's secrets, subvert the sovereign, impair national unification, or stain the nation's reputation. Internet service providers must keep all posted information, including senders' IP addresses or domain names for at least 60 days in case of investigation by 'certain governmental institutions'. Within QGLT, all postings are under the supervision of professional journalists who have been well-trained to keep online discussion on the 'right' track. Inappropriate postings like negative comments on national leaders are deleted; malign comments like supporting Tibet's or Taiwan's independence will result in the closedown of users' IDs or even the blocking of IPs.

Forming a contrast is the government's rather loose control over nationalism rhetoric online. Chinese public has been turning to bulletin boards to vent their nationalists' ranting over Japanese government's denial of the Nanjing Massacre and Japanese top officials' annual visit to the Yasukuni shrine worshiping the WWII War criminals. Apart from the call for boycotting Japanese commodities found on most Chinese bulletin boards, online nationalism discourse can go beyond rationality and turn into in hostility against Japan and aggressive sentiment over reunification with Taiwan. Thus, Hughes claims that the Communist Party has been using information communication technologies to 'mobilize nationalism to legitimate its own claim to power' (2002: 218). Such manipulation of online public opinion has been noticed by QGLT users. Dave's experience showed that when online public opinion coincides with the Communist Party's interest, the government usually use public opinion to justify their course; but when online public opinion goes against the Party's interest, public opinion will go silent in cyberspace (interview 18 April 2005).

Nationalist fervour also takes the form of flaming among users, thwarting rational critical political discussion. Political opinions different from nationalists' are labelled as 'betrayal'. Users who post pro-Japan or pro-USA opinions are called 'running dogs' and 'boot-lickers' of foreign powers, and even receive threatening messages, virtual stalking and hacking. The 'people's public use of their reason' (Habermas, 1989: 28) is key to the ideal public sphere. However, within QGLT, the public use of their reason still needs an appropriate social mechanism to regulate so that a compromised consensus can be achieved.

Another potential danger for the virtual public sphere is the speeding up commercialisation. Improving the general living standard in China, the economic reform is also widening the gap between the rich and the poor both in terms of property and information. The digital divide can demise the equal participation into electronic deliberation. Meanwhile, the opening-up policy in China invited multinational media tycoons like Microsoft, Yahoo, News Corp. and Disney as foreign investors. The virtual public sphere in Greater China faces the risk of degradation under the joint forces of political administration and global capitalism.

## Conclusion: bonding in the virtual public sphere

To a certain extent, equality in social intercourse, discussion over the common concern, and more comprehensive political participation have been partially achieved online in China. There is clear evidence that some common concerns from users such as policies regarding environment protection and agriculture were later embodied in government policies. With a growing tolerance towards politically 'constructive' suggestions, the Communist Party's tight control over communication might relax to a certain degree through citizens' involvement in political discussion. Meanwhile, Chinese diaspora's participation on Mainland-based bulletin boards has been creating a spiritual bonding, which contributes to solve problems like regional conflict and human rights abuse at the global level. To be specific, the contribution of internet bulletin boards to the constructing of a virtual public sphere in Greater China lies in the following aspects:

Firstly, public access to rational critical discussions over current issues in Greater China breaks down the Communist Party's control over press freedom by voicing grassroots public opinion, and has the potential of reversing the relationship between individuals and centralized power.

Secondly, QGLT and other internet bulletin boards are regarded by users as venues for exchanging ideas and contesting viewpoints. Online discussion based on equality promotes a gradual shift from the media's function as the Party's 'mouthpiece' to a public forum where rationality in political debate will pave the way to deliberative democracy.

Finally, a virtual-real interactive community brings about an alternative to peaceful assembly that is still lacking in the real political life in Mainland China. Cyberactivism is demonstrated in the active exploration of bulletin boards and other online communities by social movements groups, research bodies, NGOs, and so on across the geopolitical region of China, which might eventually reshape the political culture in the Mainland.

Though one has to admit that patriotism and nationalism demonstrated on QGLT are more in the Communist Party's interest, but at the same time, a manifestation of humanism and longing for democracy are also displayed within QGLT discussion. Thus, a 'public' resembling the characteristics of the public in late Eighteenth Century Europe is forming online in China and their enthusiasm in political participation can potentially lead to the tension between people and the state.

## Notes

1. 'Brief Introduction of www.people.com.cn', http://www.people.com.cn/GB/other7018/7019/20011213/626152.html [accessed: 12 Feb. 2003].
2. Ibid.
3. Ibid.
4. The concept of Greater China emerged in the 1980s and has been bearing different economical and political implications ever since. In this paper, it is used to refer to a civic sphere within which global Chinese bonded together with shared culture and language.
5. On 13–15 May, 1998, riots broke out across Indonesia after four students were fatally shot by security forces during an anti-government demonstration in Jakarta. Then looting and destruction of properties against the ethnic Chinese minority started to surface. 1229 Chinese died (including 31 missing) and at least 168 girls and women were raped with quite a proportion of gang-rape in public. President B. J. Habibie, at first denied the atrocities, later he disputed that the May Riots were racially motivated, and implied that those ethnic Chinese victims were attacked because 'they didn't give to the community' during his interviewed with the *Business Week* (3 August 1998). See also http://members.fortunecity.com/dikigoros/indonesatroc.htm [accessed: 24 Nov. 2004].
6. To protect my interviewees, I replaced some QGLT user pennames with common English names.
7. 'Understanding the WTO Basics: Principles of the Trade Systems' http://www wto.org/english/thewto_e/whatis_e/tif_e/fact2_e.html [accessed: 24 Nov. 2004].
8. http://www.huaren.org/diaspora/asia/indonesia/yelrib.shtml [accessed: 24 Nov. 2004].
9. 'Protest against atrocities targeting Chinese' http://wenhua.jztele.com/may/007.html [accessed: 24 Nov. 2004].

10. *Regulations of custody and repatriation of Wanderers and Beggars in Cities* had been put into effect since 12 May 1982. This system had been used increasingly to detain migrant workers, who come from rural area to the cities in search for employment. Others detained include beggars, vagrants and others with no fixed residence or regular employment, including people who are disabled or mentally challenged and homeless children beggars. People held in the transfer centres have to pay for their food and accommodation and for their transportation to their origin place. Those who cannot pay are forced to work instead. Many are reportedly held in such centres for months without prospect of release because they have no money and no relatives or friends to bail them out. The system effectively permits the arbitrary detention of individuals who are not suspected of committing any crime. See 'China: migrant worker dies in custody', http://web.amnesty.org/wire/July2003/China [accessed: 24 Nov. 2004].

11. 'Chinese Protest Online', *Human Rights Watch*, http://www.hrw.org/campaigns/china/beijing08/voices.htm [accessed: 24 Nov. 2004].

12. Professor He is one of the Chinese legal scholars who wrote to the Standing Committee of the National People's Congress (NPC) in May 2003 asking for a review of *Regulations of Custody and Repatriation of Wanderers and Beggars in Cities* for its human rights violation. He and other legal scholars also urged the NPC to abolish temporary residence permits and reform the migrant detention centers.

13. 'China: 10 snapshots in 2003' http://www.china-embassy.org/eng/gyzg/t57916.thm [accessed: 24 Jan. 2006].

14. 'NGOs getting more prominence', http://news.xinhuanet.com/english/2005-04/22/content_2862677.htm [accessed: 24 Nov. 2004].

15. 'Nujiang Salween River', http://www.irn.org/programs/China [accessed: 24 Nov. 2004].

16. See note 13.

# References

(1911) 'Motion Pictures', *The Outlook* 98: 381–3.

(1911) 'The Moving-Picture Shows', *Harper's Weekly*: 6.

Abercrombie, N. and Longhurst, B. (1998) *Audiences: A Sociological Theory of Performance and Imagination* (London: Sage).

About Big Noise, retrieved 25 Nov. 2002, from www.bignoisefilms.com/about.htm

Abramowitz, A. (1978) 'The Impact of a Presidential Debate on Voter Rationality', *American Journal of Political Science*, 22(3): 680–90.

Ackerman, S. (2005) 'Where Is the Brave New Digital World?' *Guardian* (Media section) 14 February, p.7.

Adorno, T. *et al*. (1950) *The Authoritarian Personality* (New York: Harper).

Ala-Fossi, M. and Stavitsky, A. (2003) 'Understanding IBOC: Digital Technology for Analog Economics', *Journal of Radio Studies* 10(1): 63–79.

Almond, G. and Verba, S. (1963) *The Civic Culture* (Princeton: Princeton University Press).

Alterman, E. (1992) *Sound and Fury: The Washington Punditocracy and the Collapse of American Politics* (New York: Harper-Collins).

Ambikairajah, E., David, A. and Wong, W. (1997) 'Auditory Masking and MPEG-1 Audio Compression', *Electronics and Communication Engineering Journal*, Aug.: 165–75.

Anderson, B. (1983, 1991) *Imagined Communities: Reflections on the Origin and Spread of Nationalism*, rev. edn (London and New York: Verso).

Anderson, K. and Goldson, A. (1993) 'Alternating Currents: Alternative Television Inside and Outside of the Academy, *Social Text*, 35: 56–71.

Ang, I. (1985) *Watching Dallas: Soap Opera and the Melodramatic Imagination* (London: Routledge).

Anonymous (Patten, S.) (1909) 'Amusement as a Factor in Man's Spiritual Uplift', *Current Literature: Religion and Ethics*: 185–8.

Ardvisson, A. (2006) *Brands: Meaning and Value in Media Culture* (London and New York: Routledge).

Arendt, Hannah (1958) *The Human Condition* (Chicago: University of Chicago Press).

Aslama, M. and M. Pantti (2006) 'Talking Alone: Reality TV, Emotions and Authenticity', *European Journal of Cultural Studies*, 9(2): 149–66.

Atton, C. (2002) *Alternative Media* (Thousand Oaks: Sage Publications).

Axford, B. and Huggins, R. (eds) (2001) *New Media and Politics* (London: Sage).

Bagdikian, B. H. (2004) *The New Media Monopoly* (Boston: Beacon Press).

Bakardjieva, M. and Smith, R. (2001) 'The Internet in Everyday Life: Computer Networking From the Standpoint of the Domestic User', *New Media & Society*, 3(1): 67–84.

Bale, J. (1993) *Sport, Space and the City* (London: Routledge).

Ball-Rokeach, S. J. (1985) 'The Origins of Individual Media-system Dependency', *Communication Research*, 12(4): 485–510.

Ball-Rokeach, S. J. (2001) 'Storytelling Neighborhood: Paths to Belonging in Diverse Urban Environments', *Communication Research*, 28(4): 392–428.

Barnard, S. (2000) *Studying Radio* (London: Arnold).

Barnhurst, K. G. (1998) 'Politics in the Fine Meshes: Young Citizens, Power & Media', *Media, Culture & Society*, 20(3): 201–18.

Baym, G. (2005) 'The Daily Show: Discursive Integration and the Reinvention of Political Journalism', *Political Communication*, 22: 259–76.

Baym, N. (2000) *Tune in, Log on: Soaps, Fandom, and Online Community* (Thousand Oaks, CA: Sage).

BBC (1928) *New Ventures In Broadcasting* (London: BBC).

BBC (1932) *Wireless Discussion Groups* (London: BBC).

BBC (2000) *English Regions Annual Review 1999/2000* (London: BBC).

BBC Written Archives Centre (WAC) R14/120/4 Central Council For Broadcast Adult Education, Executive Committee Papers, May–December 1931, File 4.

BBC Written Archives Centre (WAC) R14/124 Central Council For Broadcast Adult Education: Programmes and Publications Sub-Committee Papers, 1928–34.

Beck, U. (1992) *Risk Society: Towards a New Modernity* (London: Sage).

Benhabib, S. (1996) 'Towards a Deliberative Model of Democratic Legitimacy', in S. Benhabib (ed.), *Democracy and Difference* (Princeton, Princeton University Press), pp. 67–94.

Bennett, L. (1998) 'The Un-civic Culture: Communication, Identity, and the Rise of Lifestyle Politics', *PS: Political Science and Politics*, 31(4): 740–61.

Bennett, T. (1992) 'Useful Culture', *Cultural Studies*, 6(3): 395–408.

Bennett, W.L. (2001) *News: The Politics of Illusion*, 4th edn (New York: Longman).

Benoit, W., McKinney, M. and Stephenson, M. (2002) 'Effects of Watching Primary Debates in the 2000 U.S. Presidential Campaign', *Journal of Communication*, 52: 316–31.

Bentivegna, D. (2002) 'Politics and New Media', in L. Lievrouw and S. Livingstone (eds), *The Handbook of New Media* (London: Sage), pp. 50–61.

Bergström, A. (2005) 'nyhetsvanor.nu: Nyhetsanvändning på internet 1998–2003', [newshabits.nu: The use of news on the Internet 1998–2003] dissertation (Göteborg: JMG, Göteborgs universitet).

Berridge, V. S. (1976) '*Popular Journalism and Working Class Attitudes* 1854–1886: *a Study of Reynolds' Newspaper,* Lloyd's Weekly Newspaper *and the Weekly Times'* PhD thesis (London: University of London).

Berry, N. (2002) *Articles of Faith: The Story of British Intellectual Journalism* (London: Waywiser Press).

Bird, S. E. (1992), *For Enquiring Minds: a Cultural Study of Supermarket Tabloids* (Knoxville: University of Tennessee Press).

Bodroghkozy, A. (2001) *Groove Tube: Sixties Television and the Youth Rebellion* (Durham: Duke University Press).

Bordwell, D., Staiger, J. and Thompson, K. (1985). *The Classical Hollywood Cinema: Film Style and Mode of Production to 1960* (New York, Columbia University Press).

Bourdieu, P. (1979, 1984) *Distinction: A Social Critique of the Judgment of Taste* (Cambridge, MA: Harvard University Press).

Boyce, G. (1978) 'The Fourth Estate: the reappraisal of a concept' in Boyce, G., Curran, J. and Wingate, P. (eds) (1978) *Newspaper History: From the 17th Century to the Present Day* (London: Sage), pp. 19–40.

Brake, L. (1988) 'The Old Journalism and the New: Forms of Cultural Production in London in the 1880s', in Wiener, J. H. (ed.), *Papers for the Millions: The New Journalism in Britain, 1850s to 1914* (New York: Greenwood Press), pp. 1–24.

Brecht, B. (2000 [1932]) 'The Radio as a Communications Apparatus', In *Brecht on Film and Radio*, trans. and ed. M. Silberman (London: Methuen).

Brecht, B. (2000) 'Radio – an Antediluvian Invention?', previously unpublished 1927 typescript in *Brecht on Film & Radio*, Marc Silberman trans and ed. (London: Methuen).

Brick, H. (1998). *Age of Contradiction: American Thought and Culture in the 1960s* (Ithaca: Cornell University Press).

Briggs, A. (1961) *The History of Broadcasting in the United Kingdom, Volume One: The Birth of Broadcasting, 1896–1927* (Oxford: Oxford University Press).

Briggs, A. (1965) *The History of Broadcasting in the United Kingdom, Volume Two: The Golden Age of Wireless* (London: Oxford University Press).

Bromell, N. (2000) *Tomorrow Never Knows: Rock and Psychedelics in the 1960s* (Chicago: University of Chicago Press).

Brown, L. (1985) *Victorian News and Newspapers* (Oxford: Clarendon Press).

Brown, P. (2002) 'Commercial Radio Welcomes Communications Bill Announcement', *CRCA press release*, 14 Nov.

Brown, P. (2004) 'CRCA Welcomes New Report Which Concludes: Radio Mergers Are Not Substantial', *CRCA press release*, 10 Feb.

Buckingham, D. (1997) 'News Media, Political Socialization and Popular Citizenship: Towards a New Agenda', *Critical Studies in Mass Communication*, 14: 344–66.

Buckley, S. (1995) 'Digital Audio Broadcasting: the Politics of a New Technology', *InteRadio* 6(1): 9.

Bull, P. and Mayer, K. (1993) 'How Not To Answer Questions in Political Interviews', *Political Psychology*, 14: 651–66.

Bulmer, M., K. Bales *et al.* (1991) 'The Social Survey in Historical Perspective', *The Social Survey in Historical Perspective 1880–1940*, in K. Sklar (ed.) (Cambridge, Cambridge University Press), pp. 1–48.

Burawoy, M. (2003) 'For a Sociological Marxism: the Complementary Convergence of Antonio Gramsci and Karl Polanyi', *Politics and Society*, 31:2, June: 193–261.

Calhoun, C. (ed.) (1992) *Habermas and the Public Sphere* (Cambridge, MA: MIT Press).

Camporesi, V. (1994) 'The BBC and American Broadcasting, 1922–55', in *Media, Culture & Society*, 16: 625–39.

Cantril, H. (1940) *The Invasion from Mass: A Study in the Psychology of Panic* (Princeton, NJ: Princeton University Press).

Cantril, H. and Allport, G. (1935) *The Psychology of Radio* (New York: Harper and Brothers).

Cappella, J. N. and Jamieson, K. H. (1997) *Spiral of Cynicism. The Press and the Public Good* (New York: Oxford University Press).

Carey, J. W. (1989) *Communication as Culture: Essays on Media and Society* (Boston: Unwin Hyman).

Carter, S. (2004) 'Ofcom Receives 192 Applications for Community Radio Licences', *Ofcom press release*, 6 Dec.

Castells, M. (2000) *The Rise of the Network Society*, 2nd edn (Oxford: Blackwell).

Castells, M. (1998) *End of Millennium* (Oxford: Backwell).

Castells, M. (2001) The Internet Galaxy: Reflections on the Internet, Business, and Society (Oxford: Oxford University Press).

Chaffee, S., Zhao, X. and Leshner, G. (1994) 'Political Knowledge and the Campaign Media of 1992', *Communication Research*, 21: 305–24.

Chalaby, J. K. (1998) *The Invention of Journalism* (Basingstoke: Palgrave Macmillan).

Chen, T. X. and Deng, L. F. (2002) 'The Form and the Decline of BBS Topic: a Case Study of the Qiangguo Luntan of www.people.com.cn', in *Journalism and Communication Research*, No. 1: 11–26. [in Chinese]

Chippindale, P. and Horrie, C. (1999) *Stick It Up Your Punter!: the Uncut Story of the Sun Newspaper* (London: Simon & Schuster).

Clarke, A. (2003) *Natural-Born Cyborgs: Minds, Technologies, and the Future of Human Intelligence* (Oxford: Oxford University Press).

Clarke, John (1990) 'Populism and Pessimism' in R. Butsch (ed.), *For Fun and Profit: The Transformation of Leisure into Consumption* (Philadelphia: Temple University Press).

Clarke, P. (1996) *Deep Citizenship* (London: Pluto).

Cohen, J. (1996) 'Procedure and Substance in Deliberative Democracy', in S. Benhabib (ed.), *Democracy and Difference* (Princeton, Princeton University Press), pp. 95–119.

Coleman, S. (2003) *A Tale of Two Houses: The House of Commons, the Big Brother House and the People at Home* (London: Hansard Society).

Coleman, S. (2005) 'The Lonely Citizen: Indirect Representation in an Age of Networks', *Political Communication*, 22(2): 197–214.

Collier, J. (1908) 'Cheap Amusements', *Charities and the Commons*, XX: 73–6.

Collier, J. (1910) 'Moving Pictures: Their Function and Proper Regulation', *The Playground*, IV: 233.

Collins, R. (1993) 'Public Service versus the Market Ten Years on: Reflections on Critical Theory and Debate on Broadcasting Policy in the UK', *Screen*, 34(3): 243–59.

Conboy, M. (2002) *The Press and Popular Culture* (London: Sage).

Conboy, M. (2004) *Journalism: A Critical History* (London: Sage).

Connell, I. (1992) 'Personalities in the Popular Media', in P. Dahlgren and C. Sparks (eds), *Journalism and Popular Culture* (London: Sage), pp. 64–83.

Connell, I. (1998) 'Mistaken Identities: Tabloid and Broadsheet News Discourse', *Javnost: the Public*, 5(3): 11–31.

Corner, J. (2004) 'Afterword: Framing the New', in S. Holmes and D. Jermyn (eds), *Understanding Reality Television* (London: Routledge), pp. 290–9.

Couldry, N. (2000) *Inside Culture* (London: Sage).

Couldry, N., Livingstone, S. and Markham, T. (forthcoming) *Media Consumption and Public Engagement: Beyond the Presumption of Attention* (Basingstoke: Palgrave Macmillan).

Coyer, K. (2005) 'If It Leads It Bleeds: the Participatory Newsmaking of the Independent Media Centre', in W. deJong, M. Shaw, and N. Stammers (eds), *Global Activism, Global Media* (Ann Arbor: Pluto Press).

Cranfield, G. A. (1978) *The Press and Society: From Caxton to Northcliffe* (London: Longman).

Crisell, A. (2002) *An Introductory History of British Broadcasting*, 2nd edn (London: Routledge).

Crossley, N. (2004) 'On Systematically Distorted Communication to Bowdien and the Socio-analysis of publics', in N. Crossley and J.M. Roberts (eds), *After-Habermas: New Perspectives on the Public Sphere* (Oxford, Blackwell).

Crossley, N. and Roberts, J. M. (eds) (2004) *After Habermas: New Perspectives on the Public Sphere* (Oxford: Blackwell).

Curran, J. (1991) 'Rethinking the Media as a Public Sphere', in P. Dahlgren and C. Sparks (eds), *Communication and Citizenship: Journalism and the Public Sphere in the New Media Age* (London: Routledge), pp. 27–57.

Curran, J. (2000) 'Rethinking Media and Democracy' in J. Curran and M. Gurevitch, eds, *Mass Media and Society*, 3rd edn (London: Arnold, 2000).

Curran, J. and Seaton J. (2003) *Power Without Responsibility: the Press, Broadcasting and New Media in Britain*, 6th edn (London: Routledge).

Dahlberg, L. (2001a) 'The Internet and Democratic Discourse: Exploring the Prospects of Online Deliberative Forums Extending the Public Sphere', *Information, Communication and Society*, 4(4): 615–33.

Dahlberg, L. (2001b) 'Democracy Via Cyberspace: Examining the Rhetoric and Practises of Three Prominent Camps', *New Media & Society*, 3(2): 157–77.

Dahlgren, P. (1997) *Television and the Public Sphere: Citizenship, Democracy and the Media* (London: Sage).

Dahlgren, P. (1987) 'Ideology and Information in the Public Sphere', in J.D. Slack and F. Fejes (eds), *The Ideology of the Information Age* (Norwood, NJ: Ablex).

Dahlgren, P. (1988) 'What's the Meaning of This?: Viewers' Plural Sensemaking of TV News', *Media, Culture, and Society*, vol. 10, no.3, July.

Dahlgren, P. (1991) 'Introduction', in Peter Dahlgren and Colin Sparks (eds), *Communication and Citizenship: Journalism and the Public Sphere* (London and New York: Routledge), pp. 1–26.

Dahlgren, P. (1995) *Television and the Public Sphere: Citizenship, Democracy, and the Media* (London: Sage).

Dahlgren, P. (2000) 'Media, Citizenship and Civic Culture', in J. Curran and M. Gurevitch (eds), *Mass Media and Society*, 3rd edn (London: Arnold), pp. 310–28.

Dahlgren, P. (2002). 'In Search of the Talkative Public: Media, Deliberative Democracy and Civic Culture', *Javnost – The Public* 9(3): 5–26

Dahlgren, P. (2003) 'Reconfiguring Civic Culture in the New Media Milieu', in J. Curran and Pels, D. (eds), *Media and the Restyling of Politics: Consumerism, Celebrity and Cynicism* (London: Sage), pp. 151–70.

Dalton, D. and Cott, J. (1970) 'The Million Dollar Bash', *Rolling Stone*, 3 Sept. pp. 30–4.

Darnton, R. (2000) 'An Early Information Society: News and Media in Eighteenth-Century Paris', *American Historical Review*, 105(1): 1–35.

Dayan, D. (2005) 'Mothers, Midwives and Abortionists: Genealogy, Obstetrics, Audiences and Publics', S. Livingstone (ed.) *Audiences and Publics: When Cultural Engagement Matters for the Public Sphere* (Bristol, UK: Intellect), pp. 43–76.

Dayan, D. and Katz, E. (1992) *Media Events: The Live Broadcasting of History* (Cambridge, MA: Harvard University Press).

de Jong, W. and Stammers, N. (eds) (2005) *Global Activism, Global Media* (London: Pluto).

de Witt, P. (2005) Interview with author, 26 Feb.

DeBeer, D. (1909) 'Vaudettes', *The Banner*: 636–7.

DeKoven, M. (2004) *Utopia Limited: The Sixties and the Emergence of the Postmodern* (Durham, NC: Duke University Press).

Democracy Now!, retrieved 15 Nov. 2002, from www.democracynow.org/about.htm

Dewey, J. (1927) *The Public and Its Problems* (New York: Henry Holt).

Dewey, J. (1934) *Art as Experience* (New York: Minton, Balch & Co).

Dörner, A. (2001) *Politainment. Politik in der medialen Erlebnisgesellschaft* (Frankfurt: Suhrkamp).

Douglas, S. (2004) *Listening In: Radio and the American Imagination* (Minneapolis, MN: University of Minnesota Press).

Dovey, J. (2000) *Freakshows: First Person Media and Factual Television* (London: Pluto Press).

Downing, J. (1984) *Radical Media: The Political Experience of Alternative Communication* (Boston. South End Press).

Downing, J. (1995) 'Alternative Media and the Boston Tea Party', in J. Downing, A. Mohammadi and A. Sreberny-Mohammadi (eds), *Questioning the Media: a Critical Introduction* (Thousand Oaks: Sage), pp. 184–203.

Downing, J. (2001) *Radical Media: Rebellious Communication and Social Movements* (Thousand Oaks, CA: Sage Publications).

Downing, J. (2003a) 'The Independent Media Center Movement and the Anarchist Socialist Tradition', in N. Couldry and J. Curran (eds), *Contesting Media Power: Alternative Media in a Networked World* (Boulder: Rowman & Littlefield), pp. 243–58.

Downing, J. (2003b) 'The IMC Movement Beyond "the West"', in A. Opel and D. Pompper (eds), *Representing Resistance: Media, Civil Disobedience, and the Global Justice Movement* (London: Praeger), pp. 241–58.

Downing, John D.H. (2001) *Radical Media: Rebellious Communication and Social Movements* (Thousand Oaks: Sage Publications).

Drew, D. and Weaver, D. (1993) 'Voter Learning in the 1990 Off-Year Election: Did the Media Matter?', *Journalism Quarterly*, 70: 356–68.

Drew, J. (1995) 'Media Activism and Radical Democracy', in J. Brook and I. Boal (eds), *Resisting the Virtual Life: The Cultural Politics of Information* (San Francisco: City Lights), pp. 71–83.

DRM (2005) 'DRM Votes To Extend Its System to 120 MHz', *DRM Consortium press release*, 10 Mar.

Duke, V. and Crolley, L. (1996) *Football, Nationality and the State* (Harlow: Longman).

Duncan, T. (2002, 2005) *Principles of Advertising and IMC*, 2nd edn (New York: McGraw Hill/Irwin).

Dunne, Murphy (1970) 'Letter', *Rolling Stone*, 15 Oct., p. 3.

Durlin, M. and Melio, C. (2003) 'The Grassroots Radio Movement in the United States', in M. P. McCauley *et al.* (eds), *Public Broadcasting and the Public Interest* (Armonk, NY: M.E. Sharpe), pp. 252–64.

Eaton, W. P. (1915) 'Class-Consciousness and the "Movies" ', *The Atlantic Monthly*, 115: 48–56.

Eide, M. and Knight, G. (1999) 'Public/Private Service: Service Journalism and the Problems of Everyday Life', *European Journal of Communication*, 14(4): 525–47.

Eley, G. (1992) 'Nations, Publics, and Political Cultures:Placing Habermas in the Nineteenth Century', in C. Calhoun (ed.), *Habermas and the Public Sphere*, 6th edn (Cambridge MA.: MIT Press), pp. 289–339.

Eliasoph, N. (1998) *Avoiding Politics: How Americans Produce Apathy in Everyday Life* (Cambridge: Cambridge University Press).

Elliott, A. (1999) *The Mourning of John Lennon* (Berkeley: University of California Press).

Elliott, P. (1978) 'Professional Ideology and Organisational Change: the Journalist Since 1800', in G. Boyce, J. Curran and P. Wingate (eds), *Newspaper History: From the 17th Century to the Present Day* (London: Sage), pp. 172–91.

Elshtain, J. (1997) 'The Displacement of Politics' in J. Weintraub and K. Kumar (eds), *Public and Private in Thought and Practice* (Chicago: Chicago University Press), pp. 166–81.

Emery, E. and Emery, M. (1978) *The Press and America: an Interpretative History of the Mass Media* (Englewood Cliffs, NJ: Prentice-Hall).

Emirbayer, M. and Sheller, M. (1999) 'Publics in History', *Theory and Society*, 28, 145–97.

Engel, M. (1996) *Tickle the Public: One Hundred Years of the Popular Press* (London: Indigo).

Esser, Frank (1999) ' "Tabloidization" of News: a Comparative Analysis of Anglo-American and German Press Journalism', *European Journal of Communication*, 14(3): 291–324.

Evans, P. and Wurster, T.E. (2000) *Blown To Bits: How the New Economics of Information Transforms Strategy* (Boston, MA: Harvard Business School Press).

Fenton, N. and Downey, J. (2005) 'Counter Public Spheres and Global Modernity', *Javnost – the Public*, 10(1), 15–32.

Ferree, M.M., Gamson, W., Gerhards, J. and Rucht, D. (2002) *Shaping Abortion Discourse: Democracy and the Public Sphere in Germany and the United States* (Cambridge: Cambridge University Press).

Fiske, J. (1989) *Understanding Popular Culture* (Boston: Unwin Hyman).

Fisher, R. B. (1974) 'The People's Institute of New York City, 1987–1934: Culture, Progressive Democracy, and the People', PhD dissertation (New York: New York University) p. 468.

Fiske, J. (1992a) 'The Cultural Economy of Fandom', in L. A. Lewis (ed.), *The Adoring Audience* (London: Routledge).

Fiske, J. (1992b) 'Popularity and the Politics of Information', in P. Dahlgren and C. Sparks (eds), *Journalism and Popular Culture* (London: Sage), pp. 45–63.

Fortunati, L. (2005) 'Mediatization of the Net and Internetization of the Mass Media', in *Gazette: the International Journal for Communication Studies*, 67(1): 27–44.

Foucault, M. (1991) 'Governmentality', in G. Burchell, C. Gordon and P. Miller (eds), *The Foucault Effect: Studies in Governmentality* (University of Chicago Press), pp. 87–104.

Frank, T. (1997) *The Conquest of Cool: Business Culture, Counterculture and the Rise of Hip Consumerism* (Chicago, IL: University of Chicago Press).

Franklin, B. (1997) *Newzak and News Media* (London: Arnold).

Fraser, N. (1989) 'What's Critical About Critical Theory?: The Case of Habermas and Gender' in N. Fraser (ed.), *Unruly Practices: Power, Discourse, and Gender in Contemporary Social Theory* (Minneapolis, MN: University of Minnesota Press).

Fraser, N. (1992) 'Rethinking the Public Sphere: a Contribution to the Critique of Actually Existing Democracy', in Calhoun, C. (ed.), *Habermas and the Public Sphere* (Cambridge, Mass.: Massachusetts Institute of Technology Press), pp. 109–42.

Frazer, E., 'Teenage Girls Reading Jackie', *Media, Culture, and Society*, Vol. 9 (1987): 407–25.

Friedland, L. A., Hove, T. and Rojas, H. (2006) 'The Networked Public Sphere', *Javnost – The Public*, 13(4).

Friedland, L. A., Lang, C., Kim, N. and Shin, J. (2006) 'The Construction of the Local Public Sphere School Conflict in Madison, Wisconsin', Association for Education in Journalism and Mass Communication, San Francisco.

Friedrichs, J. (1994) 'Stresemannstraße! Eine Fallstudie zur Dynamik sozialen Protests', *Kölner Zeitschrift für Soziologie und Sozialpsychologie*, Sonderheft, 34: 359–74.

Frisch, M. (1996) 'Woodstock and Altamont', in William Graebner (ed.), *True Stories From the American Past, Volume II: Since 1865* (New York: McGraw-Hill).

Frith, Simon (1981) *Sound Effects: Youth, Leisure, and the Politics of Rock 'n' Roll* (New York: Pantheon).

Fruchter, J. (n.d.) 'FSTV Ups the Ante: Fed Up with Mainstream Media's Coverage, Media Activists Continue To Rise Up and Report the Otherwise Unreported', retrieved 2.25.2006 from www.boulderweekly.com/archive/101002/newsspin.html.

Furedi, F. (2004) *Therapy Culture: Cultivating Vulnerability in an Uncertain Age* (London: Routledge).

Gamson, J. (1998) *Freaks Talk Back: Tabloid Talk Shows and Sexual Nonconformity* (Chicago: University of Chicago Press).

Gamson, J. (1999) 'Taking the Talk Show Challenge: Television, Emotion, and Public Spheres', *Constellations* 6 (2): 190–205.

Gamson, W. A. (1992) *Talking Politics* (New York: Cambridge University Press).

Gandy, O. (2002) 'The Real Digital Divide: Citizens Versus Consumers', in L. Lievrouw and S. Livingstone (eds), *The Handbook of New Media* (London: Sage), pp. 448–60.

Gaonkar, D. P. and Kamrath, C. (1999) 'Genealogy: Lincoln Steffens on New York', in J. Holston (ed.), *Cities and Citizenship* (Durham: Duke University Press), pp. 139–54.

Gardiner, M. E. (2004), Wild publics and grotesque symposiums: Habermas and Bakhtin on dialogue, everyday life and the public sphere. In N. Crossley and J. Michael Roberts (eds), *After Habermas: New Perspectives on the Public Sphere* (Malden, MA: Blackwell).

Garnham, N. (1992) 'The Media and the Public Sphere', in Calhoun, C. (ed.), *Habermas & the Public Sphere* (Cambridge, MA: Massachusetts Institute of Technology Press), pp 359–76.

Gary, B. (1999) *The Nervous Liberals: Propaganda Anxiety from World War I to the Cold War* (New York: Columbia University Press).

Gauntlett, D. and Hill, A. (1999) *TV Living* (London: Routledge).

Gerhards, J. (1993) *Neue Konfliktlinien in der Mobilisierung öffentlicher Meinung* (Opladen: Westdeutscher Verlag).

Gerhards, J. (1997) 'Diskursive versus liberale Öffentlichkeit. Eine empirische Auseinandersetzung mit Jürgen Habermas', *Kölner Zeitschrift für Soziologie und Sozialpsychologie* 49(1): 1–34.

Gerhards, J. and Neidhardt, F. (1991), 'Strukturen und Funktionen moderner Öffentlichkeit. Fragestellungen und Ansätze', in Müller-Dohm, S. and Neumann-Braun, K. (eds), *Öffentlichkeit, Kultur, Massenkommunikation* (Oldenburg: BIS), pp. 31–89.

Gerhards, J., Neidhardt, F. and Rucht, D. (1998) *Zwischen Palaver und Diskurs: Strukturen öffentlicher Meinungsbildung am Beispiel der deutschen Diskussion zur Abtreibung.* (Opladen, Wiesbaden: Westdeutscher Verlag).

Geuss, R. (2001) *Public Goods Private Goods* (Princeton: Princeton University Press).

Giddens, A. (1991) *Modernity and Self-Identity: Self and Society in the Late Modern Age* (Cambridge: Polity Press).

Gilligan, C. (1993) *In a Different Voice: Psychological Theory and Women's Development*, 2nd edn (Cambridge, MA: Harvard University Press).

Giner, S. (1976) *Mass Society* (New York: Academic Press).

Gitlin, T. (1980) *The Whole World is Watching. Mass Media in the Making and Unmaking of the New Left* (Berkeley: University of California Press).

Gitlin, T. (1991) 'Bites and Blips: Chunk News, Savvy Talk and the Bifurcation of American Politics', in P. Dahlgren and C. Spark (eds), *Communication and Citizenship: Journalism and the Public Sphere* (London/New York: Routledge), pp. 119–36.

Gitlin, T. (1998) 'Public Sphere or Public Sphericules?' in T. Liebes and J. Curran (eds), *Media Ritual and Identity* (London, Routledge).

Gloag, K. (2001) 'Situating the 1960s: Popular Music – Postmodernism – History', *Rethinking History* 5, Winter, pp. 397–410.

Glynn, K. (2000) *Tabloid Culture: Trash Taste, Popular Power, and the Transformation of American Television* (London: Duke University Press).

Goffman, E. (1974) *Frame Analysis: An Essay on the Organization of Experience*, 1986 edn (Boston: Northeastern University Press).

Gordon, M. (1973) 'The Social Survey Movement and Sociology in the United States', *Social Problems* 21(2): autumn: 284–98.

Gorman, P. (1996) *Left Intellectuals and Popular Culture in Twentieth Century America* (Chapel Hill, NC: University of North Carolina Press).

Graber, D. A., Bimber, B., Bennett, W. L., Davis, R. and Norris, P. (2004) 'The Internet and Politics: Emerging Perspectives', in H. Nissenbaum and M. E. Price (eds), *Academy and the Internet* (New York: Peter Lang), pp. 90–119.

Greenberg, B., Sherry, J., Busselle, R., Hnilo, L. and Smith, S. (1997) 'Daytime Television Talk Shows: Guests, Content and Interactions', in *Journal of Broadcasting and Electronic Media*, 41: 393–411.

Greene, R. W. (1999) *Malthusian Worlds: U.S. Leadership and the Governing of the Population Crisis* (Boulder, Col.: Westview Press).

Greider, W. (1992) *Who Will Tell the People: The Betrayal of American Democracy* (New York: Simon and Schuster).

Grindstaff, L. (1997) 'Producing Trash, Class and the Money Shot', in J. Lull and S. Hinerman (eds), *Media Scandals* (London: Polity Press), pp. 164–201.

Grindstaff, L. (2002) *The Money Shot: Trash, Class, and the Making of TV Talk Shows* (Chicago: The University of Chicago Press).

Gripsrud, J. (2000) 'Tabloidization, Popular Journalism and Democracy', in Colin Sparks and John Tulloch (eds), *Tabloid Tales: Global Debates Over Media Standards* (Oxford: Roman & Littlefield Publishers), pp. 285–300.

Grossberg, L. (1997) *Dancing in Spite of Myself: Essays on Popular Culture* (Durham, NC: Duke University Press).

Gunning, T. (1990) 'The Cinema of Attractions: Early Film, Its Spectator and the Avant-Garde', in Elsaesser, T. (ed.), *Early Cinema: Space, Frame, Narrative* (London, BFI), pp. 56–62.

Gunning, T. (1994) *D.W. Griffith and the Origins of the American Narrative Film: The Early Years at Biograph* (Urbana, University of Illinois Press).

Gunning, T. (1998) 'Early American Film', in J. Hill and P. C. Gibson (eds), *The Oxford Guide to Film Studies* (Oxford: Oxford University Press), pp. 255–71.

Guo, L. (2001) 'Report on a Survey into the Conditions and Influence of Internet Usage', http://www.cycnet.com.cn/ce/itre/, accessed 12 May 2004 [in Chinese].

Guo, L. (2003) '*The First Day of the Terrorist Attack on the World Trade Centre: Discussion on Qiangguo Luntan*', (ms) [in Chinese].

Habermas, J. (1962/1990) *Strukturwandel der Öffentlichkeit* (Frankfurt a M: Suhrkamp).

Habermas, J. (1981) *Theorie des Kommunikativen Handelns* (Frankfurt a M: Suhrkamp).

Habermas, J. (1984, 1987) *The Theory of Communicative Action: Lifeworld and System: A Critique of Functionalist Reason*, trans. T. McCarthy, Vols I and II (Boston: Beacon Press).

Habermas, J. (1984) (1987) *The Theory of Communicative Action*, Vols I and II (Cambridge: Polity Press).

Habermas, J. (1989). *The Structural Transformation of the Public Sphere: an Inquiry into a category of Bourgeois Society* (Cambridge, MA: MIT Press).

Habermas, J. (1996) *Between Facts and Norms: Contributions to a Discourse Theory of Law and Democracy* (Cambridge, MA: MIT Press).

Habermas, J. (2001) 'The Public Sphere', in M. Durham and D. Kellner (eds), *Media and Cultural Studies: Keywords* (Oxford: Blackwell) [Originally published 1974].

Habermas, J. (2002) 'Civil Society and the Political Public Sphere', in C. Calhoun, J. Gerteis, J. Moody, S. Pfaff and I. Virk (eds), *Contemporary Sociological Theory* (Malden, MA: Blackwell), pp. 358–76.

Habermas, J. (2006 (2001, 1989)) 'The Public Sphere: an Encyclopedia Article', *Media and Cultural Studies Keyworks*, in M. G. Durham and D. M. Kellner (eds) (Oxford: Blackwell Publishing), pp. 73–8.

Habermas, J. (1964, English trans., 1974) 'The Public Sphere: an Encyclopedia Article', *New German Critique*, 1, autumn, pp. 49–55.

Habermas, Jurgen (1992) 'Further Reflections on the Public Sphere', in C. Calhoun (ed.), *Habermas and the Public Sphere* (Cambridge, MA: The MIT Press), pp. 421–61.

Hacking, I. (1990) *The Taming of Chance* (Cambridge: Cambridge University Press).

Hague, B. and Loader B. (eds) (1999) *Digital Democracy and Decision Making in the Information Age* (London & New York: Routledge).

Hale, M., J. Musso and Weare, C. (1999) 'Developing Digital Democracy: Evidence from Californian Municipal Web pages', in B. Hague and B. Loader (eds), *Digital Democracy: Discourse and Decision Making in the Information Age* (London: Routledge), pp. 96–115.

Hall, S. (1986) 'Popular Culture and the State', in Bennett, T. *et al.* (eds), *Popular Culture and Social Relations* (Milton Keynes: Open University Press), pp 22–49.

Hall, S. and Jefferson, T. (eds) (1976) *Resistance Through Ritual: Youth Subcultures in Post-war Britain* (London: Hutchinson).

Halleck, D. D. (1984) 'Paper Tiger Television: Smashing the Myths of the Information Industry Every Week on Public Access Cable', *Media, Culture, and Society* 6, pp. 313–18.

Halleck, D. D. (2002) *Hand-held Visions: The Impossible Possibilities of Community Media* (New York: Fordham University Press).

Hallin, D. and Mancini, P. (2004) *Comparing Media Systems: Three Models of Media and Politics* (Cambridge: Cambridge University Press).

Hansen, M. (1991) *Babel & Babylon: Spectatorship in American Silent Film* (Cambridge, MA: Harvard University Press).

Harrison, S. M. (1916) *Community Action Through Surveys* (New York: Russell Sage Foundation).

Hartley, J. (1996) *Popular Reality: Journalism, Modernity, Popular Culture* (London: Arnold).

Hartley, J. (1997) 'The Sexualization of Suburbia: the Diffusion of Knowledge in the Postmodern Public Sphere', in R. Silverstone (ed.), *Visions of Suburbia* (London: Routledge).

Hartley, J. (1999) *The Uses of Television* (London: Routledge).

Harvey, S. and Robins, K. (1994) 'Voices and Places: The BBC and Regional Policy', in *Political Quarterly*, 64: 39–52.

Hassan, R. (2004) *Media, Politics and the Network Society* (Berkshire Open University Press).

Hauben, M. and Hauben, R. (1997) *Netizens: on the History and Impact of Usenet and the Internet* (Los Alamitos, CA: IEEE Computer Society Press).

He, Z. (2000) 'Working With a Dying Ideology: Dissonance and Its Reduction in Chinese Journalism', *Journalism Studies*, 1(4): 599–616.

Hebdige, D. (1979) *Subculture: The Meaning of Style* (London: Metheun).

Hendy, D. (2000) *Radio in the Global Age* (Cambridge: Polity Press).

Herbst, S. (1995) 'On Electronic Public Space. Talk Shows in Theoretical Perspective', *Political Communication*, 12: 263–74.

Herd, Harold (1952) *The March of Journalism: The Story of the British Press from 1622 to the Present Day* (London: George Allen & Unwin).

Hill, A. (2005) *Reality TV: Audiences and Popular Factual Entertainment* (London: Routledge).

Hill, K. and Hughes J. (1998) *Cyberpolitics: Citizen Activism in the Age of the Internet* (Lanham: Rowman & Littlefield).

Hill, Mike and Montag, W. (eds) (2000) *Masses, Classes, and the Public Sphere*, (London: Verso).

Hills, M. (2002) *Fan Cultures* (London: Routledge).

HMSO (1925) *Report of The Broadcasting Committee*, Cmd. 2599 (London: HMSO).

Hodgson, D. (1991) 'The Ideological Origins of the Population Association of America', *Population and Development Review*, 17: 1–26.

Hoffman, A. (1969) *Woodstock Nation* (New York: Vintage).

Hofstadter, R. (1955) *The Age of Reform* (New York, Vintage Books).

Hoijer, B. (2004) 'The Discourse of Global Compassion: The Audience and Media Reporting of Human Suffering', *Media, Culture & Society*, 26(4): 513–31.

Holmes, D. (1997) 'Introduction: Virtual Politics – Identity and Community in Cyberspace', in D. Holmes (ed.), *Virtual Politics: Identity and Community in Cyberspace* (Thousand Oaks: Sage), pp. 1–25.

Holt, R. (2004) *Dialogue on the Internet: Language, Civic Identity and Computer-Mediated Communication* (Westport: Praeger).

Holub, R.C. (1991) *Jürgen Habermas: Critic in the Public Sphere* (London: Routledge).

Horrie, C. (2003) *Tabloid Nation: From the Birth of the Mirror to the Death of the Tabloid Newspaper* (London: Andre Deutsch).

Horwitz, R. (1997) 'Broadcast Reform Revisited: Reverend Everett C. Parker and the "Standing" Case '(Office of Communication of the United Church of Christ v. Federal Communications Commission)', *The Communication Review*, 2(3). 311–48.

How To Submit Programming to FSTV', retrieved 15 Nov. 2002, from www.freespeech.org/fsitv/html/howtosubmit.shtml

Huang, Y. and Lee, C. C. (2003) 'Peddling Party Ideology for a Profit: Media and the Rise of Chinese Nationalism in the 1990s', in G. D. Rawnsley and M. T. Rawnsley, (eds), *Political Communications in Greater China* (London: Routledge), pp. 41–61.

Hughes, C. R. (2002) 'China and the Globalisation of ICTs: Implications for International Relations', *New Media & Society*, 4(2): 205–24 (Sage).

Hunter, M. and Norfolk, K. (1995) 'Digital Audio Broadcasting – How It Works', *International Broadcast Engineer*, Worldwide transmission supplement, p. 24.

Illouz, E. (2003) *Oprah Winfrey and the Glamour of Misery: An Essay on Popular Culture* (New York: Columbia University Press).

Indepen (2004) *Radio Mergers Are Not Substantial: the Impact of the Communications Act and the Enterprise Act on Radio Mergers* (London: Indepen).

Inglis, W. (1910) 'Morals and Moving Pictures', *Harper's Weekly*: 12–3.

Isin, E. and Turner, B. (2002) *Handbook of Citizenship Studies* (London: Sage).

Isin, E. and Wood, P. (1999) *Citizenship and Identity* (London: Sage).

Jacobs, Norman (ed.) (1959) *Culture for the Millions?: Mass Media in Modern Society* (Boston: Beacon Press).

Jakubowicz, K. (1991) 'Musical Chairs? The Three Public Spheres in Poland', in P. Dahlgren and C. Sparks (eds), *Communication and Citizenship* (London: Routledge), pp. 155–75.

Jankowski, N., Prehn, O. and Stappers, J. (eds) (1992) *The People's Voice: Local Radio and Television in Europe* (London: John Libbey).

Jay, Martin (1973) *The Dialectical Imagination: A History of the Frankfurt School and the Institute of Social Research 1923–1950*, (Boston: Little Brown).

Jenkins, H. (1992) *Textual Poachers: Television Fans and Participatory Culture* (New York: Routledge).

Jenkins, H. and Thorburn D. (eds) (2003) *Democracy and New Media* (Cambridge, MA.: MIT Press).

Jensen, K. B. (1990) 'The Politics of Polysemy: Television News, Everyday Consciousness and Political Action', *Media, Culture and Society*, 12: 57–77.

Jensen, K. B. (1992) 'The Politics of Polysemy: Television News, Everyday Consciousness and Political Action', in Paddy Scannel *et al.* (eds), *Culture and Power* (London: Sage).

Johannesson, Eric (2001) 'Med det nya på väg (1858–1880)' [On the way to something new (1858–1880), in K.-E. Gustafsson & Per Rydén (eds), *Den Svenska Pressens Historia. Vol II, 1830–1897*. [*History of the Swedish Press. Vol II, 1830–1897*] (Stockholm: Ekerlids), pp. 126–245.

Johansson, S. (2006) ' "Sometimes You Wanna Hate Celebrities": Tabloid Readers and Celebrity Coverage', in S. Holmes and S. Redmonds (eds), *Framing Celebrity: New Directions in Celebrity Culture* (London: Routledge) 341–58.

Jones, A. (1996) *Powers of the Press: Newspapers, Power and the Public in Nineteenth-Century England* (Aldershot: Scolar Press).

Jones, S. G. (1998) 'Information, Internet, and Community: Notes Toward an Understanding of Community in the Information Age', in S. G. Jones (ed.), *Cybersociety 2.0: Revisiting Computer-Mediated Communication and Community* (London: Sage), pp. 1–34.

Jorgensen, C. (1998) 'Public Debate – An Act of Hostility?', in *Argumentation*, 12: 431–43.

Jump, R. H. A. (1910) 'Moving Picture Statistics in New Britain, Conn', *The Moving Picture World*, 7: 1541.

Jump, H. A. (1911) *The Religious Possibilities of the Motion Picture* (New Britain, CT, South Congregational Church).

Kahn, R. and Kellner, D. (2004) 'New Media and Internet Activism: from the 'Battle of Seattle' to blogging', *New Media and Society*, 6(1): 87–95.

Kang, N. (2000) 'Civic Participation, Community Networks, and News Media: A Multi-Method Approach to Civic Participation', unpublished PhD dissertation, University of Wisconsin-Madison, Madison, WI.

Katz, E. (1992) 'On Parenting a Paradigm: Gabriel Tarde's Agenda for Opinion and Communication Research', *International Journal of Public Opinion Research*, 4(1): 80–6.

Katz, E. and Lazarsfeld, P. (1955) *Personal Influence* (New York, The Free Press).

Keane, J. (1996) *The Media and Democracy* (Cambridge: Polity Press).

Kellner, D. (1992) 'Public Access Television and the Struggle for Democracy', in J. Wasko and V. Mosco (eds), *Democratic Communications in the Information Age* (Ablex: New Jersey), pp. 100–13.

Kellner, D. (n.d.) 'Globalization, Technopolitics, and Revolution', retrieved 2.25.2006 from www.gseis.ucla.edu/faculty/kellner/kellner.html.

Kidd, D. (2003) 'Become the Media: the Global IMC Network', in A. Opel and D. Pompper (eds), *Representing Resistance: Media, Civil Disobedience, and the Global Justice Movement* (London: Praeger), pp. 234–40.

Kingsley, S. C. (1907) 'The Penny Arcade and the Cheap Theatre', *Charities and The Commons*, XVII: 295–7.

Kluge, A. and Negt, O. (1972, English trans., 1993) *Public Sphere and Experience: Toward an Analysis of the Bourgeois and Proletarian Public Sphere* (Minneapolis, MN: University of Minnesota Press).

Kornblum, W. (1959) *The Politics of Mass Society* (New York: Free Press).

Koss, S. (1981) *The Rise and Fall of the Political Press in Britain. Vol 1: The Nineteenth Century* (London: Hamish Hamilton).

Kuhlmann, C. (1999) *Die öffentliche Begründung politischen Handelns* (Opladen, Wiesbaden: Westdeutscher Verlag).

Kurtz, H. (1997) *Hot Air: All Talk, All the Time* (New York: Basic Books).

Lacey, K. (1996) *Feminine Frequencies: Gender, German Radio and the Public Sphere, 1923–1945*. (Ann Arbor, MI: University of Michigan Press).

Lanfranchi, P. and Taylor, P. (2001) *Moving With the Ball: The Migration of Professional Footballers* (Oxford: Berg).

Langer, J. (1998) *Tabloid Television: Popular Journalism and the 'Other News'* (London: Routledge).

Latour, B. (2005) *Making Things Public: Atmospheres of Democracy* (Cambridge, MA: MIT Press).

Lax, S. (2003) 'The Prospects for Digital Radio', *Information, Communication & Society* 6(3): 326–49.

Leblanc, R. (1999) *Bicycle Citizens* (Berkeley: University of California Press).

Lee, A. J. (1976) *The Origins of the Popular Press in England 1855–1914* (London: Croom Helm).

Lee, A. McClung (1937) *The Daily Newspaper in America*, (New York: Macmillan).

LeMahieu, D. L. (1988) *A Culture for Democracy: Mass Communication and the Cultivated Mind in Britain Between the Wars* (Oxford: Clarendon Press).

Leurdijk, A. (1997) 'Common Sense versus Political Discourse: Debating Racism and Multicultural Society in Dutch Talk Shows', in *European Journal of Communication*, 12(2): 147–68.

Lévy, P. (1997) *Collective Intelligence: Mankind's Emerging World in Cyberspace* trans. R. Bononno (Cambridge, MA: Perseus Books).

Lewis, J, Wahl-Jorgensen, K. and Inthorn, S. (2004) 'Images of Citizenship on Television News: Constructing a Passive Public', *Journalism Studies*, 5(2): 153–64 (Routledge).

Lewis, P. and Booth, J. (1989) *The Invisible Medium: Public, Commercial and Community Radio* (Basingstoke: Macmillan).

Li, X. G. and Qin, X. (2001) 'Who Sets the Agenda for Today's China?: Electronic Forum Reconstructs the Party's Organ's Agenda During Major News Events', in *Journalism and Communication Research*, No. 3: 55–61 [in Chinese].

Liebes, T. (1999) 'Displacing the News: The Israeli Talkshow as Public Space', in *Gazette*, 61(2): 113–25.

Lin, C. F. and Zhao, L. (2003) 'Articles from People.com.cn Strengthened the Determination of Investigation of Sun Zhigang's Murder Case', http://www.people.com.cn/GB/shehui/46/20030606/1010188.html, accessed 22 Nov. 2004 [in Chinese].

Lindvall, T. (2001) *The Silents of God: Selected Issues and Documents in Silent American Film and Religion 1908–1925* (Lanham, Maryland: The Scarecrow Press).

Link, A. S. and McCormick, R. L. (1983) *Progressivism* (Wheeling, IL, Harlan Davidson).

Lippmann, W. (1925) *The Phantom Public*, (New York: Harcourt Brace).

Lipsitz, G. (1994) 'Who'll Stop the Rain?: Youth Culture, Rock 'n' Roll, and Social Crises', in D. Farber (ed.), *The Sixties: From Memory to History* (Chapel Hill: University of North Carolina Press).

Livingstone, S. (1994) 'Watching Talk: Engagement and Gender in the Audience Discussion Programme', *Media, Culture and Society*, 16, 429–47.

Livingstone, S. (2005) (ed.) *Audiences and Publics: When Cultural Engagement Matters for the Public Sphere* (Bristol: Intellect Press).

Livingstone, S. (2005). 'On the Relation Between Audiences and Publics', in S. Livingstone (ed.), *Audiences and Publics: When Cultural Engagement Matters for the Public Sphere* (Bristol: Intellect).

Livingstone, S. and Lunt, P. (1994) *Talk on Television: Audience Participation and Public Debate* (London: Routledge).

Lloyd-James, A. (1935) *The Broadcast Word* (London: Kegan Paul & Trench Trubner).

Luhmann, N. (2000) *The Reality of the Mass Media*, trans. Kathleen Cross (Cambridge, Polity Press).

Lunt, P. and Stenner, P. (2005) 'The Jerry Springer Show as an Emotional Public Sphere', *Media, Culture and Society*, 27:1, 59–81.

Lury, C. (2004) *Brands: The Logos of the Global Economy* (London and New York: Routledge).

Lydon, M. (1969) 'The Grateful Dead', *Rolling Stone*, 23 Aug., pp. 15–8.

Lydon, M. (1970) 'An evening with the Grateful Dead', *Rolling Stone*, 17 Sept., pp. 22–3.

MacDonald, M. (2000) 'Rethinking Perzonalization in Current Affairs Journalism', in Colin Sparks and John Tulloch (eds), *Tabloid Tales: Global Debates Over Media Standards* (Oxford: Roman & Littlefield Publishers), pp. 251–66.

Malina, A. (1999) 'Perspectives on Citizen Democratisation and Alienation in the Virtual Public Sphere', in B. Hague & B. Loader (eds), *Digital Democracy and Decision Making in the Information Age* (London: Routledge), pp. 23–38.

Mamoun, L. (n.d.) 'Weapons of Mass Persuasion: Anti-war TV Challenges the Corporate Media "Consensus"', retrieved 2.28.2006 from www.towardfreedom.com/home/content/view/464/69

Manoff, R. & Schudson, M. (eds) (1986) *Reading the News* (New York: Pantheon).

Marcus, G. E. (2002) *The Sentimental Citizen: Emotion in Democratic Politics* (University Park: Pennsylvania State University Press).

Marcuse, H. (1964/1991) *One-Dimensional Man: Studies in the Ideology of Advanced Industrial Society*, 2nd edn (London: Routledge).

Mattelart, A. (2000) *Networking the World 1794–2000*, trans. Liz Carey-Libbrecht and J. A. Cohen (Minneapolis and London: University of Minnesota Press).

Maxwell, R. (2000) 'Picturing the Audience', *Television & New Media*, 1(2): 135–57.

May, T. (2001) *Social Research: Issues, Methods and Process*, 3rd edn (Buckingham: Open University Press).

Mayhew, L. (1997) *The New Public* (Cambridge: Cambridge University Press).

Maysles, Albert and David (Directors) (1970) *Gimme Shelter*.

McCaughey, M. and Ayers, M. (eds) (2003) *Cyberactivism: Online Activism in Theory and Practice* (New York: Routledge).

McChesney, R. (1999) *Rich Media, Poor Democracy: Communication Politics in Dubious Times* (Urbana: University of Illinois Press).

McChesney, R. (2004) *The Problem of the Media: U.S. Communication Politics in the 21st Century* (New York: Monthly Review Press).

McGuigan, J. (2000) 'British Identity and the People's Princess', *The Sociological Review*, Feb., 1(48): 1–18.

McKee A. (2005) *The Public Sphere: An Introduction* (Cambridge: Cambridge University Press).

McLuhan, M. (1964) *Understanding Media: The Extensions of Man* (New York: McGraw-Hill).

McLuhan, M. (1967) 'The Medium is the Massage' (New York: Random House).

McLuhan, M. (1968) *War and Peace in the Global Village* (New York, McGraw-Hill).

McNair, B. (2000) *Journalism and Democracy: An Evaluation of the Political Public Sphere* (London: Routledge).

Meehan, E. (2003) 'Heads of Household and Ladies of the House: Gender, Genre and Broadcast ratings 1929–1990', in V. Nightingale and K. Ross (eds), *Critical Readings: Media and Audiences* (Maidenhead, Berkshire: Open University Press, McGraw-Hill), pp. 193–216.

Meng, J. (2000) 'The Development of Mass Communication and Progress to Democracy in China', in Yuan, J. and Hu, Z. R. (eds), *Communication Studies Towards New Century* (Beijing: Beijing Broadcasting Press), 123–38 [in Chinese].

Merritt, R. (1976, 1985) 'Nickelodeon Theaters, 1905–1915: Building an Audience for the Movies', *The American Film Industry*, in T. Balio (ed.) (Madison, WI: University of Wisconsin Press), pp. 83–102.

Merton, R. K. (1979/1949) 'Patterns of Influence: a Study of Interpersonal Influence and of Communications Behaviour in a Local Community', in P.F. Lazarsfeld and F.N. Stanton (eds), *Communications Research: 1948–1949* (New York: Harper & Brothers).

Meyerowitz, J. (1985) *No Sense of Place: The Impact of Electronic Media on Social Behavior*, 4th edn (New York: Oxford University Press).

Michalski, M., Preston, A., Gillespie, M. and Cheesman, T. (2002) *After September 11: TV News and Transnational Audiences* (ESRC, Open University, BFI, BSC, ITC).

Mills, C.W. (1956) *The Power Elite* (New York: Oxford University Press).

Min, D. H. (2001) 'The Party's Organ and the Party's Website', in *China Journalists Daily*, 10 July, p. 4. [in Chinese]

Mitra, A. (2001) 'Marginal Voices in Cyberspace', in *New Media & Society*, 3(1): 29–48.

Mittel, J. (2003) 'Television Talk Shows and Cultural Hierarchies', in *Journal of Popular Film and Television*, 31(1): 36–46.

Morris, D. (2004) 'Globalization and Media Democracy: The Case of Indy Media', in D. Schuler and P. Day (eds), *Shaping the Network Society: The New Role of Civil Society in Cyberspace* (Cambridge, MA: MIT Press) pp. 325–52.

Mouffe, C. (1993) *The Return of the Political* (London: Verso).

Mouffe, C. (1999) 'Deliberative Democracy or Agonistic Pluralism?', *Social Research*, 66: 745–58.

Murdock, G. (2000) 'Talk Shows. Democratic Debates and Tabloid Tales', in Wieten, J., Murdock, G. and Dahlgren, P. (eds), *Television Across Europe. A Comparative Introduction* (London: Sage), pp. 198–220.

Musser, C. (1990) *The Emergence of Cinema: The American Screen to 1907* (Berkeley, University of California Press).

Musson, B. and R. Grau (1912) 'Fortunes in Films: the Romance of Moving Pictures', *McClure's Magazine*, 40: 65–76.

Napoli, P. M. (2003) *Audience Economics: Media Institutions and the Audience Marketplace* (New York, Columbia University Press).

*National Readership Survey*, www.nrs.co.uk, 2004.

Negt, O. and A. Kluge (1993) *Public Sphere and Experience: Toward an Analysis of the Bourgeois and Proletarian Public Sphere* (Minneapolis, MN: University of Minnesota Press).

Negt, O. and Kluge, A. (1993, first published in German 1972) *Public Sphere and Experience: Toward and Analysis of the Bourgeois and Proletarian Public Sphere* (London: University of Minnesota Press).

Negt, O. and Kluge, A. (1972, 1993) *Public Sphere and Experience: Toward and Analysis of the Bourgeois and Proletarian Public Sphere*, trans. P. Labanyi, J. O. Daniel and A. Oksiloff (Minneapolis, MN: University of Minnesota Press).

Neuman, W.R. (1991) *The Future of the Mass Audience* (Cambridge, MA: Cambridge University Press).

Nguyen, D.T. and Alexander, J. (1996) 'The Coming of Cyberspacetime and the End of Polity', in Shields, R. (ed.), *Cultures of Internet: Virtual Spaces, Real Histories, Living Bodies* (London: Sage), pp. 99–124.

Nightingale V. and Dwyer, T. (2006) 'The Audience Politics of 'Enhanced' Television Formats', *International Journal of Media and Cultural Politics*, 2(1): 25–42

Nightingale, Virginia (2004a) 'Contemporary Television Audiences: Publics, Markets, Communities, and Fans;' in J. Downing *et al.* (eds) *The Sage Handbook of Media Studies* (Thousand Oaks: Sage Publications, 2004), pp. 227–49.

Nightingale, Virginia (2004b) 'Changing the Public: Ratings, Broadcasting and the Internet', *Southern Review*, 37(2): 22–39.

Nightingale, V. and Dwyer, T. (2006) 'The Audience Politics of "Enhanced" Television Formats', *International Journal of Media and Cultural Politics*, 2(1): 25–42.

Nimmo, D. and Combs, J. E. (1992) *The Political Pundits* (New York: Praeger).

O'Connor, A. (2004) *Community Radio in Bolivia: the Miners' Radio Stations* (Lewiston, NY: Edwin Mellen).

O'Neill, R. (2004) 'Taking Big Brother Out of the House – and Into Yours', *Sydney Morning Herald*, 24 Aug. 2004, section: next.

Ofcom (2004a) *Radio – Preparing for the Future. Phase 1: Developing a New Framework* (London: Ofcom).

Ofcom (2004b) 'Summary of Representations 25 Made During the Review of Digital Radio', *Radio – Preparing for the Future. Appendix C* (London: Ofcom).

Olon (2002) *EUREKA! Een oplossing voor digitale kleinschalige radio* (Eureka! A solution for small-scale digital radio. In Dutch, with English language summary) (Nijmegen: OLON, Dutch Federation of Local Public Broadcasters).

Olsson, T. (2004) *Oundgängliga resurser: Om medier, IKT och lärande bland partipolitiskt aktiva ungdomar* [Indispensable resources: On media, ICTs and learning among young, politically active people] (Lund: Lund Studies in Media and Communication).

Olsson, T. (2005) 'Alternativa resurser: Om medier, IKT och lärande bland ungdomar i alternativa rörelser' [Alternative resources: On media, ICTs and learning among young people in alternative movements] (Lund: Lund Studies in Media and Communication).

Olsson, T. (2006) 'Appropriating Civic Information and Communication Technology: a Critical Study of Swedish ICT-Policy Visions', *New Media & Society* 8(4), 611–27.

Opel, A. (2004) *Microradio and the FCC* (Westport, CT: Praeger).

Örnebring, H. (2003) 'Televising the Public Sphere: Forty Years of Current Affairs Debate Programmes on Swedish Television', *European Journal of Communication* 18(4), 501–27.

Örnebring, Henrik and Jönsson, A. M. (2004) 'Tabloid Journalism and the Public Sphere: a Historical Perspective on Tabloid Journalism', *Journalism Studies* 5(3), 283–95.

Pacifica Mission Statement', retrieved 16 Nov. 2002. from www.pacifica.org/about/mission/html.

Page, B.I. (1996) *Who deliberates?: Mass Media in Modern Democracy* (Chicago: University of Chicago Press).

Palmer, L. E. (1909) 'The World in Motion', *The Survey*, XXII: 355–65.

Park, R. (1904, 1972) *The Crowd and the Public, and Other Essays*, (Chicago: University of Chicago Press).

Pearson, R. (1987) 'Cultivated Folks and the Better Classes: Class Conflict and Representation in Early American Film', *Journal of Popular Film and Television*, 15(3): 120–8.

Peers, R. (ed.) (1934) *Adult Education in Practice* (London: Macmillan).

Peters, B. (2001) 'Deliberative Öffentlichkeit', in L. Wingert and K. Günther (eds), *Die Öffentlichkeit der Vernunft und die Vernunft der Öffentlichkeit – Festschrift für Jürgen Habermas* (Frankfurt: Suhrkamp), pp. 655–77.

Peters, B. (2002) 'Conceptions of Public Deliberation – Some Challenges, some Revisions'. Paper presented at the 2002 Annual Meeting of the American Political Science Association, 29 August–1 September 2002.

Peters, B., Sifft, S., Wimmel, A., Brüggemann, M. and Kleinen-von Königslöw, K. (2005) 'National and Transnational Public Spheres: The Case of the EU'. *European Review 13*, Supp. No. 1: 139–60.

Peters, J. D. (1993) 'Distrust of Representation: Habermas on the Public Sphere', *Media, Culture and Society*, 15(4): 541–71.

Petersson, B. (2001) 'Tidningar som industri och parti (1880–1897)' [Newspapers as industry and political parties], in Gustafsson, K. E. and Rydén, P. (eds), *Den Svenska Pressens Historia. Vol II, 1830–1897. [History of the Swedish Press. Vol II, 1830–1897]* (Stockholm: Ekerlids), pp. 236–342.

Plake, K. (1999) *Talkshows: Die Industrialisierung der Kommunikation* (Darmstadt: Primus).

Post Office Archives (PO), Post 89/21 Sykes Broadcasting Committee 1923, Minutes.

Poster, M. (1997) 'Cyberdemocracy: Internet and the public sphere', in D. Porter (ed.), *Internet Culture* (New York: Routledge), pp. 201–229.

Postman, N. (1985) *Amusing Ourselves to Death: Public Discourse in the Age of Show Business* (New York: Viking-Penguin).

Preston, P. (1997) *Political/Cultural Identity* (London: Sage).

Price, M.E. (1995) *Television: the Public Sphere and National Identity* (Oxford: Oxford University Press).

Pursehouse, M. (1992) 'Looking at the Sun: Into the 90s with a Tabloid and Its Readers', in *Cultural Studies from Birmingham Number 1 1991* (Nottingham: Russell Press), pp. 88–133.

Putnam, R. (2000) *Bowling Alone: The Collapse and Revival of American Community* (New York: Simon and Schuster).

Radio Authority (2001) *Local Digital Radio Multiplex Service Licences. Notes of Guidance for Applicants* (London: Radio Authority).

Radio Authority (2002) *Briefing Paper*, Feb. (London: Radio Authority).

Radway, J. (1984) *Reading the Romance: Feminism and the Representation of Women in Popular Culture* (Chapel Hill: University of North Carolina Press).

Reid, D. (2005) Interview with author, 20 Apr.

Reith, J. C. W. (1924) *Broadcast Over Britain* (London: Hodder & Stoughton).

Reith, J. C. W. (1949) *Into the Wind* (London: Hodder & Stoughton).

Rheingold, H. (1993) *The Virtual Community: Homesteading on the Electronic Frontier* http://www.rheingold.com/vc/book/index.html, accessed 25 Mar. 2003.

Rheingold, H. (2002) *Smart Mobs: the Next Social Revolution* (Cambridge, MA: Perseus Publishing).

Riismandel, P. (2002) 'Radio By and For the Public: the Death and Resurrection of Low-power Radio' in *Radio Reader: Essays in the Cultural History of Radio*, in M. Hilmes and J. Loviglio (eds) (New York: Routledge).

Robbins, B. (ed.) (1993) *The Phantom Public Sphere* (Minneapolis, MN University of Minnesota Press).

Rodgers, Z. (2004) 'A&M Records Promotes New Album in Sims Game', 27 Aug. 2004. www.clickz.com/news/article.php/3400721

Rooney, D. (2000) 'Thirty Years of Competition in the British Tabloid Press: the *Mirror* and the *Sun* 1968–1998', in Colin Sparks and John Tulloch (eds), *Tabloid Tales: Global Debates Over Media Standards* (Oxford: Roman & Littlefield Publishers), pp. 91–109.

Rorty, R. (1985) 'Habermas and Lyotard on postmodernity', in Richard Bernstein (ed.), *Habermas and Modernity* (Cambridge, MA: Harvard University Press).

Rorty, Richard (1989) *Contingency, Irony, Solidarity* (New York: Cambridge University Press).

Rose, N. and Miller, P. (1992) 'Political Power Beyond the State: Problematics of Government', *British Journal of Sociology*, 43(2): 173–205.

Rose, N. (1990) *Governing the Soul: the Shaping of the Private Self* (New York, Routledge).

Rosenberg, Bernard and White, D. M. (eds) (1957) *Mass Culture: The Popular arts in America*, (New York: Free Press).

Rossum, W. van (2004) *Meine Sonntage mit "Sabine Christiansen": Wie das Palaver uns regiert* (Köln: Kiepenheuer & Witsch).

Sabbagh, D. 2005 'Big Brother on Mobiles Earns 3 a Small Fortune', in *The Times*, Saturday, 20 Aug. 2005, Section: 'Business' p. 55.

Sakolsky, R. and Dunifer, S. (eds) (1998) *Seizing the Airwaves: A Free Radio Handbook* (San Francisco: AK Press) pp. 68–80.

Sandvoss, C. (2003) *A Game of Two Halves: Football, Television and Globalization* Comedia, (London: Routledge).

Sandvoss, C. (2004) 'Technological Evolution or Revolution? Sport Online Live Internet Commentary as Postmodern Cultural Form', *Convergence*, 10(3): 39–54.

Sandvoss, C. (2005) *Fans: The Mirror of Consumption* (Cambridge: Polity Press).

Scannell, P. and Cardiff, D. (1991) *A Social History of Broadcasting: Serving the Nation* (Oxford: Basil Blackwell).

Scannell, P. (1989) 'Public Service Broadcasting and Modern Public Life', *Media, Culture & Society*, 11: 135–66.

Schiller, Joseph Zachariah (2006) *After the Barnraising: Community Radio and the Reconstruction of the Public Sphere'*, unpublished dissertation (University of California, Davis).

Schudson, Michael (1978) *Discovering the News: a Social History of American Newspapers* (New York: Basic Books).

Schudson, M. (1992) 'Was There Ever a Public Sphere?: If So, When?: Reflections on the American Case', in C. Calhoun (ed.), *Habermas and the Public Sphere*, 6th edn (Cambridge Mass), pp. 143–63.

Schudson, M. (1998) *The Good Citizen* (Cambridge, MA: Harvard University Press).

Schudson, M. (1997) 'Why Conversation Is Not the Soul of Democracy', *Critical Studies in Mass Communication*, 14(4): 297–309.

Schudson, M. (1998) *The Good Citizen: a History of American Public Life* (New York: Simon and Schuster).

Schultz, T. (2004) 'Die Moderation politischer Gesprächsrunden im Fernsehen'. Eine Inhaltsanalyse von "Sabine Christiansen", "Berlin Mitte", "Presseclub" und "19:zehn", in *Publizistik*, 49(3): 292–318.

Schultz, T. (2006) *Geschwätz oder Diskurs? Die Rationalität politischer Talkshows im Fernsehen* (Köln: Halem).

Schütz, A. (1995) 'Entertainers, Experts, or Public Servants? Politicians' Self-Presentation on Television Talk Shows', *Political Communication*, 12: 211–21.

Sennett, R. (1974) *The Fall of Public Man* (New York: Knopf).

Seymour-Ure, C. (2000) 'Northcliffe's Legacy', in Catterall, P. Seymour-Ure, C. and Smith, A. (eds), *Northcliffe's Legacy: Aspects of the British Popular Press, 1896–1996* (Basingstoke: Macmillan), pp. 9–26.

Shattuc, J. M. (1997) *The Talking Cure. TV Talk Shows and Women* (New York and London: Routledge).

Shimpach, S. (2004) 'Attending to the Movies: Human Science, Progressive Reform, and the Construction of Hollywood's Audience', *Department of Cinema Studies* (New York: New York University).

Skovmand, M. and Schroder, K. (eds) (1992) *Media Cultures: Reappraising Transnational Media* (London: Routledge).

Slater, L. (2003) 'Democracy, New Social Movements, and the Internet: A Habermasian Analysis', in M. McCaughey and M. Ayers (eds) (2003), *Cyberactivism: Online Activism in Theory and Practice* (New York: Routledge), pp. 117–44.

Slevin, J. (2000) *The Internet and Society* (Cambridge: Polity Press).

Smeaton, B. (Director). (2004) *Festival Express* [DVD].

Smith, A. (1978) 'The Long Road to Objectivity and Back Again: The Kinds of Truth We Get in Journalism', in G. Boyce, J. Curran and P. Wingate (eds), *Newspaper History: from the 17th Century to the Present Day* (London: SAGE), pp. 153–71.

Smulyan, S. (1994) *Selling Radio: the Commercialization of American Broadcasting* (Washington, DC: Smithsonian Institution Press)

Snow, D. A., Rochford, E. B., Jr, Worden, S. K. and Benford, R. D. (1986) 'Frame Alignment Processes, Micromobilization, and Movement Participation', *American Sociological Review*, 51, 464–81.

Soley, L. C. (1992) *The News Shapers: The Sources Who Explain the News* (New York: Praeger).

Sparks, C. (1991) 'Goodbye, Hildy Johnson: the Vanishing "Serious Press"', in P. Dahlgren, and C. Sparks (eds), *Communication and Citizenship: Journalism and the Public Sphere* (London: Routledge), pp. 58–74.

Sparks, C. (2000) 'Introduction: The Panic Over Tabloid News', in Colin Sparks and John Tulloch (eds), *Tabloid Tales: Global Debates Over Media Standards* (Oxford: Roman & Littlefield Publishers), pp. 1–40.

Sproule, J. M. (1987) 'Propaganda Studies American Social Science: the Rise and Fall of the Critical Paradigm', *Quarterly Journal of Speech*, Vol. 73, Feb: 60–78.

Stacey, J. (1994) *Stargazing: Hollywood Cinema and Female Spectatorship* (London: Routledge).

Statistics of the Internet development in China', China Internet Network Information Centre, http://www.cnnic.com.cn/index/0E/00/11/index.htm. [in Chinese]

Stein, L. E. (2002) 'Off topic: Oh my God, US terrorism!: Roswell fans respond to 11 September' in *European Journal of Cultural Studies*, 5(4): 471–91.

Stein, P. (2005) 'Branded Entertainment Comes of Age', http://imediaconnection.com/content/7393.asp.

Stephens, M. (1997) *A History of News* (Orlando, FL: Harcourt Brace).

Stevenson, N. (1997). 'Media, Ethics and Morality', in J. Mcguigan (ed.), *Cultural Methodologies* (London: Sage), pp. 62–86.

Stokes, M. and Maltby, R. (eds) (2001) *Hollywood Spectatorship: Changing Perceptions of Cinema Audiences* (London: BFI).

Swidler, A. (1986) 'Culture in Action: Symbols and Strategies', *American Sociological Review*, 51(2) Apr.: 273–86.

Swingewood, A. (1977) *Myth of Mass Culture*, (Atlantic Highlands, NJ: Humanities Press).

Tang, D. Y. and Shi, J. (2001) 'Virtual Community or the Public Sphere: a Case Study of the QGLT During Plane Collision Crisis', in Deng, X. X. and Li, X. G. (eds), *Internet Communication and the News Media* (Beijing: Beijing Broadcasting Institute Press), pp. 393–411. [in Chinese]

Tarde, G. (1969) 'The Public and the crowd' (1901) and 'Opinion and Conversation' (1898) in *Tarde: On Communication and Social Influence*, T. Clark, (ed.), *Gabriele* (Chicago: University of Chicago Press).

Tarrow, S. (1994) *Power in Movement: Social Movements, Collective Action and Politics* (Cambridge: Cambridge University Press).

Tay, E. (1998) 'Global Chinese Fraternity and the Indonesian Riots of May 1998: The Online Gathering of Dispersed Chinese', http://www.sshe.murdoch.edu.au/intersections/issue4/tay.html, accessed 17 Feb. 2005.

Taylor, C. C. (1919) 'The Social Survey, Its History and Methods', *The University of Missouri Bulletin*, 20(28): 1–91.

Tenscher, J. (1998) *Showdown im Fernsehen. Eine Analyse des Diskussions- und Rollenverhaltens der Moderatoren in den deutschen Wahlkampfdebatten* (Stuttgart: Edition 451).

Thomas, M. (2002) 'T-DAB: Overcoming the Spectrum Planning and Interference Issues', *EBU Technical Review*, Jan.

Thompson, J. B. (1995) *The Media and Modernity: a Social Theory of the Media* (Cambridge: Polity Press).

Thompson, M. (2004a) 'Building Public Value', *BBC Homepage-Press Office-Speeches* [Internet], <http://www.bbc.co.uk/pressoffice/speeches> [Accessed 27 August 2004].

Thompson, M. (2004b) 'Speech given to BBC staff on Mark Thompson's first day as Director-General', *BBC Homepage – Press Office – Speeches* [Internet], <http://www.bbc.co.uk/pressoffice/speeches> [Accessed 27 August 2004].

Thornton, A. (2002) 'Does Internet Create Democracy', retrieved 28 May 2006 from http://www.zipworld.com.au/~athornto/

Tichenor, P. J., Donohue, G. A. and Olien, C. N. (1980) *Community Conflict and the Press* (Beverly Hills, CA: Sage).

Timberg, B. M. (1994) 'The Unspoken Rules of Talk Television', in: Newcomb, H. (ed.), *Television: The Critical View*, 5.edn. (New York: Oxford University Press), pp. 268–81.

Timberg, B. M. (2002) *Television Talk: A History of the TV Talk Show* (Austin: University of Texas Press).

Tocqueville, A. De. (2004) *Democracy in America*, trans. A. Goldhammer (New York: Library of America).

Tolson, A. (ed.) (2001) *Television Talk Shows: Discourse, Performance, Spectacle* (Mahwah: Lawrence Erlbaum).

Trefgarne, G. (2001) 'GWR blocks Classic clone on digital', *Daily Telegraph*, 21 Nov.

Tridish, P. and Coyer, K. (2005) 'A Radio Station in Your Hands Is Worth 500 Channels of Mush!: the Role of Community Radio in the Struggle Against Corporate Domination of Media', in E. D. Cohen (ed.), *News, Incorporated: Corporate Media Ownership and its Threat to Democracy*, (Amherst, NY: Prometheus Books).

Tsagarousianou, R., Tambini, D. and Bryan, C. (eds) (1998) *Cyberdemocracy: Technology, Cities and Civic Networks* (London: Routledge).

Tuchman, G. (1978) *Making News: A Study in the Construction of Reality* (New York: The Free Press).

Tulloch, J. and Jenkins, H. (1995) *Science Fiction Audiences: Watching Dr Who and Star Trek* (London: Routledge).

Tulloch, J. (2000) 'The Eternal Recurrence of New Journalism', in C. Sparks and J. Tulloch (eds), *Tabloid Tales: Global Debates over Media Standards* (Lanham: Rowman & Littlefield), pp. 131–46.

Turner, F. J. (1920) *The Frontier in American History* (Tucson: University of Arizona Press).

Turner, G. (1999) 'Tabloidization, Journalism and the Possibility of a Critique', *International Journal of Cultural Studies*, 2(1): 59–76.

United States Federal Communications Commission. 20 Jan. 2000. Report and Order. *In the Matter of Creation of Low Power Radio Service*, MM Docket 99–25.

Uricchio, W. and R. E. Pearson (1993) *Reframing Culture: the Case of the Vitagraph Quality Films* (Princeton: Princeton University Press).

van de Donk, W., B. Loader and D. Rucht (eds) (2004) *Cyberprotest: New Media, Citizens and Social Movements* (London: Routledge)

van Dijk, J. (2000) 'Models of Democracy and Concepts of Communication', in Hacker, K.L. and van Dijk, J. (eds), *Digital Democracy: Issues of Theory & Practice* (London: Sage), pp. 30–53.

Van Zoonen, L. (2001) 'Desire and Resistance: *Big Brother* and the Recognition of Everyday life', in *Media, Culture & Society*, 23(5): 669–79.

Wadleigh, Michael (director) (1970) *Woodstock – Three Days of Peace and Music* [DVD, *The Director's Cut*, 1994].

Walker, J. (2001) *Rebels on the Air: An Alternative History of Radio in America* (New York: New York University Press).

*Wall Street Journal Online* (May, 2005) 'How Can Old Media Survive in a New Media World?', May 23 2005, Page R1.

Walsh, G. E. (1908) 'Moving Picture Drama for the Multitude', *The Independent*, LXIV: 306–10.

Walton, D. (1989) *Informal Logic: A Handbook for Critical Argumentation* (Cambridge; Cambridge University Press).

Ward (ed.) (1970) 'Woodstock', *Rolling Stone*, 9 July, p. 38.

Warner, M. (1992) 'The Mass Public and the Mass Subject', in C. Calhoun (ed.), *Habermas and the Public Sphere*, C. Calhoun (ed.) (Cambridge, Mass.: MIT Press), pp. 377–401.

Warner, M. (2002) *Publics and Counterpublics* (New York, NY: Zone Books).

Warschauer, M. (2003) *Technology and Social Inclusion: Rethinking the Digital Divide* (Cambridge, MA: MIT Press).

Webster, J.G., Phalen, P. F. and Lichty, L.W. (2000) *Ratings Analysis: The Theory and Practice of Audience Research*, 2nd edn (Mahwah, New Jersey: Lawrence Erlbaum and Associates).

Weintraub, J. and Kumar, K. (1997) *Public and Private in Thought and Practice* (Chicago: University of Chicago Press).

Weischenberg, S. (1997) *Neues vom Tage: Die Schreinemakerisierung unserer Medienwelt* (Hamburg: Rasch und Röhring).

Wellman, B. and C. Haythornthwaite (eds), *The Internet in Everyday Life* (Oxford: Blackwell Publishing).

Wessler, H. (1999) *Öffentlichkeit als Prozess: Deutungsstrukturen und Deutungswandel in der deutschen Drogenberichterstattung* (Opladen, Wiesbaden: Westdeutscher Verlag).

Wessler, H. (forthcoming) 'Investigating Deliberativeness Comparatively', *Political Communication* 24.

What's Free Speech TV?', retrieved 25 Nov. 2002, from www.freespeech.org/fsitv/html/aboutus.shtml

Whelan, B. (1988–89) 'Further': Reflections on the Counter-culture and the Postmodern', *Cultural Critique*, Winter, pp. 63–86.

White, M. (1992) *Tele-advising: Therapeutic Discourse in American Television* (Chapel Hill: University of North Carolina Press).

White, M. (2002) 'Television, Therapy, and the Social Subject; or, The TV Therapy Machine', in J. Friedman (ed.), *Reality Squared. Televisual Discourse on the Real*, (New Brunswick, New Jersey, Rutgers University Press) pp. 313–21.

Wiebe, R. H. (1967) *The Search For Order 1877–1920* (New York: Hill and Wang).

Wiener, J. H. (1988) 'How New Was the New Journalism?', in Wiener, J. H. (ed.), *Papers for the Millions: the New Journalism in Britain, 1850s to 1914* (New York: Greenwood Press), pp. 47–72.

Wilhelm, A. (1999) 'Virtual Sounding Boards: How Deliberate Is Online Political Discussion?', in B. Hague and B. Loader (eds), *Digital Democracy: Discourse and Decision Making in the Information Age* (London: Routledge), pp. 154–78.

Wilhelm, A. (2000) *Democracy in the Digital Age: Challenges to Political Life in Cyberspace* (New York: Routledge).

Williams, R. (1974) *Television: Technology and Cultural Form* (London: Fontana/Collins).

Williams, R. (1977) *Marxism and Literature*, (Oxford: Oxford University Press).

Williams, R. (1978) 'The Press and Popular Culture – an Historical Perspective', in George Boyce, James Curran and Pauline Wingate (eds), *Newspaper History: from the 17th Century to the Present Day* (London: Sage), pp. 41–50.

Williams, S. (2001) *Emotion and Social Theory: Corporeal Reflections on the (Ir)Rational* (London: Sage).

Winnicott, D. W. (1967/2000) 'Transitional Objects and Transitional Phenomenon' in P. Du Gay, J. Evans, and P. Redman (eds), *Identity: A Reader* (London: Sage).

Wolfsfeld, G. (1984) 'Collective Political Action and Media Strategy', in *Journal of Conflict Resolution*, 28: 363–81.

World DAB (2005) 'New Wave of DAB Legislation and Developments Worldwide', *World DAB Forum press release*, 14 Apr.

Yang, G. B. (2002) 'Virtual diasporas and global problem solving project Papers', http://www.nautilus.org/archives/virtual-diasporas/paper/Yang.html, accessed 17 Feb. 2005.

Yang, G. B. (2003) 'The Internet and the Rise of a Transnational Chinese Cultural Sphere', *Media, Culture and Society*, (25)4: 469–90.

Young, I.M. (2003) 'Activist Challenges to Deliberative Democracy', in Fishkin, J. S. and Laslett, P. (eds), *Debating Deliberative Democracy* (Malden, MA: Blackwell), pp. 102–120.

Young, J. R. (1970), 'Woodstock', *Rolling Stone*, 9 July, pp. 38–9.

## Websites

www.bmwusa.com
www.cocojambo.com
www.hypnotic.com
www.journalism.org
www.answers.com/topic/porsche-design-group

# Index